Teaching Tainted Lit

Teaching Tainted Lit

Popular American Fiction in Today's Classroom

Edited by

JANET G. CASEY

UNIVERSITY OF IOWA PRESS
IOWA CITY

University of Iowa Press, Iowa City 52242
Copyright © 2015 by the University of Iowa Press
www.uiowapress.org
Printed in the United States of America
Design by Sara T. Sauers

The University of Iowa Press is a member of Green Press Initiative
and is committed to preserving natural resources.
Printed on acid-free paper

Library of Congress Cataloging-in-Publication Data
Teaching tainted lit : popular american fiction in today's classroom /
edited by Janet G. Casey.
    pages   cm
Includes bibliographical references and index.
ISBN 978-1-60938-373-2 (pbk), ISBN 978-1-60938-374-9 (ebk)
1. American literature—Study and teaching. 2. American fiction—
History and criticism. 3. Popular literature—United States—
History and criticism. 4. Literature and society—United States.
I. Casey, Janet Galligani, editor.
PS41.T43 2015
810.71—dc23   2015008714

Contents

~

Introduction

Reading, Pedagogy, and Tainted Lit

JANET G. CASEY

⁓

THE NOTION THAT popular literature is tainted has a distinguished history. What noted critic Leslie Fiedler once called "the church of True Believers"—the academic circle that interprets and canonizes "genuine" literature[1]—has long been in the business of convincing us that only a narrow group of texts is worthy of serious attention; the rest, so we have been told, are inappropriate indulgences compromised by their relation to the consumer marketplace. Yet we have indulged indeed. Like forbidden fruit, popular-but-not-quite-reputable books have seduced respectable citizens for generations, even if some of us, conditioned by the values of the literary-critical arena, have been deeply conflicted about such reading tendencies. C. S. Lewis suggested as much when he wittily observed, back in 1939, that his "highest-browed acquaintances" seemed heavily invested in discussing the "vulgarity" of the popular, "and therefore must know it well"; presumably, he argued, "they would welcome a theory which justified them in drinking freely of that fountain without forfeiting their superiority." Similarly, 1950s reviewer Carl Little characterized his enjoyment of the crime novels of Mickey Spillane with tongue firmly in cheek: "I can't recommend [Spillane's work] because I am a serious literary critic and a moral leader of the community. But confidentially, I had a hell of a swell time."[2]

Such comments, of course, underscore the cultural pressures that have urged many of us to keep our less lofty reading to ourselves. Yet they simultaneously acknowledge that *everyone* indulges, that even the highbrow reader keeps one eye on the pulpy popular (wink, wink) as s/he surveys the cultural production of and for the elite. Perhaps less telling than the extent to which one indulges, then, has been the extent to which one admits it.

Lately such admission has become downright trendy; the category of "guilty pleasure" reading has come out into the open in ways unimagined by cultural commentators of yore. Arthur Krystal recently celebrated in the *New Yorker* the sheer "yearn[ing] for a good story" that propels us into the realm of "commercial and genre novelists" whose plot-driven works adduce all sorts of heady delights, including "the knowledge that we could be reading something better." Significantly, Krystal was writing three years into National Public Radio's highly successful series, *My Guilty Pleasure*, the subtitle of which says it all: "Writers talk about the books they love but are embarrassed to be seen reading." From Peter Benchley's *Jaws* to Jacqueline Susann's *Valley of the Dolls* to Stephenie Meyer's *Twilight* series, NPR has devoted air time to the antipretensions of "serious" writers, who gleefully describe their obsessions; these include such works as the Regency romances of Georgette Heyer ("a gateway drug to Jane Austen" [Helen Simonson]) or Scott Spenser's teenage potboiler, *Endless Love* ("beneath which the burners are always set on High" [Ben Dolnick]). Even Stanley Fish weighs in on the sentimental gratifications of reading yet another predictable and "at best workman-like" biography of his idol, Frank Sinatra.[3] Veiled compulsions, it seems, at least in the literary world, are no longer so veiled after all.

What does all this fevered revelation mean? Is it, as Harold Bloom has griped when commenting on the establishment's acceptance of Stephen King, that the critical faculty has faltered, that American reading has been "dumbed down"?[4] Or is it, as Michael Chabon puts it in his extended meditation on the pleasures of books, that we are rediscovering as a culture our joy in a variety of reading options, and in the sense that reading is, after all, independent of its aesthetic valuations, a form of entertainment? (As Chabon shrewdly argues, a narrowing of the accepted literary field to, say, nurse romances would result in immediate scholarly stratification of such texts and elaborate justification of the relevant evaluative principles—but it would also create restless readers looking beyond the borders of the acceptable for something a bit different.)[5] It is a commonplace to point out that the genre of the novel itself was once a guilty pleasure, and that many a tainted popular tome has become, in time, a recognized literary classic. Who is to say, then, that today's throwaway beach novel will not be another generation's found literary gem, or that there is not a great deal to be learned—as Gordon Hutner has argued so convincingly in *What America Read*—by studying the literary preferences of the average person on the street?

If we are to judge by the academy, this last view seems to be gaining ground. The secret reading that was long hidden from parents and teachers (*Peyton Place*, anyone?) is now likely to be the very reading that appears on the college literature syllabus, and not only in classes specifically devoted to popular culture. On the contrary, such texts are at home now on mainstream reading lists for more traditionally titled courses in, say, The American Novel. This seismic shift in attitudes and teaching practices was inevitable, given the advent of cultural studies and the theoretical stance that all texts contribute to our understanding of the literary field; such developments have reshaped our understanding of how, exactly, we think about reading and writing and their roles. We have pulled the lens back, as it were, to reveal a larger cultural landscape, one in which "genuine" literature is clearly enabled by the construction of other literary categories. The very pervasiveness of the term *noncanonical* in contemporary literary studies is evidence of the centrality of popular materials and the corresponding critical impulse to study not merely texts but also the sifting and sorting processes that determine their status. Studies such as those of Janice Radway on contemporary romance readers (*Reading the Romance*) or the impact of the Book-of-the-Month Club (*A Feeling for Books*) are now standard examples of top-notch scholarship, advanced in part by vibrant professional organizations, such as the Modernist Studies Association and the Middlebrow Research Network, that explore and destabilize traditional literary-cultural hierarchies. Our collective sense of the literary has become much more capacious, and many would say more compelling, as a result of this enlarged version of what literature might be.

There are plenty of reasons to celebrate these developments and to refute the idea that they represent a "dumbing down" of literary studies. For one thing, they acknowledge what we have always known—that all kinds of people read all kinds of books, and that "good" and "bad" reading categories are overly simplistic and fail to capture the nuances of historical and contemporary constructions of the literary. If college-level work is about demystifying arenas of knowledge, we could do worse than to encourage our students to reconsider the very frameworks that have elevated and sustained the category of "academic" or "serious" texts. This is not to say that all texts are absolutely equal in some zero-sum game of literary qualification—far from it. But it is to say that different texts have different valences, different purposes, different audiences, and different relations to the larger culture—all of which reward study. Moreover, the consumer marketplace that was once scorned as the generative site of popular literature is acknowledged now as the very place where academia, too, attempts to sell itself and its values. In short, the study of literature has become nothing less than the study of culture, and the inclusion of popular materials within the mix marks the only appropriate pedagogical end to the insistence that educated citizens should be informed, broad-minded, and, above all, *critical*. As practitioners of literary studies, we have learned to turn our analytical insights back upon ourselves, questioning our past assumptions, habits, and values. In the process we have entered into a purposeful consideration of the kind of reading we were once ashamed of.

～

A couple of years back, in a course I regularly teach entitled American Bestsellers and Popular Culture, I found myself faced with an unanticipated pedagogical conundrum. Having decided that the syllabus demanded an early Western, I added Owen Wister's *The Virginian* (1902) to the reading list. I realized that it might fall flat; after all, Wister's novel seems stilted in comparison to the better-known Westerns of the 1920s and 1930s, and students were likely to find it less racy and hence far less interesting than other texts in the course (e.g., *Gentlemen Prefer Blondes* or *The Godfather*). Nonetheless, I felt that *The Virginian*'s neat establishment of some of the most cherished conventions of the genre—the cryptic but macho cowboy, the virtuous single woman, the degenerate drifter, the naïve outsider—outweighed in value any possible "slowness" of the narrative itself. Yet I was wholly unprepared for the response that I got: most of the students did not understand or even perceive these conventions at all. Their very first comments included these:

"It's pretty sexist, isn't it?"

"The characters of color are stereotyped."

"There seems to be a lot of gratuitous violence."

I quickly found myself in the rather odd position of trying to convince them of the *pleasures* inherent in a genre steeped in—yes—sexism, racism, and violence.

This experience unsettled me, and not merely because of the obvious need to historicize issues of gender, race/ethnicity, and cultural rampage. In the ensuing days I attempted to "teach" the Western by distributing handouts, showing film clips, and even addressing parodies or echoings of the genre, including TV shows such as *F Troop* and *Star Trek*. What I was trying to demonstrate is the way literary conventions work: we experience the delight of the familiar in the repetition of character types and stock scenarios as well as in their subtle and not-so-subtle deconstruction—which, of course, we can only recognize if we know the conventions in the first place. Literature thus becomes a complicated process of accrual and variation. (T. S. Eliot, talking about "serious" literature, argued something like this in "Tradition and the Individual Talent," an essay with which my English majors were conversant.) But it struck me that having to articulate the conventions of a recent popular genre was especially constraining and substantially diminished its charms; it was akin to explicating the punchline of a joke, resulting in its deflation. Surely the Western was something that students *should* know and understand; their failure to do so made me reassess not just my role as a teacher but also my own relation to the literary-cultural field. Clearly, what was general knowledge for my generation could no longer be assumed.

Readers might be tempted here to groan about students' cultural illiteracy, but that's not really my point; after all, the Western was traditionally external to academic reading and discussion, and hence was not part of the bundle of cultural materials we presumably needed students to know. Yet my experience with the Western challenges our easy assumptions that what students *do* know is popular culture; on the contrary, it highlights the historical situation of popular materials and their often rapid decline when new formats and genres take over. Significantly, my students are far more sophisticated than I concerning hypertexts and game and film narratives; many of them also know a great deal about contemporary memoir, arguably the most popular literary genre of our age. Their lack of familiarity with Westerns—while somewhat surprising, given the genre's relatively recent heyday—merely reflects a basic fact of life: that the past recedes quickly, and that students need help recapturing and interpreting it. From this perspective the teaching of the Western differs little, perhaps only in degree, from the teaching of any historically removed genre, including the Shakespearean sonnet or the early American captivity narrative—both of which, though canonical now, were part of the popular literature of their ages.

The supposed wholesale dismissal of popular literature by the academy, then, is merely an illusion, a false posture, since many now-revered canonical works were originally popular texts. This gets to the heart of the matter, which involves timing, generational perspectives, and the especially slippery nature of evaluation when one is dealing with contemporary materials. I suspect that even the most devoted upholders of the traditional canon would concede that the Western has its place, though perhaps a minor one, in the literary history of the United States, especially given our cultural investment in narratives of nation formation. (Decades of serious literary criticism have dealt with Manifest Destiny and our national mythologies, including such classic studies as Henry Nash Smith's *Virgin Land: The American West as Symbol and Myth* [1950] and Annette Kolodny's *The Lay of the Land: Metaphor as Experience and History in American Life and Letters* [1984].) Yet those same individuals may be far less likely to embrace, say, the latest romance novels, whose relation to American literary culture is more difficult to discern in this historical moment. That is, the day's popular texts, which have not yet stood the test of time, seem always already less worthy of serious consideration; they also become easily manipulated targets for "outside" commentators lamenting the disintegration of society's values, aesthetic or otherwise.

But this is hardly a new problem. Consider these remarks from the

6

American Tract Society of the early nineteenth century (emphasis in the original):

[B]*ad books* [are] whatever books neither feed the mind nor purify the heart, but *intoxicate the mind and corrupt the heart*. Works of science, art, history, theology, etc. furnish 'aliment' or 'medicine:' books of fiction, romance, infidelity, war, piracy, and murder, are *poison*, more or less diluted, and are as much to be shunned as the drunkard's cup. . . .

Familiarity with popular fiction gives a disrelish for simple truth; engenders a habit of reading merely for amusement, which destroys the love of sober investigation, and blasts the hope of mental improvement; renders scientific and historical reading tedious; gives false views of the perfectibility of human nature, thus leading to disappointments in the relations of life; and dwarfs the intellectual and moral powers, except the imagination, which is rendered morbid and unhealthy by constant excitement.[6]

Every generation has reason to distrust the incursion of new cultural modes that challenge established priorities. What's truly remarkable, perhaps, and a recent development, is that the historical distance once deemed necessary to reevaluate a work has shrunk; we no longer require a generation or more before entering into reassessment. Indeed, today we are quite likely to take seriously in college classrooms the popular works of only a decade ago, or of last week. While this speed-up may be especially threatening to the standard-bearers of the academy, it has nonetheless given us huge new areas of fascinating literary material to mine and has introduced topics—notably about the *industry* of books, including marketing, reviewing, taxonomy, censorship, and so forth—that were not usually considered in the past, when texts were studied primarily as singular works of art. And these new possibilities, connecting literature to far-reaching cultural debates and alternative knowledge arenas, have revitalized the field of literary studies, which, like the humanities more generally, has been pressured to demonstrate its relevance in our present-day world.

Of course, this newly accepted reveling in the literary vernacular is not without complications. One "problem" is that students cannot always tell which texts on a particular syllabus are canonical and which are not: what might seem to teachers to be a productive mix of canonical and noncanonical readings, creating intriguing and deliberately provocative tensions, may have little meaning to students, for whom most assigned texts exist on the same pedagogical plane. (As in my experience with the Western, what seems obvious to us is not at all obvious to them.) The onus is on teachers, then, to *teach* canonicity, which complicates the teaching task. A related issue concerns the shifting paradigms by which literary texts are read and judged, which often confound neat, predictable categories established by previous generations (again, making teaching harder, or at least more complex). For example, where exactly do we fit Harriet Beecher Stowe's *Uncle Tom's Cabin*, a popular-turned-near-canonical text if ever there was one? It would be impossible to teach Stowe's work without considering its bestselling status in its own time, and yet there is no denying that it is now a "classroom text." Indeed, its ideological contexts (e.g., mid-nineteenth-century Evangelical Christianity) and its uses of language, not to mention its length, mark it for students as "academic" (read: challenging). The shifting sands of literary status are fascinating, of course, and highly deserving of study, but there is no denying that teaching was in many ways easier when teachers agreed upon a smaller canon of "genuine" literary works and were not obligated to situate their textual choices within a dynamic and all-encompassing literary field.

Yet these perils are surely balanced by immense pleasures, notably the pleasures of fuller apprehension. When I was an undergraduate, I could not have said why a particular novel taught by my professors was superior to the books I devoured while on vacation; I simply accepted it as such. If pressed, I probably would have stated that academic texts are more "difficult" and therefore, somehow, "better" and more "valuable" than mainstream books. Did I believe this? I'm not sure; perhaps I did, since I went on to pursue a PhD in American literature. Yet in graduate school and beyond I harbored suspicions that there was a more complicated story to be told, and I relished the emerging scholarship that attempted to fill in the gaps by grappling with the literary landscape in all of its fullness. I know now that my delight in these "recovered" materials was similar to that of my students today when they, too, are granted the license to read popular books: in such moments our co-curricular reading activities—the very ones that got us interested in texts in the first place—are validated, assuring us that our instincts for sheer pleasure in narrative are not so inappropriate after all. Hence a remark by literary and cultural critic Alan Jacobs that I have lately shared with my students: "Read what gives you delight—at least most of the time—and do so without shame." Jacobs adds that "it's never too late to begin [a] new life as a free reader"—that is, one who pursues books with an open sense of what they might have to offer, and with an enthusiasm and intelligence unfettered by perceived obligations or imposed hierarchies.[7]

~

The contributors to this volume are surely among the "free readers" Jacobs has in mind; they appreciate and accommodate diverse textual materials, assuming that popular books may be not merely noteworthy but richly nuanced and deeply compelling. Even more important, they take for granted the pedagogical potential of the popular. Underlying their individual essays and perspectives are the following broad queries: How do popular texts affect the overall study of American literature? What insightful or unusual roles might the popular play in the classroom? How do college teachers handle the intersections of popularity and canonicity, and to what effect? How might the teaching of historical versus contemporary popular texts differ? What anxieties and gratifications emerge when reading the popular—for teachers as well as students?

Such questions probe the theoretical and practical dimensions of teaching this material in ways that both presume and extend its legitimacy for the college classroom. Of course, secondary school teachers have also grappled with the inclusion of popular texts in their reading lists, though they are often motivated by the perceived need to nudge high schoolers into more engaged reading postures; the constraints posed by school boards, curricular mandates, and parent concerns also permeate much of the published commentary on incorporating popular literature at the secondary level.[8] In contrast, the writers herein have the freedom and luxury—though also the responsibility—of thinking about the popular in terms related to the aims of the discipline, a disposition that necessarily furthers debates about literature's continuing roles inside and outside the academy. Collectively, then, these essayists map a terrain of inquiry that genuinely deepens our understanding not only of effective college-level pedagogy but of the literary and its multiple uses and meanings.

The contents of the volume are arranged so as to call attention to fundamental affinities among essays while also suggesting a range of thematic possibilities that might serve diverse pedagogical ends. For example, in the first section, entitled "Nineteenth-Century Popular Texts and Canon Considerations," Melissa Gniadek explores how the novels of George Lippard illustrate the serious role of sensationalism in discourses of race and nation building in the mid-1800s, while Randi L. Tanglen describes her use of "literature circles" to expand her students' exposure to the literary and cultural cross-currents of the period. Both show how the inclusion of popular nineteenth-century materials lends dimension and texture to canon-centered approaches. Kathleen M. Therrien and Antonia Losano contribute essays to "Gender, Romance, and Resisting Readers," in which they address how serious engagement with popular romances challenges readers (and teachers) in unex-pected ways; Therrien's close reading of Anya Seton's *Dragonwyck* walks us through ever-deepening stages of readerly disidentification, while Losano's experiments with integrating romances in different types of courses reveal the rather surprising fit of this genre within the theory classroom. Although Jolene Hubbs deals with Southern chick lit while Richard Schur grapples with African-American "street lit," including comic strips, together they suggest ways to approach "Race, Region, and Genre in Popular Texts," which is the title of their section. "Gothic, Then and Now" includes essays by Derek McGrath, who uses Lady Gaga's per-formances to urge students to a more nuanced consideration of Edgar Allan Poe, and Alissa Burger, who situates Stephen King's work within a broad backward- and forward-looking gothic tradition. Finally, both Michael Devine and Lisa Long address ways of "Teaching the Popular through Visual Culture": Devine investigates the influence of early twentieth-century cinema on what were originally "pop" literary texts, and Long considers continuities between the dime-novel Westerns of Thomas Chalmers Harbaugh and today's video game narratives.

This is not to say, of course, that these particular groupings exhaust the possibilities for connections among the essays; on the contrary, sub-stantive resonances abound. McGrath's essay featuring Lady Gaga could easily fit within the paradigm of "Teaching the Popular through Visual Culture," for example, while Hubbs's discussion of chick lit might be repositioned within the "Gender and Romance" section. Both Therrien and Gniadek deal with the gothic and could reasonably inhabit the ru-bric of "Gothic, Then and Now." Clearly the conceptual lines established by the section titles might be redrawn in a number of ways. (This is to say nothing of other viable alternatives, such as a period-based orga-nizational scheme, which, among other advantages, would foreground the distinctions between teaching historical and contemporary popular texts.) The idea, however, is to group essays in ways that both stage con-versations and offer a disparate range of entry points for teaching the popular—which nonetheless leaves room for multiple cross-currents to emerge. The essays are very much in conversation across as well as within categorical sections, and it is our hope that not only the indi-vidual pieces themselves, but also the section titles, will spark ongoing discussions in the field at large.

Especially instructive are the plural stances of the essays: in different ways they bring together the personal and the political, the anecdotal and the scholarly, classroom experience and research knowledge. Some model engagement with specific popular texts, demonstrating how they yield to close reading strategies; others center on broader concerns of genre or the history of canon formation. A few are quite practical, offering tips and classroom strategies, while some explore large theoret-ical claims. Many take on some combination of these approaches, and contrasting postures and concerns are also visible within the volume's individual sections. As a whole, then, this project breaks down the long-received binaries between "high" critical enterprises and "low" categories of reading and writing, and between scholarly work and teaching. In an immediate way, it performs the kind of boundary dis-solution that is its very subject, revealing the rewards of applying smart and incisive investigative strategies to texts and genres that have been routinely delegitimized in the academy.

To be sure, a volume such as this is likely to push certain buttons, appearing to invite disdain for those whom Bloom calls, in his famously negative review of J. K. Rowling's work, "the ideological cheerleaders who have so destroyed humanistic study [that] anything goes."[9] After all, even as some of our contributors unearth long-neglected novels, thereby appearing to practice a sanctioned mode of canon reconsideration, others tackle suspect and "low" contemporary narrative formations such as cartoon strips and video games. Those who subscribe to Bloom's theory that literary studies has been "dumbed down" might argue that the downward slide is fully on display here. But a volume such as this would have considerably less impact if it took a safe route. It would be less controversial, for instance, to consider only those formerly popular texts that have recently been taken more seriously as literary and cultural documents—that is, those that are historically removed from us and therefore constitute relatively tame choices for teaching the popular. In contrast, to embrace the more volatile territory of the here and now is to challenge the traditional methodology of literary studies, which has generally held that some distance is necessary for appropriate evaluation; it is also to intervene actively in the processes of culture formation. A popular text is, in a visceral sense, *for* and *about* a present moment; it actively reverberates with its time to a degree that is not always true of allegedly transcendent "high" art, and it offers the opportunity to study cultural processes not in retrospect, but as they are unfolding. Hence, to grapple with the category of the popular only from a historical remove is arguably not to grapple with it fully at all. The willingness to explore contemporary elements here—whether a Stephen King novel or a Lady Gaga video—thus marks our commitment to a thorough and appropriately provocative exploration of the category of the popular itself.

Perhaps ironically, it is in embracing *contemporary* popular culture —the very maneuver that most incites the wrath of tradition-bound commentators—that literary studies stands to reassert its relevance in an age when the arts and humanities have been grossly devalued. And this is not just a cheap strategy to purchase student interest. On the contrary, studying contemporary popular materials in earnest illuminates connections between past and present and highlights the importance of measured, intelligent interpretation of the innumerable texts in our text-saturated society. If we accept that literary studies is no longer centered on a canon of texts but on an approach to reading, then what matters most are the complex skills gained in the process—skills that translate productively to a variety of vocational lives. An ability to comprehend, deconstruct, evaluate, and translate a spectrum of written texts matters a great deal in our time; what hangs in the balance is the distinction between mastering our textual environment or being mastered by it.

And so much the better if such texts provoke fresh insights on how culture operates. Indeed, from the perspective of literary studies, popular materials provide new means of understanding the density and complexity of the cultural landscape, such that we address not just *a* literature—that is, a canon devised and sustained by others—but literature in all of its fullness and variety. This approach hardly unseats the traditional canon; rather, it situates it, revitalizes it, enriches it, all while giving us new landscapes of literary expression to ponder. If the contributors to this volume share one vision, it is surely this: that the popular greatly expands possibilities, for learning as well as for teaching.

Despite the perils, we believe, the pleasures are profound.

Nineteenth-Century Popular Texts
and Canon Considerations

"Lippard represents a drastically different literary project....and his work exposes students to a different publication history."—MELISSA GNIADEK, "'You Will Observe...': Letting Lippard Teach"

"Reflecting the ideals of a newly established democracy, 'popularity' was a major criterion for what made literature good, not evidence of its aesthetic inferiority as it is today.... Studying popular literature and using 'popularity' as a category of analysis is possibly more true to American reading choices and modes of interpretation in the nineteenth century than is the sole study of what we now regard to be the classics...."
—RANDI LYNN TANGLEN, "'Canons of Nineteenth-Century American Literature': How to Use Literature Circles to Teach Popular, Underrepresented, and Canonical Literary Traditions"

"You Will Observe . . ."

Letting Lippard Teach

MELISSA GNIADEK

⌒

GEORGE LIPPARD is a nineteenth-century popular author who captures students' attention. His cultivation of a dramatic self-image, his
ongoing exchanges with his critics, his invention of myths (like the
legend of the Liberty Bell) for a nation searching for a past, and his
commitment to exposing corruption and inequality all challenge any
preconceptions that students might have about nineteenth-century
authors. Similarly, his sensational stories and particular brand of melodrama unsettle students' ideas about what nineteenth-century American literature looks like. While many of Lippard's sprawling serialized
novels are too long to be read in a typical undergraduate course, shorter
works like *'Bel of Prairie Eden* (1848), republished in Jesse Alemán and
Shelley Streeby's collection, *Empire and the Literature of Sensation: An
Anthology of Nineteenth-Century Popular Fiction* (2007), provide rich
opportunities to bring antebellum serialized sensation fiction into the
classroom. This essay will draw on experiences teaching this particular
text in two different contexts—in a survey of American literature to 1860
and in a course explicitly concerned with gothic nineteenth-century
American literature—in order to consider how a text like *'Bel* might
be positioned and repositioned. It will ultimately suggest that not only
does *'Bel of Prairie Eden* provide opportunities to employ familiar historicist reading practices, resulting in productive conversations about
empire, race, gender, and print culture, but also that a text like *'Bel*

17

instructs students to consider how the text works on readers through its directives to "observe." It encourages students to consider questions of aesthetics and representation in ways that speak to critical concerns currently motivating and reshaping the study of nineteenth-century American literature.

~

'Bel of Prairie Eden was published serially in the Boston weekly *Uncle Sam* before being published in its entirety by Boston's Hotchkiss & Co.[1] The novel is set in Texas and Mexico in the years surrounding the United States' annexation of Texas in 1845. It tells a story of revenge between two families, one American and one Mexican. The American Grywin family has moved into the Republic of Texas following the collapse of their Philadelphia bank. Years earlier Isabel Grywin had refused Don Antonio's suit when he was the attaché of the Mexican legation in Washington, DC. Don Antonio seeks revenge for this at the same time that Mexico seeks to reclaim Texas in 1842, making the link between families and land clear. Invading the Grywin family's Texas homestead, Prairie Eden, Don Antonio drugs and rapes 'Bel, hangs her father, and later kills her younger brother. 'Bel's older brother John spends years seeking revenge for these atrocities, eventually killing Don Antonio's father and wooing his sister Isora, whose honor he plans to ruin as Don Antonio had ruined 'Bel's. John also tells Isora of the wrongs done to his family without revealing the identity of his enemy so that she, unknowingly, comes to despise her own brother. While Don Antonio is clearly evil, John replicates his wrongs, complicating the novel's stance toward these families and, consequently, toward the territories that they represent. Though Lippard himself supported expansion into western lands as a way to provide opportunities for the white working classes and generally supported the US cause in the war with Mexico, *'Bel of Prairie Eden* takes a more ambivalent stance toward the war than many of his other writings. In *'Bel*, Shelley Streeby writes, Lippard's "utopia for redeemed labor becomes a haunted homestead in the Texas borderlands."[2]

A novel like *'Bel*, then, provides opportunities for introducing students to the popular literature that surrounded the US-Mexico war and to a writer like Lippard, and also to challenge their conception of the canon in radical ways. This has been one goal of the survey course in which I teach the novel—a goal that the students themselves introduce on the first day of class when I ask them to write down the first thing that they think of when they hear the words "American literature." We then go around the room and make a list of responses, indicating when an author, text, or concept is mentioned multiple times. Not surprisingly, responses generally involve writers that students have become familiar with in high school. Mark Twain is usually mentioned several times, as are John Steinbeck and William Faulkner. Edgar Allan Poe shows up occasionally. Herman Melville sometimes makes an appearance. Events like "the Revolution" and related concepts of liberty and freedom some-times show up. If anything from before "the Revolution" is mentioned it is inevitably "the Puritans."

When we have finished compiling our list, students are generally quick to realize that most of the texts mentioned are from the twentieth century and that most of the authors are white men known for their novels. They begin to deepen the list themselves, mentioning whatever female, African American, Asian American, or Native American writers they can think of, all while marveling at the lack of diversity generated from their initial responses. But, of course, they cannot generally con-ceive of the existence of an author like Lippard, whose work lies far outside the boundaries of even the most diverse high school or under-graduate reading. As we move through the semester and students are introduced to unfamiliar voices like that of Lydia Maria Child alongside more familiar voices, from Frederick Douglass to Edgar Allan Poe, the historical reception of texts—discussion about what becomes canonical, how, and why—becomes an important part of our conversation. For example, students are always surprised to discover that *Moby-Dick* was not well received when it was first published. And they are always sur-prised to find that authors like George Lippard existed and were wildly popular. But what is just as surprising to students is how familiar aspects of a text like *'Bel of Prairie Eden* seem, even though its very existence is unexpected. While they are generally amused and disoriented by the narrative's tone, by its dramatic scenes and "heaving bosoms," they are quick to remark that it reminds them of a soap opera, providing oppor-tunities to talk about the serial form, about the gaze, about voyeurism, and about popular genres over time. Just as the survey as a whole belies their expectations about the literature of the period, *'Bel of Prairie Eden* is different from what students might expect of "American literature." Yet they are also intrigued by its familiar qualities.

～

When I have taught *'Bel* in my American Literature to 1860 course it has appeared toward the end of the semester. I have drawn attention to issues of print culture throughout the course, so Lippard represents a kind of climax regarding that particular theme. For example, when we read Anne Bradstreet poems we look at digital images of *The Tenth Muse Lately Sprung Up in America* (1650) so that students can think about how the poems reprinted in our anthology originally appeared. They think about the various legitimating prefaces placed before Bradstreet's poems and about how the addition of poems about family and domestic concerns in a second, posthumous edition changes the collection as a whole. By the time we encounter Lippard we have read parts of David Walker's *Appeal to the Coloured Citizens of the World* (1829) and have looked at facsimiles of the original text, discussing the role of its "radical typography."[3] And we have jumped ahead temporally to Emily Dickinson. We look at facsimiles of her fascicles, discussing the material history of her poems and the limited ways in which they circulated during her lifetime at the same time that we close read them. Throughout the semester we address the themes of cross-cultural contact, colonial violence, community, nation, and race that might be expected in such a survey, but we also think about how texts first appeared and why that might matter. When we approach *'Bel*, then, the text can be situated historically—for example, through debates about territory and slavery surrounding the US-Mexico war—in a way that connects Lippard to other authors that we have read and other historical problems that we have encountered. But it can also be positioned within conversations about print culture, as well as conversations about genre and about historical reception. Lippard represents a literary project drastically different from anyone else encountered during the semester, and his work exposes students to a different publication history. Indeed, any discussion of Lippard's work needs to situate his writing within the context of the explosion of newspapers and story papers in the antebellum period. Awareness of the exuberance of print culture during this period can, in turn, help students to resituate writers like Poe, Thoreau, and Dickinson within a dynamic world of print.

To that end, I try to bring students to a rare manuscript library during the class period before we begin to discuss 'Bel of Prairie Eden, if at all possible. This allows them to see what newspapers, story papers, gift books, and novels looked like during the period when Lippard was writing and helps to make more of a reality the concept of seriality —a concept that is familiar due to the current popularity of television serials—as it was experienced in the nineteenth century. (When it is not possible to view such archival materials in person, any number of online databases can stand in.) While we cannot see how 'Bel of Prairie Eden itself originally appeared, showing students how other works by popular mid-century authors were first published enables them to keep in mind that the cliffhangers and narrative leaps within 'Bel are related to a particular print history. For example, showing students how Uncle Tom's Cabin first appeared in serial form in the National Era gives them a chance to see a more familiar novel in its original context.

Though we cannot read 'Bel in a story paper, I often ask students to read half of the novel for the first class spent discussing the text, intentionally leaving them at a dramatic "cliffhanger" to replicate the experience of reading serially. That first class discussion is generally spent establishing some context for the novel. In addition to a brief introduction to Lippard, we discuss the critical reception of such popular fiction. I provide a handout with some key quotations from Michael Denning's Mechanic Accents (1987) and David S. Reynolds's Beneath the American Renaissance (1988; republished 2011). The publication dates of Denning's and Reynolds's books alert students to the fact that these types of popular, sensational texts began to receive critical attention not so very long ago, and we talk a bit about the recovery work involved in bringing texts like 'Bel of Prairie Eden into critical and classroom conversations. Reynolds, for example, shows that "major" writers like Melville, Hawthorne, Whitman, Thoreau, Emerson, and Dickinson were in dialogue with all kinds of "minor" writers and popular forms. He writes that "delving beneath the American Renaissance occurs in two senses: analysis of the process by which hitherto neglected popular modes and stereotypes were imported into literary texts; and discovery of a number of forgotten writings which, while often raw, possess a surprising energy and complexity that make them worthy of study on their own."[4] Reynolds further writes that "an understanding of the antebellum context questions the long-held notion that American authors were marginal figures in a society that offered few literary materials. The truth may well be that, far from being estranged from their context, they were in large part created by it."[5] As we discuss Reynolds's main arguments, I encourage students to reconsider the word "beneath" in his title, given the complex picture of American literature we have been developing over the course of the semester. What types of hierarchies does that concept reinforce and on what are those hierarchies based? If questions about what makes something "literature" are discussed from the beginning of the semester, students are primed to insert 'Bel into these ongoing conversations. They are eager to recognize and discuss conventional literary conceptions of "high" and "low" literature, and they are often equally willing to consider upsetting such hierarchies.[6]

It is also necessary, of course, to spend time alerting students to the novel's historical context as well as to its place in literary history. This might be accomplished through a brief historical reading on the US-Mexico war or a handout with an annotated timeline and thorough discussion of that material in class. In my case, teaching this text in Texas meant giving students the opportunity to reach back to the Texas history that many of them had learned in elementary and high school. I allowed them to take the lead in narrating the main historical events mentioned in the text, including the battles of the Alamo, Goliad, and San Jacinto, filling in gaps as necessary.[7] Including a text like 'Bel in such a survey can, then, obviously help to expose students to the diverse geographies of American literature, moving beyond the focus on New England that often continues to dominate surveys of early periods of American literature. During the same decades when Nathaniel Hawthorne fictionalized the Puritan past in his familiar novels and short stories, Philadelphia-based Lippard drew on the history of other spaces in 'Bel, in which Cortés's sixteenth-century invasion of Mexico is collapsed with the nineteenth-century US invasion of Mexico through scenes in which a reader first "watches" Winfield Scott and then Cortés arrive in Vera Cruz, or what would become Vera Cruz.

"Mapping" the novel on the board as a class, collectively working to diagram the text's various characters and their relationships, is a helpful way to reinforce its geographies and historical conflicts and allow students to begin to investigate its cultural work. *'Bel*, like Lippard's other novels, has a deep cast of characters, some of whom disappear and later reappear in disguise, and it can be easy for students to confuse some of them. Diagramming the characters and their relationships at the outset allows students to clarify any confusion regarding characters or plot points. But the diagram inevitably does more complicated work as well. As students name individual characters and indicate their relationships to other characters, they also note that many of the characters are recognizable "types." They identify the dark, foreign villain, the effeminate, angelic boy who will clearly be among the first characters to die, the virginal, wronged women who, they quickly realize, operate as metonyms for the land that is also passing back and forth between men in the text. And even as they point to the "types" at play, students use this diagram to begin to grapple with how types are blurred. They note that John's beauty is described as "Satanic." They note that over the course of the novel he becomes "Juan," and they grapple with what to make of that fact. They note that while Harry's (who is also sometimes called Henry) face had "so much of woman in its every outline," 'Bel cross-dresses as a monk, so that gender is repeatedly destabilized.[8] In other words, the simple act of ensuring that everyone understands who the characters are and what happens in the text serves to expose key mechanisms of this type of sensation fiction and begins to prompt more complicated readings of the text as a whole.

In the end, students often remain understandably confused by the novel's politics. They note that Scott is portrayed as heroic in a way that suggests the supremacy of the American cause but that the novel's awareness of past conquests complicates that heroism. And they note that this may, in fact, be part of the work that the novel does. In *'Bel* heroes are also villains, as land and women are passed back and forth in a popular, sensational narrative that leaves students rethinking the stories that are told about war as well as the stories that are told about nineteenth-century American literature.

⁓

While including *'Bel of Prairie Eden* in a survey provides opportunities to discuss a range of historical issues, to introduce students to nine-teenth-century sensation fiction, and to emphasize a print-culture approach to American literature, teaching *'Bel* in a course on nineteenth-century American gothic and sensation fiction provides opportunities to discuss American gothic in relation to the issues of empire emphasized in Alemán and Streeby's collection.[9] With its "mysterious chambers" on the "Isle of Sacrificios," its heroine disguised as a monk, its "haunted homestead," and its scenes of unspeakable horrors, the novel is more recognizably "gothic" than many other texts that one might include in such a course, giving students a chance to think about how many of the conventions that they might associate with British gothic manifest themselves and shift in a US literary context.[10]

When I taught *'Bel* in such a course, one of the arguments about American gothic that we considered from the beginning of the semester was Teresa Goddu's statement that "the gothic tells of the historical horrors that make national identity possible yet must be repressed in order to sustain it."[11] We had read excerpts from Freud's "The Uncanny"; Charles Brockden Brown's *Edgar Huntly*, in which the titular protagonist wanders the wilds of Pennsylvania becoming the very "savage" he seeks to eradicate; selections from J. Hector St. John de Crèvecoeur's *Letters from an American Farmer*; Harriet Prescott Spofford's short story "Circumstance," in which the main character survives a night in the woods in the clutches of the "Indian Devil" only to find that her ordeal saved her family from an Indian raid; Harriet Jacobs's narrative; and Edgar Allan Poe's *The Narrative of Arthur Gordon Pym of Nantucket*, among other texts. By the time we encountered *'Bel*, students were familiar with a range of narratives that use aspects of the gothic to explore issues of territory, imperial violence, and race. They were familiar with a range of narratives that highlight historical horrors as they repress them, or as they highlight their active repression.

When we approached *'Bel* with these other narratives in mind, students immediately noted how geographies are haunted by earlier histories in the novel. They noted, too, how descriptions of the land not only sexualize the landscape, reinforcing connections between the novel's women and land, but also emphasize that the land is full of "remembrance." Prairie Eden's trees, for example, resemble "solemn mourners over the dead centuries."[12] Students noted that in Vera Cruz the peak "Orizaba glares like the ghost of past ages from the western sky," and that "[t]hree hundred years ago . . . the same lone Orizaba, that towers serenely now . . . beheld a far different scene."[13] They noted that the novel's most horrific scenes of nineteenth-century revenge are set in chambers "where the priests of the forgotten creed administered their bloody rites 300 years ago."[14] They noted, in other words, that multiple pasts haunt the spaces of the present within Lippard's novel.

With these conversations behind us we were, then, prepared to read and discuss Jesse Alemán's essay "The Other Country: Mexico, the United States, and the Gothic History of Conquest" during the second class period spent discussing '*Bel*. Drawing on Freud's definition of the uncanny as *unheimlich* as he reads early nineteenth-century histories and historical romances that deal with US-Mexico relations, Alemán shows how these texts make "Mexico in particular a strangely familiar place that troubles the trans-American imaginary of the United States."[15] He develops the notion of "inter" Americanism which, he writes, "understands that the nations of the western hemisphere already contain *within* ("intra") their borders national others whose formative presence is subsequently buried (interred) but nonetheless felt and often expressed through gothic discourse."[16] While Alemán's essay does not offer a reading of '*Bel*, the concepts that it discusses are readily applicable to the novel. Students have already noted a long history of claims to land within the novel—from mention of Native Americans to Montezuma and conquistadors, to the struggle between the United States and Mexico—historical claims to land that, in Aléman's formulation, point to the various others "interred" or buried within evolving national boundaries. And they have, of course, noted how the American and Mexican families move between and within evolving national boundaries. I distribute a handout that digests some key aspects of Alemán's essay, and we discuss how his theorization of "inter" Americanism might manifest itself through '*Bel*. Alemán's essay productively complements and complicates Goddu's claim that "the gothic tells of the historical horrors that make national identity possible yet must be repressed in order to sustain it" and also provides opportunities to introduce the concept of hemispheric American studies.

⁓

Regardless of whether '*Bel of Prairie Eden* is incorporated into a course through discussion of print culture, gender, race, class (students often note that a character like Ewen MacGregor merges concerns with race, class, and national "otherness"), war, traditions of the gothic, or issues of empire and "inter" Americanism, students are always eager to discuss its sensational representations of bodies and scenes, particularly in relation to the narrative's tone. Its style inevitably feels unique and troubling to students. For example, in one class a student titled her internet forum post on '*Bel* "You will observe all these heaving bosoms . . . ," a playful reference not only to '*Bel*'s titillating scenes but also to how the narrative negotiates those scenes. This student noted that the novel's narrator gives vivid, detailed accounts of melodramatic scenes, often prefaced with phrases such as "You will observe . . ." or "You see Isabel survey . . ." She was fascinated by how "Lippard pulls the reader in (in a certain way) as he pushes the reader out." She noted that phrases like "You will observe" and "You see" give a sense of present immediacy to the story (in part because in these direct appeals to the reader the narrative shifts from the past to the present tense), yet that this idea of watching the story unfold seems to "disconnect the reader from immersing fully in the story." The reader, she wrote, is "always reminded that they are a reader."

Numerous other students have also been interested in what they have called Lippard's "interactive narrative style," his narrator's strange "self-awareness," or moments where the narrator appears to "break the fourth wall," a phrase that is certainly not narratologically conventional but that resonates with the performative and theatrical aspects of Lippard's novel. One student noted that moment when the narrator says, "Have we seen this man before?" or "The Mexican raised his hand to his eyes—was it to hide a tear?," paired with the directives to "observe" or "see" seem to indicate that the narrator and reader are "experiencing the discourse from the same vantage point and at the same time." This serves, the student continued, to enhance the "spectacle" of the story since, he noted, these moments occur "at the points in the story when something scandalous happens." The narrator is saying, "Now, look at this!" as if he too is shocked by the events that he is delivering to the reader and, according to this student, this makes the reader aware of his or her sensations or reactions.

'Bel of Prairie Eden's narrative style is, in other words, so dramatic that students cannot avoid it. I offer student reflections in their own words here to indicate that the text itself forces them to think not only about the narrative's content but also about how to negotiate its voice. Some will have a hard time taking the novel seriously because of what one student termed its "preposterous prose," but those willing to engage with the prose will be eager to discuss how the reader's emotions are engaged through questions and directives, and how the reader is made aware that he or she is engaging in voyeuristic consumption through the act of reading such sensational literature. Even before Ewen MacGregor enters Isabel's room, one student noted, "the narrator and the reader are already intruding in a way, peering through the 'slightly parted' curtains and Isabel's 'gently parted' lips."[17] Another was eager to discuss the scene late in the novel when John and Isora are at a Philadelphia theater, watching "a half-naked woman whirling over the stage, her form clothed in flesh-colored hose that clings to the skin, a piece of white gauze fluttering from her waist, her arms and bosom bare!"[18] She pointed out a central paradox of Lippard's type of sensation fiction: that a scene critiquing the objectification of female bodies operates through objectification of the female body. Readers "watch" as the woman twirls, spins, and crouches near the footlights, "her head bowed until her naked breast is revealed to the universal gaze."[19] Students are inclined to connect such scenes to the narrator's overt comments about the antebellum publishing industry—to, as one student wrote, "the novel's critiques of elitist notions of what constitutes 'good' literature." 'Bel draws attention to and comments on its status as sensation fiction in a way that students find compelling. Such moments ("Far in the corner of his cell where our author is confined, behold the magazine critic of Philadelphia; a jaunty thing, delicate in perfume, with oysterish eyes; the scissors in one hand and the scrap-book in the other") make the dynamism of the antebellum publishing world come alive as students see Lippard taking his critics to task, and doing so through the very type of sensation fiction being critiqued.[20]

Of course, drawing attention to how the reader is directed to "watch," "observe," or "see" provides opportunities to situate *'Bel of Prairie Eden* within the context of nineteenth-century visual culture, from panoramas to the illustrations that began to accompany fiction in newspapers and story papers during the years when Lippard wrote. While we do not have any illustrations to accompany *'Bel*, students might look at contemporary war pictures as well as contemporary book illustrations that capture *'Bel's* melodramatic feel.[21] But even without the historical context of particular developments in visual culture or theater or performance culture, *'Bel's* narrative style provides opportunities to discuss the mechanisms of "sensation" in ways that are not merely thematic. *'Bel's* very particular aesthetic allows students to make arguments about how narratives can make readers "feel" and simultaneously draw attention to the mechanisms by which they make readers "feel." While this is obviously a central component of sensation fiction and, in different ways, a component of its more respectable relative sentimental fiction, a novel like *'Bel of Prairie Eden* easily allows students to discover this for themselves. As Alemán and Streeby write, "Like sentimental fiction, sensational literature is a form of melodrama that aims to move its audiences to experience intense feelings, but it emphasizes thrills, shock, and horror more than virtuous and socially redemptive feelings."[22] If sentimental fiction teaches its readers to "feel right," students discover that a novel like *'Bel* might force them to "feel wrong." They recognize that they, as readers, are implicated in reenacting the voyeurism of Lippard's fiction over and over again in a way that is problematically pleasurable ("You will observe"). And they recognize the potential political, social, and ethical implications of such moves, even if those implications are not always entirely clear within Lippard's fiction or within sensation fiction more generally.

As American literary and cultural studies reflects on the historical approaches that have dominated these fields over the past decades— historical approaches that have allowed writers like George Lippard and novels like *'Bel of Prairie Eden* to be "recovered"—questions about the place of form, aesthetics, and narrative have been revived. This recent turn to form and aesthetics has worked to oppose older notions of aesthetics as empty and apolitical, pointing out that even politically engaged historicism has always engaged aesthetic questions, and that we often unite historical and formal approaches when we teach.[23] Lippard's work is "low," popular fiction brought to light by the historicist turn in American literary studies, and it is certainly antithetical to aesthetics as a term of "high art."[24] Yet we might, as Cindy Weinstein and Christopher Looby have recently suggested, return to the concept of aesthetics as a contested, imprecise term that could "include the play of imagination, the exploration of fantasy, the recognition and description of literary form, the materiality of literary inscription and publication, the pleasure of the text, sensuous experience in general, the appreciation of beauty, the adjudication and expression of taste, the broad domain of feeling or affect, or some particular combination of several of these elements."[25] Lippard's fiction can provide an accessible way for students to think about a number of these issues—to think about form, materiality, pleasure, and sensuous experience in a text that might initially seem to lend itself primarily to historicist reading practices. 'Bel instructs students to at least consider the possible politics of particular aesthetics in a way that will help them to think critically about how other texts are structured. In the classroom, Lippard's over-the-top narrative style, his narrator's directives to "observe," "watch," or "see," instruct students to think about sense, sensation, feeling, and corporeality in antebellum popular fiction in ways that encourage them to read closely and carefully what they might initially be inclined to dismiss as a scandalous popular story.

"Canons of Nineteenth-Century American Literature"

How to Use Literature Circles to Teach Popular, Underrepresented, and Canonical Literary Traditions

RANDI LYNN TANGLEN

~

BECAUSE I WAS trained in the field of nineteenth-century American women writers, I place a high value on teaching the literature that was being read by, and represents popular attitudes of, nineteenth-century audiences. So, as a new faculty member at a small liberal arts institution, I taught almost only women writers in my upper-division nineteenth-century American literature course, placing special emphasis on once-popular and best-selling authors such as Harriet Beecher Stowe, E.D.E.N. Southworth, and Elizabeth Stuart Phelps. By extension, because I was teaching a class that featured popular women writers, I also emphasized underrepresented women writers such as Harriet Jacobs, Harriet E. Wilson, and Sarah Winnemucca, who, like their best-selling Anglo peers, were using literature as a force in the world to expose and discuss social problems and to bring about change. I taught primarily popular and underrepresented women authors without much considering the need to expand the course syllabus beyond the literature that represented popular tastes and social concerns of its day. Indeed, as a feminist literary critic, the notion of a fixed canon of literature, representing "the best of the best" American literature, has always struck me as "the yawny dream of an immutable curriculum that reflects human universals," especially since the popular literature of nineteenth-century America addressed a wide range of perspectives on real-world issues such as the place of women in society, critiques and affirmations of race-based social hierarchies, and concerns about social class (Stimpson 586).

But I teach at a small liberal arts college, where I am one of two Americanists in a six-member English department. I cover all periods of American literature up until 1900, but I was hired specifically to teach courses in nineteenth-century American literature. Of course my English Department colleagues, not specialists in my area but thoroughly engaged in the larger debates in literary studies, did not question my choice to teach my upper-division nineteenth-century American literature course as a women's writers course, and even wholly welcomed and supported this approach. But because this class was the only opportunity our majors would have to study nineteenth-century American literature at all, I worried that I was privileging these popular and underrepresented authors at the expense of exposing our students to more traditionally taught authors such as Herman Melville, Nathaniel Hawthorne, and Ralph Waldo Emerson—that is, the nineteenth-century American authors canonized in F. O. Matthieson's 1941 *American Renaissance* and still the most widely taught and studied nineteenth-century American authors.

Although, as the editor of this volume explains, popular literature has secured a solid position in higher education classrooms and debates about canon formation might seem irrelevant and outmoded, I wondered what my students were missing by not being exposed to more canonical materials, especially because I appreciated the contributions of all of these authors—popular, underrepresented, and canonical alike—in my own study and scholarship. Further, as I became more acculturated into my institution and familiar with the assumptions of liberal arts education, I had to wonder if my course was contributing to the college's mission of cultivating broadly educated students in a liberal arts tradition, which, all too often, my students and some colleagues understand to be a solid training in the "Great Masterpieces."

My teaching dilemma was rooted in debates about the use and usefulness of a literary canon, especially the question of whether we have moved beyond discussions of the politics of canon formation and the canon wars. Using the literature circle approach to blend canonical, popular, and underrepresented traditions in one course is a practical way to illustrate such debates about high and low culture and to introduce students to issues surrounding their own education, particularly what they are taught and why. At this point, even my most traditional colleagues would acknowledge that privileging a canon that putatively represents literary works of great artistic merit and "the best which has been thought and said in the world" comes at the expense of excluding the valuable perspective of popular and underrepresented voices (Arnold 5). Yet they would argue that an established canon of classic texts is central to the intellectually "liberating" mission of the liberal arts, as they see teaching canonical works of cultural distinction and high artistic quality as a way for students to transcend the social, political, and religious status quo. From a more practical perspective, some college trustees, parents, and alumni might want students to benefit from the cultural and academic capital that comes from studying a curriculum of canonical works. They assume that such a background will ensure students' future social and professional success.[1]

But even a defender of a more canonical curriculum, philosopher John Searle, acknowledges the unfixed (if not arbitrary) nature of canon formation as he points out the false dilemma of a bifurcated canon: "In my experience there never was, in fact, a fixed 'canon'; there was rather a certain set of tentative judgments about what had importance and quality. Such judgments are always subject to revision, and in fact they were constantly being revised" (37). The issue, then, has to do with who gets to make these judgments. Searle was writing at a time when scholars of the "cultural left" were opposed to the more conservative curricular agenda represented by Allan Bloom and other pundits. At this point, though, I want my students to move beyond the stalemate of the earlier canon wars, but not necessarily because the issues surrounding those debates have gone away. Rather, I hope to organize my classes so that students can be part of the debates about their education and make these judgments for themselves, that is, to apply their critical thinking skills to larger and real world questions—the actual goal of a liberal arts education. Many of my students are surprised to learn, for example, that until recently American literature was not considered part of the tradition of serious or high art that would be included in the canon of texts representing the best of western civilization and its intellectual traditions. Or that literature they might have been taught as "classics" in high school—such as *Uncle Tom's Cabin* or *A Narrative of the Life of Frederick Douglass*—hasn't always been part of the canon of American literature traditionally taught and studied.

Yet some scholars find it easier to just eschew the politics of canon formation altogether. Some colleagues have advised me that since the boundaries between high and low culture have been so blurred in this generation of students' experiences with culture, they won't know something is canonical unless I tell them it is. So by just mentioning the word "canon" in my course title—even as a way to question and critique its relevancy—I am affirming its legitimacy as metanarrative and perpetuating its hegemonic, limiting assumptions. This postmodern approach to popular culture celebrates the lack of distinction between high and low culture and has the basic assumption that such distinctions are political and not actually based in a work's artistic merits. Therefore, this line of reasoning sometimes follows that since these distinctions are now blurred and proven to be invalid, students no longer need to be introduced to the debates of the earlier canon wars or grapple with the politics of canon formation. But I see this perspective as the postmodern annex of the traditional argument for a fixed and transcendent western canon. While not necessarily insisting on transhistoric and universal human values, the spurious multiculturalism sometimes implied in this perspective too easily makes it possible to set aside the realities of social difference and political inequality in the production and reception of literature in its own day and ours.

In the nineteenth century, popular women writers were marginalized due to gendered sanctions that women not speak or act publicly as well as assumptions of womanly intellectual and artistic inferiority. African American and Native American writers—like those from other marginalized racial and ethnic groups—were not able to access the mainstream educational opportunities and artistic networks that would allow them to publish and circulate their writing.[2] These nineteenth-century social and material realities are still being played out today, since through-

out my students' educational lives they may not have been exposed
to literary traditions that represent their own experiences as African
Americans, American Indians, women, members of the working class,
and members of other historically marginalized and underrepresented
groups. More inclusive and representative literature anthologies such
as the *Heath Anthology of American Literature* have attempted to address this issue in terms of coverage, but the classroom practicalities of
teaching an integrated canon can still be challenging.

Popularity in the Nineteenth Century

In the study of nineteenth-century American literature, the "popular"
is often tied to the study of women's writing, as women writers wrote
some of the best-selling fiction of the day. The most cited example is,
of course, Harriet Beecher Stowe's *Uncle Tom's Cabin* (1851–52), which
eventually became the second best-selling book of the century, sur-
passed only by the Bible and selling 300,000 copies in the first year of
its publication. Not close to *Uncle Tom's Cabin*'s run-away success but
popular nonetheless was Elizabeth Stuart Phelps's 1868 *The Gates Ajar*,
a Spiritualist response to the Civil War's massive death toll that struck
a chord with the nation's women, selling 80,000 copies in the United
States and 100,000 copies in Europe. And E.D.E.N. Southworth's fiction
was so popular that she was able to give up her work as a schoolteacher
and support herself as a professional writer. She eventually wrote sixty
novels, and her sensational novel *The Hidden Hand* (1859) supposedly
sold 2 million copies in the nineteenth century. As many feminist critics
have illustrated through recovery work and scholarship, much of the
popular sentimental, domestic, and sensational fiction of the nineteenth century was written by women writers with women readers in
mind, with plots and characters that focused on religious, domestic,
and heterosexual love themes.[3] Similar to Janice Radway's study of the
readers of popular, mass-produced romance novels, these scholars of
nineteenth-century sentimental and domestic fiction by women have
indicated that female reading practices had political, even subversive,
possibilities.

Yet even though these popular nineteenth-century authors and texts have become fairly commonly taught and studied, and in many cases almost canonical themselves, all too often popular literature is overlooked in the teaching of nineteenth-century American literature. Although we would like to think we have moved beyond having to defend "noncanonical works," still informed by a modernist aesthetic that privileges psychological complexity and depth and doesn't tend to see such depth in women's experiences in general, "twentieth-century critics have taught generations of students to equate popularity with debasement, emotionality with ineffectiveness, religiosity with fakery, domesticity with triviality, and all of these, implicitly, with womanly inferiority" (Tompkins 123). Further, high school English curricula and textbooks, much to the chagrin of many high school English teachers I know who feel constrained by homogenous standards and state-mandated testing schedules, still present literature from a formalist perspective, in which students are trained that"[l]iterary text . . . that make continual and obvious appeals to the reader's emotions and use technical devices that are distinguished by the utter conventionality, epitomize the opposite of everything that good literature is supposed to be" (125). Of course those of us who teach popular literature aren't as concerned with determining if a work of literature is "good," but rather what it was trying to do as a work of art in a specific historical and cultural context. Yet, as a result of my students' earlier training in the study of literature, I spent a lot of time not having these types of conversations with my students but rather trying to make a case for including entire courses in our curriculum on popular authors, especially as students thought they were signing up to study the "classics" when they became English majors.

I explain to my students that studying a more integrated canon— one that represents popular and canonical traditions alike—reflects the realities of print culture at the time, when "emerging distinctions among a largely non-popular highbrow literature, middlebrow sentimentalism, and a lowbrow sphere of story paper fiction and dime novels began to stratify the literary field" (Alemán and Streeby xvii). And although it is true that Hawthorne now famously railed against the "damned mob of scribbling women," the stark divide between "popular and high culture had yet to be drawn," until the creation of American literature anthologies in the late nineteenth century (Bennett, Kilcup, and Schweighauser 4). Reflecting the ideals of a newly established democracy, "popularity" was a major criterion for what made literature good, not evidence of its aesthetic inferiority as it is today. If, through the process of democratic elections, the people could vote for their own leaders and rule themselves without the mediation of a monarch, couldn't the people, too, determine what makes "good" literature, without the mediation of a critic? Nineteenth-century readers and critics alike insisted that "[p]opularity is, generally speaking, a sure test of merit," and "popularity," in many cases, was viewed as a sign of literary excellence (qtd. Bennett, Kilcup, and Schweighauser 4). Studying popular literature and using "popularity" as a category of analysis is possibly more true to American reading choices and modes of interpretation in the nineteenth century than is the sole study of what we now regard to be the classics of nineteenth-century American literature.

Jane Tompkins and others have provided us with strategies for teaching the ways in which popular fiction "is remarkable for its intellectual complexity, ambition, and resourcefulness and . . . in certain cases . . . offer[ing] a critique of American society far more devastating than any delivered by better-known critics such as Hawthorne and Melville" (124). While in some cases popular fiction might affirm or remain ambivalent on social issues, as Davidson points out, it often offered an assessment of the existing social order that "proclaim[ed] a socially egalitarian message. It spoke for . . . orphans, beggar girls, factory girls, or other unfortunates, and it repeatedly advocated the general need for 'female education'" (73). The sensational newspaper literature and popular dime novels of the nineteenth century often brought up issues of slavery, empire expansion, frontier violence, and Indian removal and represented a wide range of perspectives on these contentious issues.[4] The popular literature of the nineteenth century was often speaking to cultural concerns that were, in return, shaping ideas about what it meant to be an American, which was really at the heart of the artistic goal of many American authors, at least in the early nineteenth century when authors and critics were trying to develop an American literature that would distinguish the young republic from the nations of Europe.

Because teaching nineteenth-century popular literature means teaching the social and political debates of the day—usually concentrated around issues of gender, class, race, and ethnicity—the literatures of minority authors and experiences are also associated with the teaching of popular literature. With a few exceptions, most of the Native American and African American authors writing in the nineteenth century didn't receive the popularity of some of their white peers. Making students aware of the stigma of popular literature—why many best sellers have been dropped from the canon of literature that is most often taught and studied—can also help them see why critiques of the dominant culture offered in the highly structured and sophisticated work of authors such as William Apess, Harriet E. Wilson, and Sarah Winnemucca ensured that their work was never widely circulated in the first place.

But I found that teaching popular and underrepresented literature in its historical, cultural, and political contexts made it difficult to place the literature within larger literary and artistic frames of reference. Due, perhaps, to the increasing demands on high school teachers and changes in curriculum standards, I found that my students had a limited background in the literary traditions these popular and underrepresented authors were shaping and responding to. My college is located in Texas, and many of my students were educated in the Texas public schools. A quick analysis of the table of contents of the Texas Grade 11 American Literature textbook reveals that the only literary traditions many of my students probably learned about in high school (if they remembered them at all) were very narrowly defined definitions of romanticism and the American gothic. Without a background in literary traditions and movements, how, for example, could students understand the role of women writers such as Caroline Kirkland and Harriet Beecher Stowe in anticipating the realism of the late nineteenth century, if they weren't aware of the male authors who later received recognition for developing that tradition? Or how could they appreciate sentimentality as a set of tropes and conventions not only used by popular women authors but also folded into the work of their now-canonical peers?[5]

I initially spoke to these issues of coverage and gaps in student knowledge by alternately teaching the course on more canonical authors one semester and then teaching a course on women and other underrepresented writers the next.[6] That way, I thought, my small department's overall curriculum in the major would still expose students to a wide range of nineteenth-century American authors and texts. But depending on which semester a major took my course, she or he would each receive a very different—yet still limited—perspective on the literary history of the United States in the nineteenth century. And by emphasizing the difference between canonical and popular traditions in the different versions of the course, I didn't want to reinforce the notion of a bifurcated canon, perpetuating the old idea from the Culture Wars that these traditions were somehow in opposition with and in competition with each other, in their own day and even in ours. I was also concerned that "bracketing off" popular writers from canonical writers might make women and minority writers seem like anomalies—and "how can the popular be anomalous?"—thereby leaving untouched assumptions about canon formation that privilege the already canonical white, male authors (Kolodny 297). As Paul Lauter puts it, I wanted to present the course material in such a way that students would understand that "the cultures and literatures of nineteenth-century America have to be seen not as separate, isolated enclaves but as changing, intermingling, growing organisms that—often to the grief of editors and teachers—simply will not altogether fit into any single organizational format" (1464).

I realized that in order to teach a representative literary history of the United States, fulfill my department's curricular needs, address my students' coverage issues, and stay true to my values as a teacher and a scholar, I needed to find a way that would allow me to teach an integrated literary history of the nineteenth century, *all in one course.* Using a classroom strategy called "literature circles," I was able to add several canonical texts without taking away too many popular and underrepresented texts from my original course syllabus. I have developed the course as a series of literature circle units that now makes it possible for the class to collectively read three different novels—one representing a popular, underrepresented, and canonical tradition—at the same time. I eventually changed the name of the course to Canons of Nineteenth-Century American Literature and used the literature circle format to make my students aware of multiple literary traditions that might have distinctive characteristics but that were often feeding off of and blending into each other. Through the course structure and assignments, I make my students aware of the idea of a shifting canon that reflects changing aesthetic values and contingencies of historical, social, and political mores of critics and audiences of various times, including their own.

What Are Literature Circles?

The literature circle format is a student-centered, collaborative approach to teaching literature originally developed for and primarily utilized in elementary and middle school classrooms. The objective of literature circles is to promote in-depth, student-driven discussion and higher-order thinking skills in younger students. Because literature circles promote "collaborative classrooms where students take increasing responsibility for choosing, reading, and discussing books," I have found that the literature circle class structure can be successfully adapted to the college classroom as well (Daniels).[7] Teachers use the literature circle format in a variety of ways (certainly I have adapted the format for my own purposes), but Harvey Daniels explains that they usually exhibit several distinctives, including students first choosing their own reading selection and then coming together in "small temporary groups . . . formed based on book choice" (18). One class of students might be separated into several small groups, with each group reading a *different* book. Another unique characteristic of this teaching strategy is that students use written responses to guide their reading and discussion; the fact that "discussion topics come from the students" means that "[t]he teacher serves as a *facilitator*, not a group member or instructor" (18). When they go well, literature circles promote student-centered and student-led discussion. The proponents of literature circles claim that as a result of students having choice in their reading materials and more autonomy in discussion, they are more likely to continue reading outside of class and to become lifelong readers.

Literature circles make it possible for one class of students to read several different books at the same time. Therefore, literature circles created the opportunity for students in my nineteenth-century American literature course to read several different novels simultaneously—although the small groups would read different works representing different literary traditions. This was the perfect way to showcase the many traditions of American literature and to expose one class to a wide range of authors and texts, without having to cut any one author, work, or tradition from the version of my syllabus that favored women and popular writers or the version that featured canonical authors traditionally associated with the "masterpieces" of nineteenth-century American literature.

In my class, we devote two weeks to each literature circle unit. I usually integrate three to four units into each semester and use the other class sessions for the study of shared texts or to read critical texts. What distinguishes the literature circle format from other small-group discussion formats is that each member of the group has a specific role and prepares an assignment before the class session. The students assign themselves one of five roles and prepare a brief, one- to two-page paper based on their role that they bring to class to guide their group discussions. The idea behind the specific group roles is that "readers who approach a text with clear-cut, conscious purposes will comprehend more" (Daniels 13). Before we begin the first literature circle, I give students a handout that explains each role and my expectations for the short paper each group member will write:[8]

1. Summarizer: Prepares a brief and concise summary of the day's reading assignment;
2. Question Asker: Develops about ten higher-order discussion questions to promote critical and analytical thinking about the literature;
3. Connector: Finds connections between the book and other literature and literary movements studied in this class or other courses;
4. Close Reader: Locates significant passages and analyzes them in relation to the larger work, the unit theme, and the overall concerns of the course;
5. Researcher: Finds background information on the author or historical or cultural contexts that will enhance the group's understanding and interpretation of the literature.

In the class sessions over each two-week unit, each group reads and discusses their own novel, but in class discussions and writing assignments, students look for connections among the texts that speak to the larger concerns of the unit and the course, specifically, "what is gained and lost by expanding the canon of literatures traditionally taught and studied to include popular and underrepresented literary traditions." I will occasionally provide supplemental mini-lectures that draw all three works together, and at one point during each unit each group will give an informal presentation on their novel to the other groups, followed by a student-led discussion that gets the students to see linkages between each group's novels and, over the course of the semester, the fluidity between canonical, popular, and underrepresented literary traditions.

Literature Circles and an Integrated Nineteenth-Century American Literary History

Using literature circles in this class, I was able to add several canonical texts to my course syllabus without taking away too many popular or underrepresented texts. Every thematically based unit contains one novel that might come from a canonical, popular, and/or underrepresented tradition. Of course these categories themselves are ahistorical and somewhat arbitrary, and my choice and placement of novels within these categories could be called into question. These units and categories aren't perfect and themselves represent a perspective full of thoroughly modern assumptions and values. But this actually leads to rich class discussion about the fluidity and arbitrary nature of some of these categories and placements and points toward larger issues I want my students to think about as English majors, such as the shifting nature of aesthetic values, critical categories, and canon formation. Nevertheless, I attempt to organize the unit themes around literary movements or the major social, historical, and artistic concerns that were prompting authors to write and compelling audiences to read their work. Before each unit begins, I provide a list of overarching questions that frame the small group discussions and guide students as they write their short, role-based essays (see "Supplement to Tanglen Essay" in the appendix).

In a unit I call "National Romance and the Historical Novel," I aim to get students to think about the role of the novel as nineteenth-century authors worked with the goal of creating a distinctively American identity, literature, and culture. One literature circle group reads Nathaniel Hawthorne's 1851 *The House of the Seven Gables* (a canonical author), another group reads Lydia Maria Child's 1824 *Hobomok* (an underrepresented author and text, at least in our day), and yet another group reads James Fenimore Cooper's 1826 *The Last of the Mohicans* (a popular author and text, especially in the nineteenth century). Another version of this unit, called "Romance, National History, and the Indian Reform Novel," keeps *Hobomok* and *The Last of the Mohicans* but replaces the Hawthorne novel with Catherine Maria Sedgwick's *Hope Leslie* (1827). Yet another configuration of this unit, which drops the focus on the portrayal of American Indian characters and issues, focuses more on various nineteenth-century interpretations of "romance" and "romanticism"; it blends *The Blithedale Romance* (1852), *The Hermaphrodite* (c. 1840s) by Julia Ward Howe (an underrepresented work by a popular author), and *Woman in the Nineteenth-Century* (1845) by Margaret Fuller. This version of the unit tends to lend itself to discussions of gender roles in society and artistic communities.

The next unit, "Literatures of Slavery, Race, and Abolition," emphasizes the role literature had in instituting ideas about slavery and race-based social prejudice. This unit includes Harriet Beecher Stowe's *Uncle Tom's Cabin*, Harriet Jacobs' *Incidents in the Life of a Slave Girl* (1859), and William Wells Brown's *Clotel* (1853). I might include Martin Delany's *Blake* (1859–1862) in this unit, and I sometimes integrate Herman Melville's *Benito Cereno* (1855) into it or have the class read the Melville together after we have completed the unit. In this literature circle, we consider the relationship between literature and history, especially the way that distinctions between "literature" and "history" can blend into each other. The fact that nineteenth-century audiences and authors expected literature to have an effect on social outcomes is a contrast to the present-day expectation of many of my students that "good" literature and art would have no social objectives.

Another unit, representing literary movements at the end of the nineteenth century, is organized around the topic "Realism, Naturalism, and Social Reform." This unit is meant not only to introduce students to the traditionally understood notions of realism, naturalism, and regionalism but also to promote the idea that realism was a means for some authors to bring about awareness of social problems, and to advocate for reform. Configurations of this unit have included Theodore Dreiser's *Sister Carrie* (1900), representing a traditionally understood example of realism, along with Elizabeth Stuart Phelps's 1871 *The Silent Partner* and Sarah Winnemucca's *Life among the Piutes* (1883), both of which use realistic strategies to bring awareness to the plight of factory girls or the United States government's unjust American Indian policies. Other iterations of this unit have included Charles Chesnutt's *The Marrow of Tradition* (1901), which presents the daily realities of African Americans in the post-Reconstruction South. By combining texts that hope to leave a mark upon the world with realistic authors who claimed to simply and "realistically" hold up a mirror to nature, students see a variety of interpretations of the same literary movement. The formations and pairings in this particular unit make students rethink the notion of "genre" as a fixed category, especially as I ask them to consider the distinction Kenneth Warren makes between realism and sentimentality, one of the more popular literature genres of the nineteenth century, when he claims that in realistic fiction "the redemption of the individual lay within the social world," whereas in sentimental fiction "the redemption of the social world lay within the individual" (75–76).

One unintentional, yet nonetheless significant, coincidence in using this classroom approach of discussing nineteenth-century American literature in small groups is that it possibly mirrors the reading and interpretation strategies of nineteenth-century audiences. The women's book club was an institution in the nineteenth century, with groups of women meeting to discuss literature becoming a "vital element in the women's intellectual tradition in America" (Daniels 30). From the more formal salons in New England, to the small book clubs that popped up in the Midwest and on frontier settlements, throughout the nineteenth century, collaborative and group experiences of reading were valued by many nineteenth-century readers.[9]

Advantages and Limitations of Literature Circles

Along with solving the pedagogical and critical dilemma of my course, I found that literature circles promoted the type of student-centered discussion that I valued as a feminist teacher and scholar. Often the students run the class sessions themselves, and I fade into the background as they explore their own ideas about the literature. Yet that isn't to say that there aren't potential drawbacks to integrating literature circles into a college literature classroom. While the student-centered discussion promotes deeper thinking about the literature, it does take control away from the professor. Since I'm not leading discussions or preparing the daily discussion questions that students explore in class, I'm not always sure if students are catching on to the key passages or nuances in plot and character that affect the cultural work and meaning of the text. But I can check for student comprehension by reading their daily responses and then supplementing gaps in that comprehension with facilitative comments on those daily papers. I try to anticipate information that students will need to fully understand their texts by framing each unit with discussion questions and augmenting some of the discussion sessions with occasional mini-lectures to provide appropriate background and contextual information.

Another possible concern—from a practical perspective—is that literature circles create a lot of reading, prep work, and grading for the professor. It is true that I need to be prepared to discuss and answer questions about three different novels in any given class session. This is something that was difficult the first few times I taught this course using the literature circle structure, but heavy preparation is typical for any new iteration of a course. At this point I can now pull from several semesters' worth of course notes to help me prepare for students' questions and to provide relevant background information. But the point of structuring the class like this is to place the responsibility of the discussion on the students, so that they end up doing most of the intellectual work of the course. Once I step back, I find that the students are usually capable of filling in the gaps and making the connections that I would usually make for them in a traditional lecture or professor-facilitated classroom format. The daily grading of group-member short essays does begin to get onerous. However, as these are shorter essays that don't always require a lot of revision and feedback, I have found that they can be graded quite quickly. And the constant writing and feedback (even minimal), over the course of the semester, does make students better writers and promotes the development of sharper arguments in their final essays.

But what the students get from the literature circle format far outweighs any of these drawbacks and possible inconveniences. First, although students won't read all of the literature circle novels on the syllabus, this expanded syllabus does provide them with a more extended reading list and bibliography of primary sources useful for their own reading and study, especially for students preparing for graduate work and studying for the GRE, which still does emphasize more canonical authors and texts over popular and underrepresented authors and texts. But rather than pursue graduate study, many of the English majors at my institution will go on to become language arts or high school English teachers in the state of Texas. Literature circles are identified by the National Council for Teachers of English (NCTE) as a "best practice" in the teaching of reading and writing (Daniels 7).

Popular and noncanonical works by women and minority writers tend to address issues of racial, class, ethnic, and sexual difference, all contentious issues in curriculum battles in places like Arizona and Texas. This is especially relevant in the context of teaching high school English in Texas (where many of my students will become certified to teach), a national battleground for textbook formulation and public school curriculum.[10] For my students, who in their future classrooms might be limited in what they teach based on a narrow and ideologically formed curriculum, being exposed to a wider range of literature and possible strategies for integrating these literatures into their classes could be a possible benefit.

My students have told me they like being able to choose their own texts and come up with their own reading schedule, and that they are more likely to do the class reading because they have to answer to their classmates and group members if they don't. Indeed, the collaborative benefit of literature circles shouldn't be overlooked. The Association of American Colleges and Universities (AAC&U), a clearinghouse for liberal arts education research and advocacy, has identified ten high-impact educational practices, including "collaborative projects and assignments," which promote students' "learning to work and solve problems in the company of others, and sharpening one's own understanding by listening seriously to the insights of others, especially those with different backgrounds and life experiences" (AAC&U). But as a teacher of literature, the primary benefit of the use of literature circles in this course is that it allows the students to be exposed to both "popular" and "canonical" authors and texts, and most important, provides opportunities for students to engage in the debates surrounding the politics of canon formation, to become aware of the arbitrary nature of aesthetic values and assumptions, and to articulate *for themselves* what is gained and lost by expanding the canon of American literature to include popular and underrepresented texts and multiple literary traditions.

Gender, Romance, and Resisting Readers

"[*Dragonwyck* shows that] if trouble lurks in popular fiction, it resides in *reading* in [a particular way], not in the books themselves."
—KATHLEEN M. THERRIEN, "'One Would Die Rather Than Speak . . . about Such Subjects': Exploring Class, Gender, and Hegemony in Anya Seton's *Dragonwyck*"

"In the end . . . it proved most effective to incorporate romance fiction into a theory classroom—already a space of discovery, debate, and (often) bewilderment."—ANTONIA LOSANO, "Sneaking It In at the End: Teaching Popular Romance in the Liberal Arts Classroom"

"One Would Die Rather Than Speak . . . about Such Subjects"

Exploring Class, Gender, and Hegemony in Anya Seton's Dragonwyck

KATHLEEN M. THERRIEN

⌒

THE TITLE OF this collection, *Teaching Tainted Lit*, gave me pause. As an academic who wrote her dissertation on mass-market romance novels and has focused largely on popular texts from the nineteenth and twentieth centuries, I long ago abandoned any sense that reading and teaching popular literature are outré, improper, or unacceptable. I am, of course, fully aware that a diet of nothing but Twinkies, *Twilight*, and Top Twenty can produce a nasty sort of intellectual anemia, but I am also convinced that popular texts are not merely empty-calorie literary junk food or the equivalent of textual botulism—poisonous to the intellect. In doing initial research for this essay, however, I came upon a stunning reminder of just how powerful, how resonant, the "tainting" concept can be. First I discovered that, according to the MLA Bibliography database, almost no sustained critical work has been done recently on Anya Seton, let alone on her novel *Dragonwyck*. And second, I found that one of the few articles that mentioned her positioned her novels as, essentially, exemplars of the "tainted."

In her 1958 article "Teaching Judgment of Prose Fiction," high school teacher Elizabeth Williams laments "an embarrassing experience" of seeing "three girls and a boy from the previous year's senior class, all with B-plus grades, . . .with armfuls of books by Anya Seton, Grace Livingston Hill, and Florence Means" (495). Williams "restrained [her] impulses to give a postgraduate lesson then and there" (495), but she was motivated to create a program to mold students' taste. They would be informed of what readers *really* like: "[M]ost readers enjoy prose writing that flatters them with subtleness—not everything labeled and told obviously; that we like, too, enough vividness and reality or realism to fit the purpose—even in fanciful tales—to hold our belief" (498). They would be given the powers of "discrimination" (497) to rate books as "inferior, middling, or superior" (498) and to select "the rewarding, better book" (496). Even teachers would be encouraged to take standardized tests of taste and discuss the results with students to "show how insufficient scrutiny gives wrong results" (497).

In Williams's eyes, her students' selection of popular texts is evidence of insufficient and improper cultivation of "taste," since enjoyment of popular novels like Seton's is a self-deluded illusion at best—after all, one could not truly *enjoy* such a text—and a guilty pleasure at worst, an experience rife with "wrong[ness]," "mistakes," and even "hazards" (497). Within this paradigm, a Seton novel is clearly positioned as tainted—as something that has the power to lead readers to be "wrong" and make "mistakes" and that can even, ultimately, cause harm to the reader.[1]

More than fifty years have passed since Williams's moment of dismay at the library, and while her primary conviction—that popular fiction must be avoided—may have faded within the academy, her secondary conviction—that popular novels, or at least certain kinds of popular texts, cannot be truly *read* and can offer no "reward"—still has resonance. It can be detected in the simple fact that despite decades of scholarly work on women authors and popular texts, almost nothing has been published on Seton, whose novels were very popular indeed in the mid-twentieth century. It can be sensed in the fact that mass-market romance novels are still rarely addressed in the scholarly arena.[2] It can be seen in the frequent use of the word "consume" (as opposed to "read") when popular fiction is discussed. It can be heard when my honors students ask me whether the brightly illustrated graphic novel listed as a required text for my course is *really* the book they need.

And it can be felt strongly in our initial discussions of Seton's *Dragonwyck* in my Women's Popular Fiction course. Once students see the phrases "gothic romance," "dark, terrible secrets," and "remarkable passions" on the back cover,[3] they tend to slide into autopilot reading mode, focusing on their enjoyment of the plot and some of the text's more obvious cultural critiques. But by reading this way they miss a fascinating glimpse at some ways in which certain powerful ideologies were being identified (or not), contested, valorized, and negotiated at the time of the novel's production.

I have found that the best way to address this—and, in the process, enhance students' understanding of a key concept in cultural studies—is to utilize Dick Hebdige's immensely useful framing of hegemony in his classic study *Subculture: The Meaning of Style*. Hebdige draws particularly upon the work of Stuart Hall, Roland Barthes, and Louis Althusser to craft a discussion of ideology and hegemony in the Birmingham School tradition that is highly accessible (and often highly appealing) to students. Quoting Hall, he explains that "[t]he term hegemony refers to a situation in which a provisional alliance of certain social groups can exert 'total social authority' over other subordinate groups, not simply by coercion or by the direct imposition of ruling ideas, but by 'winning and shaping consent so that the power of the dominant classes appears both legitimate and natural'" (15–16). Again quoting Hall, he argues that "hegemonic power, precisely *because* it requires the consent of the dominated majority, can never be permanently exercised by the same alliance of 'class fractions.' . . . 'Hegemony is, as Gramsci said, a "moving equilibrium" containing relations of forces favourable or unfavourable to this or that tendency'" (16).[4]

I would argue that in a thoughtful and self-reflexive reading of *Dragonwyck*, two crucial dynamics within this argument—the "provisional alliances" of "class fractions" and dominant social groups and the continually moving equilibria both between those groups and between those groups and the people they dominate—may be seen with remarkable clarity. They become visible within the plot itself, wherein continually shifting alliances of cultural forces exercise power, and within the reader's recognition of the heroine's consent to various forms of power. They may also be seen within the reader him/herself, who, like the heroine, may unwittingly consent to dominant ideologies even while assuming that s/he is resisting them.

In her essay "'At last I can tell it to someone!': Feminine Point of

View and Subjectivity in the Gothic Romance Film of the 1940s," which touches very briefly on *Dragonwyck* and its filmic adaptation, Diane Waldman affirms that wartime and postwar gothics "dramatize the attempts of a patriarchal order to achieve hegemony over feminine perception and interpretation" (34), and she argues that they utilize a series of generic textual elements to do so: the heroine's doubting of her own perceptions of her husband's actions, the husband's attempts to manipulate the heroine's understanding, the isolated heroine's inability to contextualize and reality-check her perceptions, and the presence of a secondary male character who at least appears to validate her.[5] But while Waldman emphasizes the husband's active subversion and redirection of the heroine's perceptions of her situation, I will argue that the *heroine*, located within an ideological and discursive matrix that informs her sense of reality and logic, actually subverts and redirects her own perceptions—and does so even at the end.[6] To understand how my readings of and subsequent pedagogical approaches to the text work, however, one must first understand the inner dynamics of the text itself and the ways in which *it* explores reading—and misreading. And I believe that such understanding is best achieved through a close reading that unpacks the text's internal dynamics and then examines them in light of Hebdige's paradigm of hegemony.

∽

Dragonwyck, a best-seller upon its publication in 1944, is the story of Miranda Wells. Unlike Amber St. Clare, the clever and bold heroine of Kathleen Windsor's contemporaneous *Forever Amber*,[7] Miranda is neither particularly sharp nor unconventional. She is, however, romantic and highly attuned to beauty; she therefore feels like a fish out of water on her family's small farm, where her natural "fastidiousness and dainty ways" (7) lead to ridicule and alienation. She wishes desperately to leave and to marry a wealthy, glamorous man. These inchoate dreams arise in part from her reading of novels such as *The Beautiful Adulteress*, which she does not entirely understand—"she had not the vaguest notion of the horrifying behavior that resulted in one's becoming an adulteress" (2)—but which she loves for their "glorious palpitating romance" (2). *Dragonwyck*'s treatment of Miranda's reading could be read as an (albeit ironic) metafictive indictment of "tainted" literature and its attendant perils, since *The Beautiful Adulteress* clearly falls into the gothic genre that *Dragonwyck* itself draws upon. But I would argue that this scene serves a very different cautionary function. It is Miranda's essentially clueless reading of novels and lack of intellectual engagement with them that the text highlights here: if trouble lurks in popular fiction, it resides in *reading* the way Miranda does, not in the books themselves. This calling of attention to the ways that popular fiction is read—particularly at the outset of the novel—is particularly striking because it sets up, or at least suggests, both a strategy for engaging with the rest of the novel and a remarkably astute and self-referential commentary on the reading of popular fiction itself. In other words, *Dragonwyck* poses a pointed riposte to the Elizabeth Williamses of the world: while it is certainly not a didactic text, it does implicitly argue that popular fiction, if read thoughtfully and with self-awareness, allows the reader to recognize, consider, and engage critically with the world—particularly with the ideological structures that, left unheeded and unseen, inform Miranda's own tumultuous, and in many ways tragic, narrative and questionably happy ending.

By playing out the idea of Miranda as uncritical reader of the texts—literary, social, and personal—set before her, the novel creates a complex tripartite approach by which it contests and negotiates ideologies of identity and power. It allows the critically engaged reader to enter into those negotiations, pressing him or her all the while to not behave like Miranda—to not merely absorb what is presented unquestioningly, evaluate it thoughtlessly, and repress nascent insights about it but instead to be, and remain, aware of his or her own reading process. Intriguingly, though, the third stage of the text's exploration of structures of power actually *relies* upon the reader's falling into precisely the sort of reading that Miranda does in order to generate the imaginative resolution of ideological conflict required for a generically conventional conclusion. And the reader who does not do so may find, instead of a "happy ending," a remarkably chilling depiction of the self-preserving power of hegemonic structures.

⌢

The text's first level of ideological critique, which focuses upon gender, is quite explicit. At the novel's outset, Miranda's father Ephraim attempts to exercise absolute control over his family and regards dissent, especially from women, as "foolish" (11). When Miranda tells him that she'd like to leave the family farm, he insults her roundly for not wanting to settle down with a local boy and informs her that "[her] opinion is of no consequence whatsoever" (12). His authority is predicated upon a hegemonic structure wherein patriarchy and conservative Protestant theology are allied and mutually reinforcing, one shifting into a position of power when the other is challenged: "God's will usually seemed to coincide with her father's, and against this partnership there was no hope of appeal" (10).

Even if she is not initially "consciously critical" (25), Miranda is able to recognize her father's authoritarian attitudes toward women, and his unconscious but self-serving imbrication of theology and misogyny, for what they are. This consciousness allows her to subvert Ephraim's power by using one of his own tools against him when he denies her request to leave the farm. She claims to have "a leading" (13) during family prayer and asks her father if she can perform a "test" to see if her revelation is correct. Knowing perfectly well that the much-read old family Bible will fall open to one of her father's favorite passages, she pretends to randomly open the book and point toward the passage in which Abraham sends Hagar away (13–14). Since God seems to confirm Miranda and her mother's desire for her to depart, and since resistance would pull back the curtain on how very "coincidental" God's agreements with Ephraim are, Ephraim is trapped into allowing her to go.

Miranda assumes that life on her cousin Nicholas Van Ryn's estate, Dragonwyck, will be an escape from attitudes like her father's. In her mind, a "very grand personage . . . lord of a large manor" (5) could be nothing like the small-minded, small-farming Ephraim, and when she meets Nicholas, her logic seems to be confirmed. While Ephraim is devout, frugal, and suspicious of what he considers "foolish extravagance" (23), Nicholas enjoys luxury; he is both "a hedonist and an atheist" (28). And when Ephraim, disconcerted by Nicholas's assertion that "his" tenant farmers cannot buy the land they work, says "I would rather . . . own one half-acre of barren stony land myself free and clear, than work the richest farm in the country for someone else," Nicholas retorts, "Then you're very foolish" (29).

What Miranda does not recognize as she listens to their conversations and compares her father unfavorably to her glamorous relative is that *both* of their personal philosophies devolve upon the ability to exercise authority in one's perceived realm of power. Both see that ability as resting in ownership of property, control of resources and of others, alignment with (and the approval of) powerful institutional structures of authority, and male privilege. In other words, Miranda misreads their dialogue—and Nicholas; in doing so, she begins to ally herself with him, a position within which she implicitly consents to his view of the world and his exercises of power. This dynamic of generated consent is grounded, in large part, in another alliance of cultural and political-economic forces—in this case, class and popular media.

Miranda's perceptions and readings of the world have been shaped by discourses and mass media, such as *Godey's Lady's Book* and sensational novels, that validate, celebrate, and naturalize class-based attitudes like Nicholas's and class-marked aesthetic objects, such as gourmet foods and luxurious decor. The Astor House, where Nicholas lodges his visitors en route to Dragonwyck, stands in Miranda's mind as an exemplar of aesthetically pleasing space, and his access to this institution is wonderful to her. It is therefore unsurprising that Miranda does not question whether Nicholas is, in fact, as wonderful as he appears; she simply sees him as doubly validated—first, by the seemingly seamless garment of approval created by allied media and class forces, and second, by his apparent difference from that which she knows is oppressive.

Unfortunately and ironically, given her clever recognition of her father's conflation of himself with the Lord, Miranda does not consider that the "lord of a . . . manor" may *not*, in fact, be all that different from Ephraim. Her misreading is confirmed when she boards ship for Dragonwyck:

> They reached the gangplank, an ornate affair of mahogany and red plush carpeting. Miranda stopped uncertainly at its foot, instinctively waiting for Nicholas to lead the way.
>
> He shook his head. "You must go first. Always a lady precedes her escort."

"Oh, to be sure," she said quickly. Pa had always led his flock but this was different, the ways of gentry. She would not make that mistake again. (33)

What Miranda sees as "different" behavior is actually just a different manifestation of the same core assumption: that a man has the right to determine where a woman walks and that a woman "must" conform to that determination (failure to do so is a "mistake"). Such a determination is based upon the man's assumed power in relation to the woman,[8] and Nicholas's positioning within and embrace of that patriarchal mindset is made explicitly clear in the preceding passage:

Her naïveté amused him. It would be interesting to form this immature mind, to teach it and mould it. She would have much to learn before she would do him credit as his cousin. Those hideous clothes must be rectified. She must lose the flat drawl that proclaimed her Yankee upbringing. . . . her table manners in general needed correction. She must learn how to walk with dignity. . . . She was unpoised. . . . But she would learn easily. (32–33)

Nicholas assumes that he both can and should determine Miranda's "location" in both space and culture; he has the right, he believes, to quite literally reposition and reconstruct her, changing the signifiers—accent, clothing, behaviors—that make her who she is, both in terms of self-signification and cultural affiliation. But since he frames his sexist behavior as a sort of benevolent deference, Miranda, who is accustomed to and identifies sexism as the explicit imposition of power within a context of directly articulated assumptions of masculine superiority, is unable to see it. And because she has internalized ideologies that conflate certain kinds of chivalrous behavior with romance, heroism, and love, she actually thinks that Nicholas's attitudes and actions are grounded in respect for women, not an assumption of power over them. Therefore, rather than resenting being led, she cherishes being directed to the front.

～

While Miranda is not able to see that she has simply moved from frying pan to fire, students often are. Both Nicholas's own thoughts and the narrative voice's tone and descriptions invite the reader to step back and read Nicholas differently than Miranda does. This second level of the novel's engagement with ideologies of gender—one in which the reader is able and invited to recognize oppressive attitudes when the primary character cannot—is not merely an advisory to read everything carefully and critically. It also continues the exploration of hegemony initiated in the opening chapters, suggesting that when one reinforcing ideology (in this case, theology) is delegitimated, another (in this case, class) may slot into place, ultimately maintaining the core power structure by making it appear to be something quite different from, and less oppressive than, what it actually is. The text also opens up this critique by creating an elaborate textual pun on Nicholas's weaponizing, as it were, of class-based discourses of civility and aesthetics.

Nicholas's home, Dragonwyck, is a fictionalized version of a Hudson Valley hereditary estate controlled by an ethnically Dutch owner, or patroon (69),[9] and Nicholas takes this term quite literally: "true to his birth and an upbringing far less democratic than that of an English nobleman, [he] delighted in the rôle of patron. He had patterned himself half-consciously on a Lorenzo de Medici or a Prince Esterhazy" (36). Just as he feels entitled to direct and remake Miranda, he feels entitled to control the lives and work of the tenants he calls "[m]y farmers" (28) and to promote and assist certain artists, effectively shaping and controlling the physical and cultural landscapes. But since Miranda cannot see his behavior toward her for what it is, it's not surprising that she also misreads his attitudes toward those he patronizes. Deeply invested in ideologies of class, she sees Nicholas as someone who has the right to codify what is "right" and "wrong" in any given situation and to legislate behavior.

She views Nicholas's patronage in a purely pragmatic light as well: he is her ticket off the farm and away from a world she experiences as stultifying. Miranda, with her love of beauty and dislike of manual labor, feels trapped by more than her father; she has been born into a world that provides no space for her to—to use a cheesy modern term—self-actualize. It is not surprising, then, that in her desperation to find a world into which she can fit and to receive some sort of validation for herself as herself, Miranda reads wealthy, sophisticated, educated Nicholas as a means to an end and embraces the attitudes that, at long last, privilege her way of being.

Caught in this web of powerful ideologies and her own needs,

Miranda is unable (and, perhaps, unwilling) to see that Nicholas views her as a project, not a person needing space to grow and thrive: like a commissioned painting, she is a work of art being created to his specifications, one that will "do him credit as his cousin" (32). She therefore eagerly absorbs Nicholas's amused and patronizing tutelage, assenting to his will and consenting to his direction of nearly all of her actions. When he purchases an entirely new wardrobe for her, providing everything from dresses and "more intimate garments" (53) to perfume and tooth powder, she initially blushes at "an unpleasant aspect of charity to this gift" (53); she senses the power dynamic implicit in it and recoils at it. But in a moment of what Waldman calls the classically gothic "hesitation between two possible interpretations of events" (31), she quickly persuades herself that Nicholas "would be annoyed if she made a fuss . . . think her countrified and silly. And the clothes were so beautiful" (53). Similarly, when he informs her that she is "rather ignorant" and that he will "map out a plan of reading for [her]" (36), she is temporarily hurt but soon stops reading the Bible, seeing it as "coarse and uninspiring" (98), and reads Hawthorne instead because Nicholas recommends him. She also embraces Nicholas's political and economic positions.

By quashing her nascent resistant readings of Nicholas's actions and instead unquestioningly aligning herself with him—and, by extension, consenting to the institutions and cultural forces that inform and maintain *his* power—Miranda feels, for the first time in her life, empowered. Ephraim had always insisted that her attitudes toward beauty and labor, her Otherness, made her undeserving of autonomy and unqualified to make judgments about herself or the world. But with these same qualities now aligned with and given the stamp of "approval" by a powerful man widely recognized as having what Williams might call "taste" in both aesthetic and social matters, Miranda finally feels able to take the upper hand in social relations. When she meets a number of men involved in the tenant rent revolts, for example, she chastises them, and in a move eerily reminiscent of Nicholas's treatment of her, informs them of how they should see themselves, saying, "I should think you'd be ashamed" (106).[10] She also overcomes the insecurity she feels when she hears several of Nicholas's old-money party guests criticizing her, silencing them when she returns to the party with an "erect, defiant back" (82).

Furthermore, as she becomes more and more aligned with Nicholas and his ideologies, she begins to read her home community and family in much the same way he first read her. She "notice[s] things that had never bothered her before. Had the boys always gulped like that, and wiped their mouths on the back of their hands? And after Nicholas's chivalrous politeness, it was disconcerting to see that her mother and sister must wait for each dish until the hungry males had helped themselves" (145). Reading in alignment and alliance with powerful class forces, Miranda is no longer "namby-pamby" and "mincing" (12); instead, her family is "uncouth" (144). And in her newly critical and patronizing survey of her family, she does not see the parallels between Ephraim's behaviors and attitudes and those of the people in her newly adopted world—people now including herself.

For, just as her father undergirds his patriarchal power by aligning himself with the Lord, she now allies herself with the lord of the manor to shore up her perceptions of herself as empowered, superior, and authorized to judge. Unlike Ephraim, however, Miranda does not possess any real, culturally sanctioned power of her own. She is a woman, she does not possess any property or financial resources of her own, and she does not have any innate talent for performing respectable, marketable work (unlike her sister and mother, who are savvy farm workers and managers). Her delusions of power therefore render her painfully vulnerable: the only way she can continue to feel empowered is to entirely ally herself with Nicholas, believe that he is right in what he thinks and does, and remain in his favor by consenting to both his demands and his vision of the world.

The text makes this vulnerability, and the power relations undergirding it, explicit in its abuse subplots. Nicholas, convinced that the power granted to him as a wealthy, sophisticated man is natural and right, feels entitled to use that power any way he sees fit. Furthermore, he enjoys feeling powerful and seeks out ways to feel dominant and in control of others and his world; such ongoing exercises, in turn, help to naturalize power relations, rendering them part of the texture of everyday life and making them "just the way things are." Not surprisingly, given the patriarchal nature of his culture and power, one of the ways in which he exercises power is abuse of the women in his life. He disregards his daughter, Katrine, feeling that only sons matter. He neglects and emotionally abuses his wife, Johanna, for Nicholas values women only in relation to what they are able to provide him personally or socially; because Johanna has not produced a male heir, is not sophisticated company, and is no longer beautiful, the only "use value" she still possesses lies in her illustrious family background and concomitant social position, both of which reflect well on him.

Johanna quite literally embodies the ramifications of Nicholas's attitudes. Spurned, lonely, and starved for affection—"[f]or three years [Nicholas] had not shared her bed" (65)—Johanna overeats to the point of morbid obesity. The local doctor, Jefferson Turner, recognizes that, "[b]aulked of other passions, she had gradually poured all her desires into one channel. It's a form of lust, he thought with pitying distaste, and in itself a disease" (128). But while he recognizes the sad truth of Johanna's situation, Jeff actually sides, at least in part, with Nicholas: when Johanna speaks wistfully about the oleander flowers Nicholas has given her, he thinks, "Evidently the patroon did not often trouble himself to bring his wife flowers . . . and in truth, were I married to this lump of suet, I wouldn't either" (128).

Such a reading dehumanizes and condemns Johanna while exonerating Nicholas, leaving him not only free to continue his emotional abuse but supported in it. This, in turn, feeds Nicholas's vision of his own rightness, a vision he maintains even when he kills Johanna by feeding her poison in a cake: as far as he is concerned, *she* is responsible for her own death; she chose to eat the cake, so "[h]er foul gluttony has killed her" (134). In his own eyes, he is not only innocent but benevolent. Nicholas, not surprisingly, is a eugenicist, and he had previously proclaimed that "[i]t would be far better for the race if the ugly and useless ones were eliminated" (62). His murder of Johanna suggests, again, an elision of gender and class ideologies: just as he sees himself as entitled and able to deploy his class- and gender-based power to remake Miranda, control his tenants, and patronize artists to create an aesthetically pleasing world that serves and advances his purposes, he sees himself as entitled to remove his "ugly and useless" wife.

Miranda, like Jeff Turner, is unable to sympathize with Johanna, let alone empathize with her. She views the older woman's obesity with disgust, and her negative response is fanned by Johanna's own barely concealed resentment of the girl.[11] Any moments of connection Miranda does feel with Johanna are quickly undermined by her increasing identification and alliance with Nicholas. When, for example, Miranda witnesses Johanna's "expression of helpless bewilderment" (102) during a marital spat and thinks, "Can it be that she's frightened?" she quickly revises her initial—and, sadly, accurate—reading: "Nicholas was always so courteous . . . he usually did exactly as Johanna wished. . . . What a fool she is! thought the girl impatiently, and forgot Johanna, whose wishes were negligible now that Nicholas had taken hold of the situation" (102).

The text clearly suggests that because the women see each other as rivals for a valued resource (Nicholas's attention and validation and their concomitant social power), Nicholas subtly positions them to turn on each other, not on him, strengthening his own position and weakening their own. Also, each reads the other through differing facets of the same set of class-based social paradigms and coded differences: Miranda sees Johanna as fat, lazy, demanding, and snobbish, all of which she—and much of dominant society—condemns; Johanna, in turn, sees Miranda as common, ineffectual, graspingly ambitious, and a tart-in-the-making, all of which she—and much of dominant society—condemns. Unable to recognize and aid each other as potential allies—as women suffering the effects of patriarchal power—Miranda and Johanna are instead isolated, each seeing the other as Other and herself as concomitantly empowered, each thereby coopted into and participating in the very structure that is harming her.

⌒

After Johanna's death, the narrative takes what appears to be a classic romance plot turn: beautiful, young, naïve, essentially penniless Miranda marries handsome, wealthy, powerful, saturnine Nicholas. But marriage does not somehow "rescue" Miranda, giving her autonomy and value. Instead, any power she has gained is contingent upon her connection to Nicholas and his "approval" of her; were she to recognize his oppressive behavior and patriarchal attitudes for what they are and rebel against or reject him, she would lose it. So, in her desperation, Miranda quashes her growing recognition of the reality of her situation. Each time she reads Nicholas and his actions correctly, she convinces herself that she has actually *mis*-perceived, *mis*-read, rewriting reality to fit the ideological structures of Nicholas's world, implicitly consenting to his power and paradigms.

And the reader is once again positioned to recognize more than Miranda does, both about Nicholas and herself. Nicholas feels that, in marrying Miranda, he has simply gained a valuable resource that he can exploit for his own purposes and aggrandizement. He makes this frighteningly clear in the sexual dimension of their relationship. When he first proposes to Miranda,

> [w]ith one violent motion he jerked her up against him. He kissed her savagely, and against her shrinking breasts she felt the pounding of his heart.
>
> "No, no—" she whispered, terrified, struggling to push him back.
>
> He raised his head. . . . He stood up, gave a short laugh. "If I wished 'Yes,' do you think your silly 'No, No' would stop me?" (138)

Unable to fit this overtly abusive Nicholas into her vision of him, distrusting her own perceptions, and frightened of losing him and everything he represents, Miranda quickly revises her response: "[N]ow that he stood apart from her, again cool and controlled, her eyes filled and she looked at him with pleading" (138).

Not surprisingly, after they marry, Nicholas's behavior takes a turn for the truly brutal. When he first approaches her on their wedding night, she again says, "No, no, please—" but this time "[h]e picked her up and threw her across the darkened bed" (173). The next morning, it is clear that she has been brutally raped; she acknowledges the "livid marks" (174) on her arms and breasts, and the memory of the abuse she has endured prompts her to try to flee. Even when she looks at her sleeping husband and thinks, "This was not the same man who had inflicted on her the lurid-streaked blackness of those hours just past, who had violated without pity her soul as well as her body" (174), she remains "poised for flight" (174). However, Nicholas ties her back to him with a double knot: he reminds her of her legal status, saying, "You can't leave me. . . . Don't you know that? Nothing but death will ever separate us" (175), and he gaslights her by behaving like a tender lover. He makes her once again doubt her own perceptions, and she tells herself, "This is the way he really is. . . I must never forget that no matter what he does or says, he's really good and he does love me" (175).

At this point, the narrative voice intervenes, shattering any (mis)readings that concur with Miranda's: "[Her thoughts were] the beginning of a long and painfully maintained self-deception, for the precise type of goodness and love for which her heart yearned had not existed in Nicholas since he was twelve, and his mother died" (175). So Miranda's ongoing self-deception—her misreading—may be frustrating to the reader. But having committed herself entirely to both Nicholas and his world view, Miranda cannot, at this point, *not* deceive herself. Her inability to accurately read her situation is also compounded by her isolation, both literal and discursive. Waldman notes that "[a] necessary condition for the husband's success or failure in invalidating the heroine's experience is his ability to isolate her within the nuclear family" (35), and Nicholas, like many abusers, cuts Miranda off from contact with others; eventually she recognizes that he "wanted her to have no intimacies whatsoever . . . he had discouraged her acceptance of any invitations from the young matrons she had met . . . she seemed to be permanently cut off from her mother as well" (225).

This process of experience-invalidating isolation is effective because it is reinforced and rendered essentially unquestionable by a powerful, interlocking alliance of ideologies and discourses of class, marriage, and sexuality. Miranda's participation in the very upper-class life that she seeks, for example, isolates her even as it immerses her in a busy loneliness; its "ceaseless activities" (266) leave her with "no time to consult her soul, and no privacy. Outside of her room there were people, and within it there was always Nicholas" (266). Even when she does reflect upon her situation, the romance paradigm that a woman's world should focus entirely on her husband and that he should be the source of all her happiness intervenes. It renders her initially "happy to be . . . islanded with Nicholas" (225) and believing that "it proved his love for her that he wished to share her with no one" (225); it rewrites other, more accurate perceptions, as when Nicholas forbids her from dining with other tourists at a hotel: "If only I had someone to talk to, she thought, and then reproached herself. A bride did not yearn for outsiders" (214). When she regards her expensive and beautiful new clothing, she is similarly disquieted and self-quieting:

> She had her heart's desires, everything that the Miranda of two years ago would have considered a paradise—wealth, position, and Nicholas. Why then should she suddenly remember a Spanish saying she had read long ago in "The Gipsy's Revenge," one of those idiotic books she used to borrow from Debby Wilson: "May all your wishes come true, and may they all curse you!"
>
> I don't know what's the matter with me, she thought impatiently, and turned from the rail. (211)

She is perhaps most forcefully isolated, her own recognitions of reality most powerfully silenced, by a powerful cultural taboo against discussing sexuality. For example, when, early in their marriage, "Nicholas' comparative indifference to the marriage relation, an indifference which had lasted for weeks and which she in her innocence assumed to be normal, gave place again to violent passion" (213), Miranda misreads her situation once again: "Marriage, she thought, must always be like this, and if it weren't, there was no way of finding out. One would die rather than speak to anyone about such subjects" (213–14).

This point is critically important, for Miranda does not just lack a frame of reference through which to interpret her experience; she truly believes that it is impossible to obtain one. She could not even speak openly with her beloved mother about sex before her marriage. Abigail herself, though in many ways Miranda's greatest champion and sympathizer, inadvertently participated in Miranda's silencing and isolation, clearly communicating the idea that sex is shameful and quite literally unspeakable in her attempt to have "the talk":

> Abigail had tried to talk to her. "Ranny—I hardly know how to— how to prepare you—" . . . slow color flush[ed] her thin cheeks. She had turned from Miranda, fixing her unhappy eyes on the room's farthest corner. "You must submit to your husband, even if it—no matter what—you must do as he wishes. You see—"

"Yes, Ma—I know," Miranda had interrupted. She too was
embarrassed. (171)
Abigail's language of submission, chilling "even if it—," and "unhappy
eyes" all suggest that she too knows something of abusive sexual activ-
ity. But she is rendered inarticulate by her shame at talking about the
matter, and that shame is contagious, leading Miranda to cut off the
very information she needs; Miranda also feels that Abigail's words are a
"desecration" of the "miracle that was occurring" (171). In this exchange,
the ongoing silencing of women's discourse on sexuality and abuse
emerges from a "provisional alliance" with at least three other powerful
discourses: conservative Protestant Christianity (submission of wives
to husbands), gender (ditto), and romance (the idea that marriage will
be perfect and that any questioning of that is a "betrayal" of love).

The impact of this powerful alliance of silencing forces is seen explicitly when Miranda reflects upon her own sexuality: "Often there
was the dark shamed pleasure, but always there was pain, and she felt
that her body was to him only an instrument without personal identity.
But one must submit, out of fear—for the slightest resistance increased
his brutality; out of duty—a wife should always obey her husband.
Under these lay like a layer of granite beneath quicksand the fundamental reason—the willing enslavement of her senses and soul" (214).
Miranda has no context for understanding the existence or dynamics
of healthy, consensual sexuality that involves play between pleasure,
power, and pain; she therefore has no way of differentiating between
physical responses to a certain set of stimuli and acceptance of mis-
treatment. Ultimately, then, Miranda is left in a situation in which she
rereads her pleasure as consent to abuse, her doubts as disloyalty, her
fear and anger as unwomanly. This surrendering of her own physical
and emotional perceptions coalesces with the other forms of hegemonic
consent—other "willing enslavement[s]"—that Nicholas has obtained
from her to deepen the vicious paradox she finds herself in.

But the fictional relations between herself, her husband, and the
world that Miranda has constructed and maintained at such a cost
cannot hold, and they finally begin to crumble in earnest after the
Astor Place Massacre. Nicholas shoots and kills a boy at the theater.

Afterward, Miranda is horrified and tries to reconcile his actions with her vision of him; "[t]he conviction grew upon [Miranda] that Nicholas too was suffering and that he felt remorse" (279), but his "moroseness" (280) is elicited only by his own injury at the hands of the crowd. He has become, in his own eyes, "a man whose invincibility had been scathed by a chance blow" (279)—and such vulnerability, particularly at the hands of the lower classes, utterly upends Nicholas's conception of himself and his place in the world.

Nicholas decides to reassert his sense of dominance in the most brutal way: he physically injures and rapes his wife, telling her when she resists, "Ah, but you don't want to go, my darling. Your soul and body are only a reflection of my will" (282). Overwhelmed by undeniable evidence of Nicholas's view of her (and supported by her outraged maid/friend Peggy), Miranda finally allows herself to read his attitudes and behavior the same way she once recognized her father's sexism. Her first step in working within this new reality is talking to Jeff about Nicholas's growing opium addiction, which is difficult for her, since she codes it as a betrayal—especially when Jeff, seeing her swollen wrist, gets her to admit that Nicholas inflicted the damage. She quickly reverts to rereading Nicholas, saying, "I couldn't desert him, he needs help. Underneath he's really fine and good" (290). But a seismic shift has occurred.

This is why, when she discovers Johanna's diary, she is finally able to, quite literally, read Nicholas and her own situation accurately. Miranda recognizes clues that there was more to Johanna's death than anyone thought; she immediately brings the diary to Jeff, who finishes putting the pieces together and realizes that Nicholas killed Johanna with oleander sprinkled on a piece of cake. This killing, however, does not get rewritten in Miranda's mind. And she accepts an even greater truth: when Jeff tells her about the murder, she says, "I think I've always known . . . not consciously. But in the dark, secret part of my soul where I never dared look" (302). She finally acknowledges the trade she has made—the terrible calculus by which she has continually deemed her own knowledge misreading, tucked it away, and replaced it with convenient and sanctioned fictions.[12] And she realizes, in an inchoate way, the consent to power both rooted and culminating in her "[e]njoying the results of that murder" (302). Armed with this knowledge, empowered by recognizing and relinquishing her consent to power structures, she finally makes plans to break away.

The text, in accordance with the traditions of sensation and gothic fictions, frees Miranda only after a dramatic showdown between Jeff and Nicholas and Nicholas's eventual death after a steamboat explosion—he commits suicide by deliberate drowning after saving other passengers (including Miranda, who had boarded the boat to escape her husband). But escape she does, and she eventually marries Jeff, providing the novel with what appears to be a conventional romance ending.

⁓

At this point, the reader may be wondering, "But where is the third part of the tripartite structure mentioned at the beginning of the essay? We've seen the first, in which both reader and Miranda are able to recognize and resist oppression and hegemony; we've seen the second, in which Miranda does not perceive the structures and ideologies she's imbricated in while the reader sees both them and her misreadings of them. Where's the third?" It's lurking in that allegedly happy ending—or, more precisely, in the entirety of Jeff and Miranda's relationship. More precisely still, it resides in the reader's probable misreading of them.

If Nicholas is a critical revision of the gothic hero who appears villainous but is proved innocent, Jeff appears to be a "real" romance hero—a man who is both powerful and gentle, brave and thoughtful. He resists gender-based oppression: he acknowledges and condemns Nicholas's behavior, rejects conventional ideologies of wifely submission, urges Miranda to flee and protect herself, and intervenes at the risk of his own life to help her escape from her husband. And while Nicholas considers his tenants "his" and praises the Southern "plantation system and slave labor, of which he heartily approved" (170), Jeff's political and economic positions champion a sort of de Crèvecourian ideal, one in which hard-working people toil on farms (or in small medical practices) that they own and keep their profits. Jeff is aligned with the fiery anti-renter Dr. Boughton, who shouts at Miranda, "Your forefathers left the old country . . . to find freedom and be quit of tyranny. All the length and breadth of this great land white men are free, except here on these manors. . . . A stinking survival from the past!" (106–07).

Clearly, Jeff's embrace of democracy and free enterprise is valorized in comparison to Nicholas's backing of a system coded as a hangover from a feudal, aristocratic European (read: un-American) past. Jeff is therefore doubly validated in many readers' eyes: he actively, consciously, and, at times, daringly works against ideologies and practices that are oppressive and damaging, and in doing so he aligns with what many readers would consider positive, or at least acceptable and non-oppressive, values or positions. [13]

However, it is precisely in its contrasting of Jeff and Nicholas that the text should be prompting the reader to tread carefully. For there was another reader—Miranda—who was deceived by the apparent Otherness of her father, Ephraim, and Nicholas, who actually shared many characteristics and whose actions and attitudes were informed by similar ideologies. And I would argue that the apparent Otherness of Jeff and Nicholas, in combination with the apparent generic "requirement" of a happy ending, may deceive the reader as it does Miranda, leading to a misreading of Jeff.

Jeff's initial thoughts about Miranda, for instance, are wrapped up in a "diagnosis" of her situation:

Affected little ninny! Perversely clinging to that atmosphere of decadent luxury, pretending she was an aristocrat. . . . Honest work, she needed, with those smooth white hands she was so obviously vain of, honest work and a simple, honest man to knock the nonsense out of her and give her a houseful of babies. She's healthy enough for all that she needs a bit more meat on her bones, thought Jeff irritably. (121)

Though the overall construction of Jeff's character suggests that no literal abuse is implied, in the context of the larger narrative, the phrase "knock the nonsense out of her" takes on rather a dark cast indeed. It is also clear that Jeff's thinking is rooted in much the same ideological soil that Nicholas's is. Jeff, as a man and a doctor, is convinced that he knows what's best for the "little ninny,"[14] has the authority to "approve" or "disapprove" of certain courses of action, and can "place" her where she should be. Jeff even, like Nicholas, believes that he has the right to determine the "proper" appearance for her—in this case, weighing more than the fashionable ideal she currently embraces.[15]

This patriarchal attitude surfaces again when Miranda goes to Jeff for help with Nicholas's opium addiction and increasingly bizarre and violent behavior. When she expresses ambivalence about leaving her husband, Jeff's response is startlingly Nicholas-like: "He wanted to shake her, he wanted to kiss her pathetic swollen arm. . . . To his own dismay he suddenly leaned over and kissed her hard on the lips" (290). Unlike Nicholas, he does not actually shake her and does not continue his sexual aggression, assuring her, "I [am not] going to force on you any indecent proposals" (290). But he does continue to behave in a strikingly paternalistic fashion. When Miranda admits that she had inklings of the realities of Johanna's death, Jeff, sounding alarmingly like Dr. John of Charlotte Perkins Gilman's "The Yellow Wall-Paper," belittles and dismisses them promptly, telling her what to think and how to feel instead. "This is morbid, Miranda. Let's try to be sensible and face together what must be done. We must keep our heads and use them," he insists, adding, "[Y]ou must rid yourself of these morbid feelings of guilt" (302). Though he says, "[W]e must keep our heads and use them," he really means that *he* must. He devises an escape plan for her to follow, continues to tell her how to feel, and after he finally frees her from the manor, puts her on a boat and tells her how to behave. She acquiesces to his suggestions, and when it is time for her to depart, "[s]he nodded like an obedient child and walked slowly up the gangplank" (320).

Even as he infantalizes her, Jeff does have some respect for Miranda and her abilities. For example, unlike Nicholas, who isolates Miranda and strips her of agency by making her the pampered and purely decorative lady of the manor, Jeff really does believe that she needs "[h]onest work" (121); he tells her that "[w]ork's not such a bad thing… There's joy in getting things done, in being useful" (161). After she returns to her parents' farm, where she demonstrates "quiet strength and a seriousness of purpose in everything she did . . . [including] the most distasteful tasks" (334), he realizes that she has the makings of a good nurse; when Jeff operated on Miranda's maid's leg, "it had been Miranda—white as the sheet which covered the little body on the scrubbed table—who had held the ether cone, steadily pouring the merciful drops in obedience to Jeff's terse orders" (334). Shortly after this, she herself proposes a professional partnership: "I've been thinking, Jeff, I could help you. In California they need doctors" (335).[16] It is obvious that their marriage will be very little like her first.

It is therefore remarkably easy for the reader, like Miranda, to imaginatively reconstruct Jeff's paternalistic, patriarchal attitudes as benevolence, to write off his language of "knocking" and "shaking" her, to brush aside the fact that she responds to him "like an obedient child," and to ignore the moment in which he, like Nicholas, tells her when and how to ascend a gangplank. Even Waldman includes Jeff in her list of male characters who "corroborate[] the heroine's experience, and, in true gothic tradition, come[] to her rescue" (36). It is easy, in other words, to consent to patriarchy in the guise of Jeff. And it is in that ease that, I believe, the text performs its strongest critical move. Even having seen Miranda misreading Nicholas in comparison with her father, even having seen the text problematize uncritical readings of popular novels, even having seen how a character's alignment with dominant, valorizing ideologies can lead others to overlook or misread warning flags about said character . . . even with all of this, the reader misreads.

And it is precisely this misreading that grounds the text's final vision of the power of Hebdigian hegemony. When Nicholas dies, one version of allied patriarchy and economic privilege—a patronizing, aristocratic one that maintains its power through the explicit exercise of physical and economic power—is overturned. But another version of the same core power structure takes its place—a version Waldman, quoting Reuben Hill, describes as "semi-patriarchal" (37).[17] This version maintains its power through just enough distribution of wealth to keep the laborers complacent, but not too much, and through just enough partnership with and respect for women to keep the women happy and consenting, but not too much. For example, when Miranda proposes turning the Dragonwyck land over to the tenants, saying, "It's only the workers who have a right to things," Jeff's response is telling: "'My dear girl!' protested Jeff, smiling. He did not believe that she meant it" (332). The kind Dr. Francis agrees, calling her plan "childish nonsense" (333) and accusing Jeff of filling her head with "Brook Farm communal-living trash" (333), a charge he quickly denies. Jeff clearly has no compunction in dismissing Miranda's re-vision of economic relations as the daydream of an ignorant "girl," and he is quick to repudiate his own radical ideas when a chance to put them into action—a chance that would involve losing out on the wealth that his new wife brings to the marriage—is actually available. Waldman ultimately argues that the gothics of the 1940s "hold out the possibility" (38) for more egalitarian relations between the sexes, and yes, Miranda's life is changing. But, I would argue, the reader is left wondering just how much.

At this point, it is (I hope) clear that, in both its subject matter and its positioning of the reader in relation to its ideological content, *Dragonwyck* provides students a fine entrée into exploring the "moving equilibria" and "provisional alliances" Hebdige maps out. One of my former students, Samantha Klein Latham, developed her reflections upon these concepts into an excellent essay examining the dynamic alliance between ideologies of class and gender within the text. One of her key points is that both deploy the concept of the "moving finish line," in which an abused person is never able to fully satisfy the demands and expectations of the abuser. The bar of expectations is continually raised just enough that the abused either fails or is immediately met with another challenge, so the abuser is always withholding approval, and the victim feels responsible for trying to meet the demand. Klein Latham notes that Nicholas expects Miranda to, for example, read and understand increasingly sophisticated literature and to understand high-culture jokes and references. This sets her up for continual failure and humiliation, for he always finds ways for her to need to master something just beyond her grasp. Similarly, no matter how well Miranda dresses or how perfectly she masters etiquette, the aristocratic women of her new social circle will never fully accept that she is "one of them." Therefore, the possibilities of both genuine class mobility and gender equity are simultaneously stifled. And as long as Miranda can be made to feel that it is she who has been inadequate, the mutually reinforcing power structures that set her up to fail are protected from critique.

The text's dynamics also provide students a way to explore their own reading strategies and relationships to the concepts. For example, just as Miranda sees and acknowledges the combination of forces undergirding her father's authoritarianism, students are able to easily recognize the alliance of cultural forces maintaining that power structure; since I teach at a school on the buckle of the Bible Belt, this section is often particularly resonant for students, and the discussions are often lively. The abuse narrative also tends to resonate strongly. For some students, the novel's presentation of an abused main character who creates a "long and painfully maintained self-deception" (175) about her situation is particularly important, for it creates a safe space for revealing and discussing responses that may be incomprehensible to those who have never experienced or witnessed abuse. Conversely, students who have maintained a "Why doesn't s/he just leave?" stance toward abuse—and there are many—are able to dig into precisely that question. As they recognize the confluence of sociopolitical, economic, and emotional forces acting upon Miranda, they can begin to understand her staying with her husband and not discussing the situation with outsiders; they can also then reflect back on why they initially responded the way they did—why they, in effect, consented to the abuse of others by deeming it the fault of the abused.[18]

Because the novel is a work of historical fiction, some students may have a "back in the day" response as they engage with these issues: they may understand the logic of Miranda's behavior and acquiescence in light of nineteenth-century legal and ideological constraints but then argue that "things are different now." Such a response can sabotage the novel's larger critique of hegemony, reinforcing current norms and practices by making them look benevolent by comparison (much as Nicholas looks terrific upon initial comparison to Ephraim and Jeff seems great in comparison to Nicholas). However, students can be prompted to think about historical fiction, like science fiction and fantasy, as a mode of displacement—as a way of detaching contemporary cultural anxieties from the "here and now" in order to create a context within which difficult questions and realities can be confronted without activating the sorts of knee-jerk, "painfully maintained self-deceptions" that Miranda resorts to. In this light, examining both the origins and the results of the "Why doesn't she leave?" response dovetails with discussion of hegemonic consent, illuminating ways in which subjects of power (read: readers) can be positioned to accept and even valorize oppressive structures.

That discussion, obviously, also intersects with the novel's presentation of Jeff Turner as a very problematic hero indeed. Most students read him positively, not noting the parallels between his attitudes and Nicholas's. Those who pick up on the tensions in his construction tend to be tentative in their responses, suspecting that they, like Miranda, are misunderstanding a heroic man. Discussions of my reading of the Jeff subplot tend, not surprisingly, to be lively, for some students really want a happy ending to the novel. Others are very uncomfortable with recognizing that they either did not pick up on or imaginatively neutralized textual hints that patriarchal ideologies inform all relationships in the text (albeit in differing ways and to different degrees).[19] A similar pattern can also often be seen in students' responses to Johanna. Many respond negatively to her, in part because information about her is filtered through the narrative voice, Miranda, and Jeff, whose perceptions are rooted in cultural paradigms that devalue obesity, greediness for food, certain kinds of snobbery, detached motherhood, and weakness, and in part because those paradigms are still powerful and shape their own thinking. While students may intellectually understand that much of Johanna's behavior is in response to emotional abuse, they still tend to side with Miranda and Jeff, regarding Johanna as fully agentive in her situation and not realizing that by reading this way, they, too, are consenting to and participating in oppressive patterns of thought—patterns that they decry when viewed in another light.

~

When Elizabeth Williams lamented the fact that students were reading novels by Anya Seton, assuming that they could get nothing from the texts, she was, perhaps, the reader committing the most egregious misreading. Students may have gravitated to those novels for precisely the reasons that most of my students ultimately end up appreciating *Dragonwyck*. The novel presents, in an abstracted, distanced way, difficult realities: sexism, emotional abuse, domestic violence, classism. And this, I would argue, is precisely what makes the novel compelling—and popular. It articulates and validates suspicions that the reader, like Miranda, may have buried in layers of denial or counter-reading. It is a "popcorn escapist fiction" that, in a sense, leads readers right back into the world, asking them to take another look at their own haunted mansions of culture. When readers hear the voice of the novel's ghost, Azilde, laughing from the past when the disastrous results of abuse, oppression, and corruption become undeniably visible,[20] they too may hear voices from the past asking them to see those patterns playing out today as well. Azilde's laughter is, ultimately, the libratory force in the text, paralyzing Nicholas in a moment of deadly violence rooted in generations of unquestioned class, ethnic, and gender privilege and power. And students, too, may find themselves pressed to stop and reconsider, seeing their own patterns of reading and finding their own ghosts, the long history of ideologies and ideas that inform those readings.

Sneaking It In at the End

Teaching Popular Romance in the Liberal Arts Classroom

ANTONIA LOSANO

◞

WHILE SOME GENRES of popular fiction—science fiction and graphic novels in particular—have in many cases secured a position on college and university syllabi, popular romance fiction decidedly has not. When compiling a list of US institutions of higher education that teach the genre, popular romance scholar Pamela Regis found just over a dozen schools in which romance fiction was taught—mostly tucked into the margins of thematic courses or tangentially referenced in popular culture courses. Only in two cases were romances taught in stand-alone romance fiction courses.[1] Romance fiction is arguably the last barbarian pounding on the gates.

Part of this, scholars of the genre argue, is a simple matter of sexist discrimination; part is a misunderstanding (and misinterpretation) of the generic characteristics of popular romance; part is an Adorno-like reaction to mass culture more generally.[2] Historically, academia has tended to devalue genres that are written largely by or for women or "the masses" (the novel itself suffered this fate on and off throughout the history of literary criticism), and genres that are slow to innovate formally are similarly dismissed. As Barbara Fuchs writes, the popular romance is "iterable and predictable" (128). Others use words such as "formulaic" or "stock." Horkheimer and Adorno, while not addressing romance fiction specifically, found mass culture in general to be dangerous because of its homogeneity: "Under monopoly all mass culture

77

is identical"(121); later they remark on the "ruthless unity" of mass culture (123).

Works like Jan Radway's groundbreaking *Reading the Romance* did little to raise the canonical stock of romance fiction; her goal, laudable at the time, was more sociological than literary critical. Another early work, Tania Modleski's *Loving with a Vengeance: Mass Produced Fantasies for Women*, actively disparaged the genre even as it sought to validate aspects of it. As Eric Selinger writes, "The first twenty years of serious analysis of romance fiction treated it and its readers with ambivalence at best, and often with undisguised contempt" (310).

Subsequent scholars followed their lead; the title of the excellent collection *Empowerment versus Oppression*, for example, signals its investment in the conversation about the genre's sociocultural import begun by Radway and Modleski. Other treatments of the genre tend to fall similarly one way or the other: either romance is dangerously conservative (see Daphne Watson, Ann Cranny-Francis, and Bridget Fowler) or potentially subversive and liberatory. For example, in the latter vein Jay Dixon argues that romance fiction represents "female power" (177). George Paizis, similarly, argues that women achieve success in popular romance by being able to control their passions and those of the hero; such control is rewarded by social success and personal fulfillment (f117). (For other arguments on the subversive side, see the collection *Romance Revisited*, ed. Pearce and Stacey). The wide and often surprisingly disparate arguments about romance fiction serve to suggest, as Lisa Fletcher rightly notes, that "the ideological foundations of romance are unstable and uncertain" (2).

Slowly, however, literary scholars have over the past thirty years begun intermittent considerations of the romance novel as a literary artifact worthy of scholarly attention—and hence pedagogic attention as well. Recently critics have attempted to bring romance fiction more decisively into the literary fold. Seeking to reveal the stylistic conventions and literary precursors of the genre, numerous articles in the collections *Romantic Conventions* (ed. Kaler and Johnson-Kurek) and *Dangerous Men and Adventurous Women* (ed. Krentz) treat romance novels as both a species of literature and as cultural documents. Jayne Ann Krentz, herself a romance writer, specifically addresses the issue of predictability, asking, "Are we woefully derivative and unoriginal?" (21). She officially answers "No," but in fact her answer is really "Yes, because it works." Her point is that stock phrases and repeated plot elements carry emotional and narrative weight because of centuries of accretive use—just as in canonical literature, which has its share of repeated tropes and narrative structures. Lisa Fletcher writes "The 'logic of iterability' which the concept of performativity [from Butler as well as semiotic theory] names and recognizes allows us to consider anew the ubiquity and apparent inexhaustibility of the romance genre as a result of an inhering failure ever to secure its terms with any finality" (2). The mere fact that the "happily ever after" must be reiterated, Fletcher argues, says something about its inherent instability; we are not done with writing and reading romances because true love remains an unfulfilled and probably unfulfillable fantasy.

In a similar vein, Diane Elam argues that the romance genre is actually defined by inexhaustibility; its excess, in terms of sheer number of volumes but also in its formulaic repeatability, is one marker of the genre's postmodernity (3ff). The iterability of the romance form, of course, has always been the blackest mark against the genre. Yet in the context of literary history the logic of this claim is questionable. Literary historians will admit that much of what we now call canonical literature is based, often entirely, upon previous sources, stock characters, traditional formulas, and so forth. It is illogical and possibly ingenuous to dismiss genre fiction for its iterability while praising Shakespeare's reliance upon Thomas Kyd and the *Gesta Danorum*. As these recent scholars suggest, romance fiction is arguably no more or less dependent upon repeated codes and traditions than any other genre.

The scholarly discourse has continued to expand impressively, as the essays in Sarah Frantz and Eric Selinger's recent volume *New Approaches to Popular Romance Fiction* attest. Like Regis, whose *A Natural History of the Romance* paved the way for much of the most recent scholarly analysis of romance, Frantz and Selinger attempt to turn romance scholarship toward the specific, individual artistry of romance novels and away from the previous tendency to lump all romances together. As such, they advocate a move from structuralist or generic criticism toward a theoretically informed close reading, which is fundamentally necessary for the development of this field of study. The genre is by no means coherent or univocal, these critics argue.

Pedagogically, this varied scholarly history can be extraordinarily useful. Most teachers of popular culture encourage their students to weigh the ideological force of the cultural texts they study and to ascertain their level of "containment or resistance," to use Stuart Hall's terms in "Notes on Deconstructing the Popular." Romance fiction is an eminently valuable repository of cultural beliefs about gender, sexuality, love, and narrative itself—as well as a host of other sociocultural constructions. As such, while romance scholars might justifiably choose to move beyond discussions of the genre, teachers of popular romance would be ill served by neglecting the cultural work of the romance genre *as a whole* in favor of close-reading individual texts. Yet, as recent scholarship makes abundantly clear, many contemporary romances stand up extremely well under close textual analysis.

As a representative example of the conflicts and complications inherent in the teaching of popular romance, I offer in this essay a brief account of my varied endeavors to introduce romance fiction into the classroom at a small, prestigious, rural liberal arts college. When I began working seriously on popular romance as a scholarly pursuit, the thought of teaching one of the novels in an academic context never crossed my mind. After several years of taking the genre seriously, and after meeting like-minded academics who had successfully taught popular romance in their university classrooms, I decided to make the attempt. I was first confronted by a problem common to those who teach popular genres of any kind: *in what context* do we teach it? Should I try to create a new course just on romance fiction, or should I incorporate one or more romances into a preexisting course with a particular thematic focus? Mounting innovative new courses on popular literature arguably is always challenging, but the endeavor has particular tensions at a small liberal arts college. The English Department at NYU, for example, lists over fifty course offerings for fall of 2011 (*not* including creative writing courses, listed elsewhere). Middlebury College, where I teach, on the other hand, was offering twenty, including six creative writing courses and two courses cross-listed with other departments (Film and American Studies), plus four first-year seminar courses not designed for majors at all. We have a small department, and our major requirements include extensive period and genre coverage, two "gateway" courses, and a standard theory course.

If I were to offer a course solely on popular romance, then one of the gateway courses or a seminal survey or the Victorian literature course, which is my bailiwick, wouldn't get taught that year. Colleagues in other disciplines (such as Film or American Studies) face similar problems: courses in popular culture would displace "core" curricular offerings. Liberal arts English majors, too, are often highly invested in the literary canon (although more radical in their politics): they want Shakespeare, and they want Joyce; they justifiably want to feel that they have studied the classics. Those who teach at any small institution will understand the situation: there's often less flexibility in course offerings than can be found at the larger universities. I opted in the end, then, to incorporate a romance novel into another course, initially a senior seminar course on canonicity and literary aesthetics. We read a series of literary pairings—Benjamin Franklin's *Autobiography* alongside Momaday's *The Way to Rainy Mountain*, the *Odyssey* and Atwood's *Penelopiad*, as well as *Hamlet* and the film *Strange Brew*. We ended the semester with *Pride and Prejudice* and Georgette Heyer's regency romance, *Frederica*.

I dutifully and systematically pointed out the similarities in narrative structure between these two texts, which feature contrasting sister narratives: the unconventional Frederica and the lovely Charis in Heyer's novel are clearly modeled on the unconventional Elizabeth and the lovely Jane from Austen. Likewise, both novels feature two families with financial troubles, unimpressive suitors for the heroine's hand, and an upper-class hero who must be taught the value of untraditional females and middle-class family values. Both novels also arguably contain "extras" designed to mark the historical setting—hot air balloons and technological innovation in Heyer, military structure in Austen. I hoped to show students that in this one example at least, romance fiction could be a rich repository for social critique. I also offered them Harrington and Bielby's observation that because popular culture fails in some way to achieve the aesthetic standards that mark "high art," it therefore reveals the "relations of power" embedded in the distinction between high and low (10).

Unfortunately, Heyer's novel was received with only derision and contempt. "The easiest weighing job of the whole semester," one student claimed; "*Frederica* has no redeeming features save entertainment," wrote another. The kicker came, however, when one student confessed that he didn't actually think much of *either* book, *Pride and Prejudice* or *Frederica*. Maybe if he'd read *Pride and Prejudice* in a different context, he argued, he wouldn't have noticed that it was *just* about romance and not much else. Much of the rest of the class nodded in agreement.

Having ruined Austen for a group of college seniors rather than successfully engaging them with popular romance, I gave up the idea of including romances on my syllabi for several years. But when I taught a course on the historical development of the marriage plot narrative, beginning with Richardson's *Pamela*, I took a risk and ended the course with Susan Elizabeth Phillips's *Nobody's Baby but Mine*. Students liked *Pamela* better, an opinion I found frankly astonishing. I had framed the course as a historical development narrative, a teleology that inadvertently opened the floodgates for students to argue for cultural *devolution*; the marriage plot novel, they concluded, had become trite, relegated to chick lit, no longer central to the literary tradition. As with the course on canonicity, I tried to suggest to students that the boundaries between romance fiction and canonical fiction are more permeable than critics of the former would like to admit. As Pamela Regis demonstrates in the opening five chapters of *A Natural History of the Romance*, almost any definition of "romance" will be both overly reductive and yet simultaneously overly inclusive—that is to say, it's hard to come up with a reasonable definition of "romance novel" that includes Susan Elizabeth Phillips but excludes Austen's *Pride and Prejudice* or Richardson's *Pamela*.

This emphasis on permeability and overlap is prevalent in the critical discourse. Like Regis, Lisa Fletcher compares what one might call "literature" with romance fiction, "exposing their common ground" (7). And Barbara Fuchs's introductory volume *Romance*, although ostensibly about medieval romance, makes it clear—though entirely inadvertently and unwillingly—that this common ground is solid, deep, and wide ranging. While Fuchs tries hard to argue that popular romance is not "Romance" in the literary sense, she nevertheless repeatedly must admit similarities, and she comes up with a surprisingly long list. She also fails to see the irony in her statement that popular romance relies on "formulaic construction" and is hence *bad*, while a hundred pages earlier she has claimed that Romance with a capital R—the medieval French tradition—is characterized by a reliance upon traditional constructions and repeated thematics, which is somehow more worthy than "formulae."

These theoretical supports notwithstanding, I failed to convince students that popular romances are part of a long literary tradition; indeed, I failed to engage them with the popular romance in any meaningful way. The moral seemed to be that if I assigned a romance novel *qua* romance novel I was destined to fail because students in English classes want "great literature."[3] In retaliation, so to speak, I next taught a course on love and romance in which I didn't teach *any* popular romances but only well-respected canonical literature—Shakespeare, Keats, Tennyson, Henry James, Arundhati Roy. This went quite well; students were happy to argue about love and romance if they knew they were safely discussing "literature." But of course it didn't solve the problem. Undaunted, I tried again two years later and taught *The Sheik* in a unit on Orientalism. That went over well, but it is perhaps not surprising, since the point of the course was to critique western authors who systematically misrepresent nonwestern cultures and peoples. We weren't criticizing *The Sheik* any more or less than we were criticizing *Heart of Darkness*, so the fact that the novel was something called a romance passed largely unnoted.

This gave me an idea to test out what we might call the "don't ask, don't tell" method. Last year I taught Nora Roberts's *The Search* in a new course titled Animals in Literature and Culture. We'd read *The Call of the Wild* the week before, Haraway's *When Species Meet* the week before that, and Derrida's *The Animal That I Therefore Am* earlier in the semester. We followed it up with Vicki Hearne's work on animal training and psychology, *Adam's Task*. In my lectures, I consciously avoided mentioning that *The Search* is a romance, and I did not discuss Roberts as a writer; I merely presented the text as a contemporary book with animals in it. And nobody scoffed; nobody made dismissive comments.

At that point I concluded that, at least for the students I teach, this method is the most successful. We might even view this approach—what we might call the "incorporation" method—as a positive constraint. If we teach stand-alone courses on popular culture (whatever the genre), we run the risk of isolating and encrypting the very genres we are trying to validate; my course in Victorian adventure and science fiction has suffered that fate, as it is understood by students and colleagues to be the repository of "fun" fiction rather than "great" literature. To avoid this problem, I would argue that romances (and by extension other forms of popular literature) can and should be folded into the fabric of the academic canon. A course *just* on popular romance runs the risk of isolating and marginalizing the genre—as if we were trying to keep it from infecting the canonical survey.

Yet if we do decide to incorporate examples of the genre into existing courses, do we *foreground* its popular-genre characteristics or gloss over them, as I did in my Animals in Literature course? If we foreground genre issues, do we thereby neglect a text's other characteristics—namely, those things which we might ordinarily discuss if we were discussing, say, James Joyce (narrative style and structure, theme, figurative language, sociopolitical ideology, etc.)? Teaching Roberts's *The Search* without bringing up issues of canonicity, gender politics, and the history of literary genre felt to me both irresponsible and unethical (even if the students responded positively). How can we validate both the specifics of an individual romance novel (in the case of *The Search*, for example, the focus on animal training and development and the links Roberts draws between that and human "training" and development) *and* the cultural importance of the genre as a repository of a wide range of ideological debates?

In an attempt to bridge this gap I decided next to use a romance novel in my section of our undergraduate literary theory course. I assigned Jennifer Crusie's *Welcome to Temptation* (along with *Robinson Crusoe*, *Lyrical Ballads*, and *To the Lighthouse*) as a "touchstone" text, a text students read at the outset of the semester and then return to repeatedly throughout the term; as new schools, paradigms, theorists, or essays are introduced, students are asked to consider the touchstone texts in the light of these new theoretical ideas. The approach is a little bit like that early theory "introduction," *The Pooh Perplex*, in which Frederick C.

Crews creates fictional theorists who each "write" an essay about the Pooh stories in the characteristic style of a number of theoretical schools. What would Derrida say about Crusie, for example? What would Lacan say? Judith Butler? Cognitive science theorists? New Historicists? Queer theorists? Eco-critics?

This was by far the most successful approach to teaching popular romance in my experience. To begin with, students were stunned that they could actually *find* something in Crusie to discuss during each new theoretical unit. While Marxism, feminism, psychoanalysis, cultural materialism, and cultural studies turned out to be better friends of the romance novel than, say, high Derridean deconstruction, it was still the case that *any* theoretical approach could fruitfully be brought to bear on the romance—and thus legitimate the genre as part of literary history. Arguably, the full usefulness or relevance of a theory has not been developed until it has been brought into contact with the widest possible range of literary and cultural artifacts.

Significantly, in this course *Welcome to Temptation* quickly became the go-to touchstone text and provided a common language for every class discussion; its narrative bones were more readily visible to students, and they felt less reserve in making critical commentary about Crusie's work than they did about the canonical texts. Students invariably started comments about *Robinson Crusoe*, for instance, by saying, "I might have misunderstood this part of the novel, but . . ." In contrast, when they spoke about Crusie, they were firm, confident, and forceful.

But the full use-value of the text truly became apparent when we began the unit on gender studies. After a series of lectures on the history of feminist literary criticism and contemporary gender studies, I offered students a brief history of feminist responses to romance fiction. Students were asked, first, to determine whether Crusie's novel and others like it were feminist, antifeminist, or somewhere in between. Then I asked them to evaluate the history of critical discourse on the romance itself, to be aware of the ways criticism changes over time, and to consider what might motivate literary or cultural critics to make certain assessments of the romance genre. Writers on the romance have struggled consistently with the genre's vexed relation to feminism; the history of that struggle offers an excellent opportunity to show that critical discourse is rarely objective and is always subject to change based upon changing historical situations.

This is, in essence, the story I tell my students: before 1990 (as I mentioned in my introduction), early scholars of popular fiction in general and romance fiction in particular were concerned with gauging the sociological, economic, or historical import of the genre rather than examining works in particular detail. Early classics in the field such as Radway's *Reading the Romance* and Modleski's *Loving with a Vengeance* come to different conclusions but ask similar questions: why do people (mainly women) read so many of these things? What cultural and economic work do they do? Radway acknowledges that the genre can be a force of patriarchal indoctrination, forcing women to believe that they cannot be happy as autonomous individuals but must exist in relation to a man, but she leaves space open for romance's subversive side and readers' "resistant" readings. Modleski argues that the genre has more subversive potential, as it expresses women's frustration with their social powerlessness by rewriting male behavior into something more bearable as well as creating narratives in which women often have a good deal of power (sexual and otherwise) over their own lives and over the hero figures in the novels. But both of these foundational texts find romance novels, in the final analysis, to have an essentially *negative* impact on the female reading public.

Dawn Heinecken notes astutely that Radway's and Modleski's work is based on romantic narrative conventions that have changed dramatically in the years since they studied the genre, and hence their conclusions need to be reconsidered. Indeed, we might be ready to jettison the dualism between romance's alleged conventionalism and its supposed subversiveness, which has been a standard feature of scholarship on the genre but which arguably limits and oversimplifies analysis (Heinecken 150ff). Of course, Heinecken's analysis is itself now more than ten years old—a fact which does not diminish its force but, by its own logic, suggests that another reevaluation may be needed. The second half of Merja Makinen's chapter on the romance in her *Feminist Popular Fiction* is an excellent example of what such new textual analysis might look like, and I would argue that even more recent romance novels, especially of the paranormal variety, offer visions of female empowerment in which women are rewarded for *unleashing* (not controlling) their passions.[4]

With this critical history under their belts, students are able to make impressive statements not only about *Welcome to Temptation* but about the inner workings of literary and cultural criticism—much of which did not seem as clear when looking at the critical history of *Robinson Crusoe*, for example. My experience in this course brought home the truth of Brenda Weber's argument that popular culture is the ideal locus for any pedagogy which desires to operate on feminist principles. She writes:

Every person in the room both interacts with and in many respects creates popular culture. Also, popular culture is perhaps the single-greatest influence in how members of a particular culture learn to, as Judith Lorber phrases it, "do gender." Popular culture is, as Tasker and Negra as well as Douglas note, the primary mechanism through which postfeminist ideas are communicated. In this regard, both male and female students enter the popular culture gender studies class with certain forms of literacy and knowledge that can contribute to the professor's expertise. But they also hold many unexamined biases. It is therefore important that a gender studies course in popular culture—as distinct from a similar themed course in mass communication or journalism— mindfully authorizes, yet also problematizes, the knowledge that students bring to the topic rather than simply reverting to a model of "professing" that results in rote learning and text/lecture/test assessment strategies. Indeed, if part of how we understand the "popular" stems from the ways in which a populace has agency in the making of its own cultural artifacts (rather than simply as passive consumers of cultural products made by artists), then the classroom itself must be structured in ways that foster interactive expressions and multiple sites of epistemological agency, including, quite often, how the body is central to learning. (129)

Weber's words were not meant to apply to romance fiction specifically, yet in a gender studies context they are eminently applicable.

In the end, and in my particular academic circumstances, it proved most effective to incorporate romance fiction into a theory classroom—

already a space of discovery, debate, and (often) bewilderment. Crusie's *Welcome to Temptation* became a surprisingly valuable workhorse, a way to introduce students to a whole array of critical issues: feminism, canonicity, popular culture, patriarchy, sexuality, and more. (It was also a great deal sexier to read than *Robinson Crusoe*.) The romance genre may be slow in benefiting from the burgeoning pedagogic interest in popular culture, but it will amply recompense whatever attention we choose to pay it in the future.

Race, Region, and Genre
in Popular Texts

"Chick lit can help us move beyond the idea that, in the South, [in Faulkner's words], 'The past is never dead. It's not even past.' . . .
[Lockwood's *Dixieland Sushi*] may offer fusty visions of womanhood and romance, as some of the genre's critics contend, [but] its picture of the South is fresh."—JOLENE HUBBS, "Chick Lit and Southern Studies"

"Too often the turn to popular texts seeks to activate notions of 'cool' and to find new ways to energize class discussions. But hostility, not cool, is what we need to be exploring with our students. The popular is and always has been a place for marginalized groups to challenge hegemony. . . . Black popular texts can help reveal how popular culture structures limit what we know and the kinds of voices we get to hear."
—RICHARD SCHUR, "'A Right to Be Hostile': Black Cultural Traffic in the Classroom"

Chick Lit and Southern Studies

JOLENE HUBBS

$\sim$

IN SOUTHERN STUDIES courses, it can be hard to get a bead on the contemporary South. The reason, as sociologist Larry J. Griffin observes, is that time and again "the region's history, that very particular Southern past, is evoked in the present: the South of *then* is recreated and oddly memorialized, concretized in a sense, in the South of *now*" (5). As a result, hot-off-the-press literature often treats Southern history. Kathryn Stockett's bestselling novel *The Help* (2009), for example, depicts Mississippi in the early 1960s. Alice Randall's *The Wind Done Gone* (2001), another recent bestseller, rethinks the Civil War–era story of Margaret Mitchell's Depression-era novel. Movies including *The Help* (2011), *Django Unchained* (2012), and *12 Years a Slave* (2013) also take up the South's past. These works, like so many fictional treatments of Southern experience, return to the watershed Civil War and civil rights eras—periods that, while unquestionably formidable, are called upon too often to define Southern experience writ large. How can we adjust the payload of what historian C. Vann Woodward once called "the burden of Southern history" to get a solid grip on the present?

Chick lit, contemporary fiction about "contemporary women and contemporary culture," can help (Ferriss and Young 2). Yet chick lit comes with its own concerns, including "its dubious status as feminist and as literature" (Wilson 85). Scholar Stephanie Harzewski takes these popular novels seriously in her book *Chick Lit and Postfeminism*, yet she acknowledges that other novelists, journalists, and scholars have blasted chick lit, concerned "that frothiness might once again come to seem the hallmark of female literary expression" (3). To its detractors, the genre's protagonists present "a passive and disempowered image of womanhood that has simply been revamped for a postfeminist era" (Genz and Brabon 85). Looking at its story lines, these critics find that "the codes of traditional romance are reinstated 'through the backdoor,'" maintaining "transcendent love and sexual satisfaction" as characters' ultimate aims despite their attention to careers, consumer culture, and friends (Gill and Herdieckerhoff 494). On the question of literary merit, columnist Maureen Dowd declares this type of fiction "all chick and no lit" (A15). But chick lit's value in Southern studies courses emerges from its contemporaneity. Chick lit can help us move beyond the idea that, in the South, "The past is never dead. It's not even past" (an often-cited line from William Faulkner's fiction [92]) and toward analyzing contemporary Southerners grappling with contemporary concerns.

In this essay, I use my experiences teaching Cara Lockwood's novel *Dixieland Sushi* (2005) to illustrate how chick lit can enrich courses on the literature and culture of the US South. *Dixieland Sushi* tells the story of Jen Nakamura Taylor, a half-Japanese, half-white woman who grew up in the tiny town of Dixieland, Arkansas, but moved to Chicago to take a job as a television producer. The novel's romantic story line unfolds when, having returned to the South for a cousin's wedding, Jen finds herself torn between feelings for her coworker (and wedding date) Nigel Riley and her childhood crush (and cousin's bridegroom) Kevin Peterson. The conclusion ties these personal and professional narrative threads into a neat bow: in the end, our heroine not only gets the guy—Riley—and the promotion but also, as the back cover blurb puts it, "learns to come to terms with her heritage, her love life, and herself." While Lockwood's novel may offer fusty visions of womanhood and romance, as some of the genre's critics contend, its picture of the South is fresh. *Dixieland Sushi* offers us novel ways to approach questions that come up in teaching about the contemporary South: Why does the Southern past so forcefully inform representations of its present? And how should we define Southern distinctiveness for the twenty-first century?

The Real South and the Reel South

Chick lit's insistent contemporaneity throws into sharp relief the way in which other popular cultural representations of the South define the region not by its present but by its past. For this reason, the novel can help students critically engage the question of why the picture of the South repeatedly used to sell books, films, and television programs is an image of the old South.

In an op-ed article on chick lit, Maureen Dowd observes that "cartoon women, sexy string beans in minis and stilettos, fashionably dashing about book covers with the requisite urban props—lattes, books, purses, shopping bags, guns and, most critically, a diamond ring" adorn the fronts of countless chick lit novels and define the form's cover art aesthetic (A15). Southern fried chick lit, one of several subgenres of chick lit, deviates from this pattern in some respects. Southern cover girls swap lattes for sweet teas and surround themselves with signifiers of the South: peaches on some covers, plantation houses on others. To open our discussion of *Dixieland Sushi* in my Women in the South class, I show students a selection of covers from chick lit and Southern fried chick lit novels and ask where Lockwood's novel fits. Respondents usually propose that it falls somewhere in the middle. The cover's cartoon woman, drawn by artist Anne Keenan Higgins, is the prototypical sexy string bean described by Dowd. Indeed, as the cover illustrator for a number of chick lit novels—including books by Sophie Kinsella, author of the bestselling Shopaholic series—Higgins in no small measure defines the chick lit aesthetic. But the image also features symbols of the South—a red pickup truck with a license plate that reads, "I (heart) Dixie," for example—as is characteristic of Southern fried chick lit.

This analysis reveals how the text is positioned to corner two markets: buyers of both mainstream chick lit and a Southern subset of the genre. This marketing strategy aligns Lockwood's novel with the contemporaneity of chick lit. While Southern fried chick lit tells stories about women's lives in today's South, these modern tales can be masked behind covers ornamented with old emblems of the region: the peach, a symbol of Georgia since the nineteenth century, or the antebellum plantation house. In contrast, chick lit covers regularly spotlight *à la mode*

93

accessories, using trendy status symbols like Hermès Birkin bags and Christian Louboutin stilettos to signal the protagonists' (and authors') up-to-the-minute chic. Comparing and contrasting these cover art styles helps students see how the past—signified by peaches and plantation houses—is used to sell stories of the South. And after determining *how* the past defines the South in popular culture, students are ready to tackle the question of *why* this is the case. For this analysis, we move from *Dixieland Sushi*'s cover art to its engagement with the celluloid South.

In novels, movies, and television shows, the popular culture South is often both distinctive and dated. Whether a dream awash in moonlight and magnolias or a nightmare teeming with moonshine and misfits, the cinematic South is frequently out of step with contemporary American life. In *Dixieland Sushi*, narrator Jen ponders the discrepancies between Hollywood's South and her South, concluding, "I can only imagine the image of the American South being broadcast to hundreds of countries across the world" (119). The novel's engagement with late-twentieth-century movies and television shows provides a platform for considering how and why popular media commonly present an outdated South.

"Dixieland would never be chosen for the setting of one of those endearing Southern movies like *Steel Magnolias* or *Fried Green Tomatoes*," Jen observes, because it was too contemporarily Southern: filled with Burger Kings and Dairy Queens rather than folksy beauty salons and quaint cafés (169). The iconic films Jen mentions offer up not the real South but the reel South—the region as pictured in the American cinematic imaginary. For example, the place called Whistle Stop, Alabama, in *Fried Green Tomatoes* is in fact Juliette, Georgia, a dilapidated one-horse town that was "nearly forgotten" until the moviemakers "discovered Juliette and reconstructed the existing buildings into the fictional community of Whistle Stop" ("Juliette"). These cinematic examples enrich class discussions by bringing into focus the salable South: the picture of the region capable of earning praise and profits from a national audience. These two comedy-drama films, each of which garnered Oscar nominations and grossed over $80 million at the domestic box office, render Southern distinctiveness a visible feature of the landscape. Small towns with two-lane main streets dotted with distinctive mom-and-pop stores, not communities brimming with internationally known franchises, define the South in these movies. *Dixieland Sushi* defines its setting in contradistinction to cinema's time-capsule South. Lockwood's Dixieland is an up-to-date place whose skyline is marked with "giant golden arches": a feature of the built environment that links contemporary cities from Tupelo to Tokyo, showcasing global interconnectedness rather than regional distinctiveness (169).

Riley's visions of the South, gleaned from movies and television shows, offer the novel's most vivid examples of popular culture's picture of the region. Riley reports that "everybody watched" *Dallas* and *The Dukes of Hazzard* when he was growing up in England (119). He calls the impending nuptials of Jen's cousin "the Hee Haw wedding" (58) and declares that his outfit for the occasion will be "overalls. Without a shirt. Like Jed Clampett from the *Beverly Hillbillies*" (108). He accounts for his desire to attend this wedding in Dixieland by explaining, "I've always wanted to visit the set of *Deliverance*" (58). While encompassing a varied swath of 1960s–1980s Americana, Riley's media consumption yields a consistent portrait of the South. With the possible exception of *Dallas*, these cultural productions depict the US South as rural and retrograde. The characters on *Hee Haw* and *The Beverly Hillbillies* are yokels. The Dukes, eponymous heroes of their series, and the menacing hillbillies in *Deliverance* live in rural Georgia. Riley's tongue-in-cheek interest in visiting the set of *Deliverance*, in particular, calls to mind media-born images of rabid rusticity, because the 1972 film adaptation of James Dickey's 1970 novel "entered popular consciousness as a cautionary tale of the unrepressed savagery awaiting civilized white men just off the road in the southern wilderness" (Graham 182). These movies and television shows make manifest what Tara McPherson calls "our cultural schizophrenia about the South" (3). McPherson identifies this schizophrenia in representations of the antebellum South, epicenter of both the horrors of slavery and nostalgic conceptions of plantation life. But this schizophrenia also impacts depictions of the postbellum South, home to both the doltish Jethro of *The Beverly Hillibillies* and the demonic rapists of *Deliverance,* and thus a rustic enclave simultaneously simpler and scarier than the rest of the nation.

While the late-twentieth-century South was more rural than the nation at large, this fact alone cannot account for the horde of hayseeds in movies and television shows. In the last decades of the twentieth century, the region did not lag far behind the nation in rates of urbanization. In 1980 (when Jen would have been six years old, and Riley somewhere around that age), one-third of Southerners lived in rural areas, compared to one-fourth of all Americans. Were *The Dukes of Hazzard* striving for realism rather than ratings, then perhaps Bo and Luke Duke would have been running maple syrup rather than moonshine, because the state with the most significant rural population during the show's heyday was Vermont, where 66 percent of people lived in the country (US Census Bureau).

These media-made Southerners offer a jumping-off point for talking about viewers' appetites for backwoods folks with backward ways. While students may not be familiar with every example Riley mentions, introducing a few still images or video clips can lay the groundwork for analyzing more recent shows that perpetuate Southern stereotypes— and the redneck reality programming currently in vogue affords a treasure trove of material that students are eager to discuss. In my classes, we interrogate specific elements of these television shows to consider how and why rural Southerners are depicted as riveted to the past. For instance, I ask, Why is the Dukes' car called the General Lee? Why are performers on so many of these programs costumed in overalls? Why do commercials for and articles about MTV's reality show *Buckwild* repeatedly feature cast member Shain Gandee's statement, "I don't have no phone. I don't have a Facebook. I don't have none of that Internet stuff" (qtd. in Bradner)? By considering possible answers to questions like these, we grapple with why, whether positively spun as quaint or negatively depicted as queer, media's contemporary Southerner is often an out-of-date hick.

Yet Lockwood's aim in deploying references to popular culture is to create "common ground." As she explains in an afterword titled "Up Close and Personal with the Author," popular entertainment "can cut through traditional boundaries, because it's not generally divisive, but inclusive since its primary purpose is to entertain." And, indeed, the film most central to the novel—*The Karate Kid*—works in this way, crossing boundaries and forging links. For one thing, references to Jen's favorite childhood movie create connections between the 1980s film and this 2000s novel. Pearls of wisdom from Mr. Miyagi, the karate master played by Pat Morita in *The Karate Kid* trilogy, serve as chapter epigraphs, offering inspiration and advice germane to Jen's career, familial relationships, and burgeoning romance. For another thing, the film strengthens ties among facets of Jen's identity. Because Jen looks to American mass culture to understand both her Japanese and her Southern heritage—mixing Mr. Miyagi's maxims with Daisy Duke's Southern belle blandishments—the novel ultimately can move class discussions beyond regional stereotypes into broader questions of identity construction and identification. Jen recounts that her paper on "Mr. Miyagi as a Japanese American culture icon" was censured by a professor as a poor way to get in touch with her "'authentic' Japanese self" (18). Yet Jen knows the power of imaginative identifications, explaining that her family members were devotees of the television show *Dallas* because "we saw ourselves in their struggles, even though we weren't rich, white, or from Texas" (99). My students and I talk about how identifying with imaginary others can move viewers beyond their own ethnic and regional identities, and how this move can open up new perspectives on the South and its people.

Contemporary Southern Distinctiveness

Whether we address it explicitly or implicitly, and regardless of the ways we work to complicate or trouble it, the idea of Southern distinctiveness is the raison d'être of Southern studies. But in educating our students about what makes the South unique, we part ways with earlier generations of Southern scholars who worked to root Southern distinctiveness in a single idea or experience—whether white supremacy, or yeoman culture, or familiarity with poverty, guilt, and defeat. Instead of trying to trace it to a single source, we teach Southern distinctiveness as an evolving set of ideas about and aspects of Southern places and populations reflective of the region's ethnic, racial, religious, sexual, socioeconomic, and topographic diversity.

The most famous works of Southern literature—novels like *Adventures of Huckleberry Finn* (1884), *Gone with the Wind* (1936), and *To Kill a Mockingbird* (1960)—dramatize lives defined by a binary opposition between blackness and whiteness. One way that blind spots can develop from reading lists dominated by these kinds of works, as legal scholar Juan F. Perea argues, is that "because the Black/White binary paradigm is so widely accepted, other racialized groups like Latinos/as, Asian Americans, and Native Americans are often marginalized or ignored altogether" (346). By moving beyond the black/white binary that still dominates much popular Southern fiction (including the recent best-seller *The Help*), *Dixieland Sushi* helps in teaching about the social and political complexity of the multiracial South.

In the past decade, Southern voters elected the nation's first Indian American governor and first Vietnamese American member of Congress. In 2000, 19 percent of America's Asian population lived in the South (Barnes and Bennett 4). Arkansas, the setting for Lockwood's story, saw its Asian population double between 1990 and 2000, with 20 percent of those 2000 respondents using the Census's new "mark one or more" (MOOM) option to identify as both Asian and at least one other race (5).[1] Centered on a character who consistently conceives of her racial and regional identities in both/and (rather than either/or) terms, *Dixieland Sushi* offers concrete examples that can ground in-class discussions about these cultural and political shifts.

Protagonist Jen stresses fusion—a both/and approach—at every turn. Her family creates Asian-Southern hybrid cuisine by, for example, putting soy sauce on chicken fried steak. When her college roommate calls her a Twinkie, declaring her "yellow on the outside, white on the inside," Jen rejects this bifurcation of her racial identity (38). Indeed, Jen backs away from all efforts to pigeonhole her into a single race or ethnicity. When a date refers to her as Japanese, she corrects him, explaining that she's "half, actually" (33). His subsequent assumptions—that Jen will be interested in hearing about his visit to Tokyo, will enjoy sake and sushi for dinner, and will speak Japanese—ensure that, as far as Jen is concerned, their first date will be their last one. Nationality, too, is treated as a both/and rather than an either/or proposition. Riley, Jen's coworker and eventual boyfriend, is the son of an American mother and an English father. Born in Dallas but raised in London, young Riley was humiliated when his kindergarten teacher informed his classmates that he was "a Yank from America" (114). Lockwood's central characters embrace their racial or national hybridity rather than cleaving to only one part of their identities.

Approaching identity as a both/and proposition opens up new ways of talking about Southern distinctiveness. Students who enroll in Women in the South after taking my Introduction to Southern Studies course have read the work of historian C. Vann Woodward. Writing in the 1950s, Woodward argues that Southerners' "un-American experience" with guilt, poverty, and defeat makes them unique in a nation associated with innocence, wealth, and success (17). My students understand the utility of Woodward's definition of Southern distinctiveness even now, more than a half-century later, but they also see its limitations. Like Lockwood's protagonist, my students embrace a both/and identity paradigm. That is, they identify as both Southerners and Americans, merging regional traditions with national trends. For instance, a typical day might see them grabbing breakfast at Starbucks but then heading to the 15th Street Diner for a meat-and-three lunch, thereby enjoying both national foodways and regional ones. Talking about Lockwood's both/and approach to identity establishes a context for understanding and talking about their own both/and forms of identity.

This both/and construction of Southern identity paves the way to understanding a both/and definition of Southern distinctiveness. In an article published around the same time as Lockwood's novel, Larry J. Griffin contends that formulating a singular definition of the region— or the nation, for that matter—means imposing an order "artificially devoid of significant internal diversity and schism" (14). He closes his essay with a crescendo of both/and observations that echoes in-class conversations about racial and regional diversity:

> [The South] and America are both rural and urban, cosmopolitan and provincial, moral and immoral, radical and reactionary, rich and poor, brown and red, and yellow and black and white, and when the issue of Southern distinctiveness is raised . . . it is both useful and fair to ask, *Which* America? *Which* South? To ask, Why *this* South? Why *that* America? (19)

Griffin's closing questions are the same ones raised by efforts to define Jen's both/and identity in either/or terms. For Jen, identifying as Asian *or* Caucasian would mean choosing one side of her family over the other, a move she eschews early in the novel: "If I embrace one half of my heritage over the other it seems like I'm playing favorites" (17). Studying the novel's treatment of mixed-race identity opens up opportunities for talking about recent regional and national shifts in racial demographics and definitions.

In *Dixieland Sushi*, white characters' responses to Asian foods—sushi in particular—illustrate how an "us" versus "them" dichotomy takes shape. While sushi moves from unique to ubiquitous in the United States from Jen's childhood to adulthood, it is used to distinguish Jen from other people in both periods. Getting students to discuss this seeming paradox—that the volte-face from foreign to familiar does not diminish sushi's Othering potential—lays the groundwork for tackling an issue that hits closer to home: while the past century has seen the South change from a place of starvation to a land of obesity in the American cultural imaginary, either of these conflicting images can be used to position the region as a "negative standard" for the rest of the country (Griffin 11). The novel's treatment of sushi thus offers a useful model for thinking through the double-edged politics of Southern distinctiveness.

Sushi serves as a barometer of people's ideas about Jen's Japanese ancestry. The text opens with Jen's tenth birthday party, held at the Dixieland Roller Rink. Everything at the bash is cool to its 1980s preteen attendees: the decorations are puffy stickers and gel icing, the fashions are Gloria Vanderbilt jeans and Members Only jackets, and the video games are Ms. Pac-Man and Frogger. Everything is cool, that is, except the food. The snacks—cucumber rolls, rice-stuffed tofu sacks called *inari*, and pickled vegetables—are Japanese delights made by Jen's mother and grandmother or "ordered especially for the occasion from San Francisco" (5). While normally appealing, these birthday treats become appalling in this context—capable of, as Jen puts it, "Ruining My Life As I Knew It" (5).

> Now, in the privacy of my own home, away from the questioning eyes of Kevin Peterson, I would gladly have devoured the sushi and pickled treats. But under his gaze, as I saw the look of horror and surprise as the pungent combination of smells reached his nose, I found myself frozen with mortification.
>
> "Ew," he breathed, his nose wrinkling, ... "WHAT is THAT?" (5)

What is familiar and fondly consumed at home with her family becomes foreign and foul when served in the Dixieland Roller Rink to
her friends. Here difference is incarnated in ethnic foodstuffs, and Jen's
own vision is distorted as a result of Kevin's "questioning eyes." Looking
at these foods, Jen watches them transform from the yummy morsels
she knows to the unappetizing objects Kevin must see: the dried fish
"look surprisingly like shriveled monkey claws," while the inari "in the
roller disco light, looked suspiciously like cat livers" (5). In this moment,
Jen sees her cultural heritage take tangible form and differentiate her
from her peers—an unwelcome instance of Othering for Jen who, like
so many children, desperately wants to fit in.

While sushi next appears in the novel as a food served by—rather
than scorned by—a white man, it again functions to Other Jen. In the
two decades between Jen's roller rink birthday party and her date with
John, sushi has become, as Jen observes, "as common as hot dogs" in
the United States (35). As a result, the sushi John serves isn't the "gourmet delicacy" that Jen's grandmother says it should be but instead stale
sushi "probably bought from a chain grocery store" (36). Although it
has moved from niche Japanese delicacy to ubiquitous American food,
sushi still inspires an Othering gaze. John is what Jen calls "an AO blood
type, meaning Asian Obsessed," and his fixation is evinced by his taste
for sushi, his apartment filled with Asian-inspired tchotchkes, and his
interest in Jen, which grows after he learns of her part-Asian heritage
(33). In discussing how John exoticizes Jen—viewing her through an
"AO" lens that makes her look like "a two-dimensional sex fantasy"—
students conclude that while Kevin and John respond to Jen in opposite
ways, the effect is the same for Jen (34). Whether exorcized from her
childhood cool kids' circle or eroticized by her date, Jen is differentiated
from those around her.

In discussing how sushi can go from unique to ubiquitous yet still
be used by others to mark out Jen, we establish a paradigm for tackling
a touchier subject: how Southerners morphed from famished to fat in
the American imaginary, yet remain stigmatized in either incarnation.
A recent *Time* article rather indelicately called "Why Are Southerners
So Fat?" answers the question its title poses by noting, "Southerners
have little access to healthy food and limited means with which to

purchase it" (Suddath). These same access and resource limitations plagued Southerners a century ago.

> Socioeconomic factors, environment, and food security are issues as influential to the well-being of southerners today as they were more than 100 years ago. It is still primarily the low-income residents of remote, rural areas who are struggling for access to fresh foods, but instead of the cornbread and fatback that was popular during the early 20th century, southerners today have an array of quick, processed meals at their disposal. (N. Brown 123)

Poverty-induced nutritional imbalances afflict twentieth- and twenty-first-century Southerners alike. But while the inexpensive foodstuffs of the last century produced starvation, today's cheap foods lead to obesity. Both bodily states can inspire responses of disgust and dissociation. As scholar Kathleen LeBesco writes, "[F]at people are widely represented in popular culture . . . as revolting—they are agents of abhorrence and disgust" (1). But the gaunt, bony bodies of underfed Southerners inspired similarly harsh and distancing responses. In her autobiography, Virginia Foster Durr describes how her parents taught her to understand the poor people she encountered as a child in early twentieth-century Alabama: "If they had pellagra and worms and malaria and if they were thin and hungry and immoral, it was just because that was the way they were" (31). Southerners are represented as revolting both when depicted as a headless bulging belly next to a colossal container of French fries, as in the photograph that accompanies the *Time* article, and when described as a "thin and hungry" composite of disorders born of poverty and poor nutrition, as in Durr's autobiography. Here, then, the double-edged nature of Southern distinctiveness is made clear to students. As something defined both within and beyond the region, Southern distinctiveness is a set of ideas giving rise to both association and dissociation. And while the characteristics seen as Southern may evolve or even do an about-face, the stigma surrounding what is Southern may persist.

Maureen Dowd concludes her critique of chick lit with a barbed zinger: "The novel was once said to be a mirror of its times. In my local bookstore, it's more like a makeup mirror" (A15). Yet *Dixieland Sushi* does serve as a mirror of its times for my classes, offering a reflection of contemporary US culture conducive to interdisciplinary analysis. In Women in the South, the book provides a springboard for discussing how contemporary novels target their audiences as well as how contemporary movies depict the South. The novel also affords a vantage point onto how racial hybridity and ethnic Othering shape the experiences of contemporary Americans. Tara McPherson observes that fictional representations can "open the space for imagining other ways of being southern" (11), and *Dixieland Sushi* does just that, pointing us to some of the ways that regional distinctiveness can shape the lives of contemporary southerners.

"A Right to Be Hostile"

Black Cultural Traffic in the Classroom

RICHARD SCHUR

KENNELL JACKSON USES the metaphor of "black cultural traffic" to describe the interactions between texts and contexts in African American life. He writes, "[W]hen we speak of the traffic in Black cultural material, we often refer to fragments of cultural complexes that break loose and assume a life of their own" (11). For Jackson, the metaphor of traffic suggests how texts ebb and flow through culture and place, can move in multiple directions, and are comprised of an almost infinite number of competing desires, goals, and objectives. In other words, black popular culture is not a destination or a specific place but an exchange of ideas, images, texts, and practices, some of which began their journeys outside of the black community while others were initially rejected by many African Americans only to gain acceptance later. Jackson's understanding of black cultural traffic suggests that there can be at least two potential "traffic jams" when bringing black popular culture into the classroom. There is the potential conflict within the black community about the meaning and value of a specific text and a second venue for contestation and resistance when black texts travel to outsider audiences.

This concept of cultural traffic builds on the work of cultural studies scholars from the past few decades. Challenging the idea that popular culture is merely fun or entertainment, cultural studies scholarship has brought new depth and nuance to the study of popular culture.

Stuart Hall, who helped revise Marxist approaches to popular culture, argued that cultures should be "conceived not as separate 'ways of life', but as 'ways of struggle'" (451). For Hall, popular culture is "the arena of consent and resistance. It is partly where hegemony arises, and where it is secured" (453). This means that the study of black popular culture necessarily invokes and involves contemporary social cleavages. For Hall, the significance of black texts is their ability to protect or challenge existing power relationships. Hall helped transform how scholars understood the relationship between leisure activities and cultural power. In particular, Hall argued that cultural texts do not produce or support specific hegemonic structures but are an integral part of the war of positions that is happening within a society.

Janice Radway applied Hall's and the Birmingham School of Cultural Studies' understanding of popular culture to the romance novels consumed by women. She found that women readers frequently read these books in ways that challenged traditional female roles, despite the seemingly patriarchal nature of the plots (11). Radway's methodology encouraged scholars to understand romance readers as active participants, not mere passive consumers (221). Similarly, in a series of essays in the 1980s and 1990s, bell hooks explored how many texts from both dominant and black popular culture were doing important cultural work, sometimes challenging racist, sexist, and classist narratives but even more frequently reinforcing hegemonic power. hooks tried to teach her readers how to become "critical spectators" who could "resist the dominant ways of knowing and looking" (*Black Looks* 128). Indeed, in *Teaching Critical Thinking: Practical Wisdom*, hooks writes that "imagination is one of the most powerful modes of resistance that oppressed and exploited folks can and do use. In traumatic situations, it is imagination that can provide a survival lifeline" (61).

During the early 2000s, I wanted to bring this exciting scholarly work into my classrooms. Sharing the assumption with Hall, Radway, and hooks that popular cultural texts constituted key sites in the battle for hegemony, I wanted to encourage my students to become critical thinkers based on this emerging approach to popular culture. I came up with the idea of beginning my survey courses in African American literature and ethics with popular contemporary African American texts. My hypothesis was that using these texts would allow my classes to explore issues of justice, hegemony, and inequality, thus engaging my students and bringing the history of African American literature and ethics alive. I thought that if we could begin the surveys with the current controversies, our journey backward would seem more familiar as we could see the origin of contemporary issues in those older texts. I also thought that these texts would be entertaining and perhaps even more engaging than more traditional and canonical texts.

My experiment, however, did not quite go as planned. My use of popular black writing seemed to provoke either confusion or hostility from my mostly white students. They thought I was describing a "noteworthy" place/space with these texts rather than a series of oppositions and conflicts. Jackson's concept of black cultural traffic helps provide some strategies for effectively incorporating black popular texts in the college classroom. In this essay, I am arguing that scholars of popular culture and African American literature would be wise to develop pedagogies that attend to the cultural traffic around these texts as much as the texts themselves. Because race, gender, sexuality, and socioeconomic status shape the construction, journey, and reception of black cultural texts, these must be part of class discussion.

My Experiment

For a couple of semesters in the early 2000s, I began my African American literature courses by assigning a collection of *The Boondocks* comics by Aaron McGruder entitled *A Right to Be Hostile*. Teaching at a historically and predominately white institution, my students were not quite sure what to make of the comic strips, but they loved the idea of reading a comic strip in a literature class. Riley, Huey, Jasmine, and the whole *Boondocks* world of young African Americans in a white suburb, being raised by civil rights and post–civil rights-era parents, struck a chord with my students, even if they didn't quite understand it all. The ensuing class discussions were marked by both belly laughs and awkward silences; my mostly white students did not understand a significant number of the jokes, and trying to explain why they were funny proved quite challenging. The gap between what *The Boondocks* assumed its readers knew about the world, especially about the ordinary lives of African Americans, and the lives of my mostly rural white students revealed to them—and me—just how important a course like African American Literature might be. I hoped that the course, if successful, could help bridge the chasm between black and white points of view that reading *The Boondocks* exposed.

Although things did not go perfectly with *The Boondocks*, they went well enough that I decided to use Sister Souljah's *The Coldest Winter Ever* as an introductory text for my general education course in ethics. Souljah's novel tells the story of Winter Santiaga, the daughter of a drug dealer who must fend for herself once her father goes to jail. From my perspective, the novel explores how Winter navigates the morally ambiguous world of street drug culture in urban America. Moreover, the story describes how Winter's concept of the good life and her moral code have been shaped by her neighborhood. To my surprise, however, the students hated the book and its main character and struggled to see how her choices to become a drug dealer and engage in premarital sex were anything but unethical, and therefore not fodder for discussion in an ethics class. Even more damning, the students found the writing and the story too "lowbrow" and not worthy of their attention. Their reaction surprised me because it was quite different from their response to *The Boondocks*. While the students found some common ground with Huey, Riley, and their granddad, they did not feel any sort of connection with Winter.

As I have reflected upon these divergent responses, I have come to realize that I had been merely teaching the texts, not the texts as illustration of black cultural traffic. I needed to focus more on texts' journeys and the traffic jams they encountered. The paths to "popularity" for *A Right to Be Hostile* and *The Coldest Winter Ever* were quite different ones and are worth contemplating. *A Right to Be Hostile* began in 1997 in a student newspaper at the University of Maryland, where Aaron McGruder, author of the *Boondocks* strip, majored in African American studies. In 1999 the Universal Press Syndicate picked up his work, which soon began appearing in newspapers across the United States. At the height of its popularity, the *Boondocks* comic strip appeared in more than three hundred daily newspapers, including the *Los Angeles*

Times, *Chicago Tribune*, and *Washington Post*. It is not accidental that the majority readership of these papers is white, nor is it unremarkable that the black readers of these publications were likely to have more formal education than many African Americans.

The Boondocks gained popularity through traditional print media and frequently explored the challenges and humor of growing up black in the suburbs; hence it was read by and resonated with those of a certain class and educational status. To speak of *The Boondocks* as a popular text is, of course, correct, but it is equally essential to identify with whom the strip was popular. Or, in Jackson's terms, it is not enough to identify *The Boondocks* as popular; rather, we must chart its starting point at a major state university and explore its travels through American culture.

By contrast, *The Coldest Winter Ever* has taken a very different path in its journey to becoming a popular text. The author, Sister Souljah, became nationally known during the 1992 presidential campaign. Talking about the Los Angeles riots, the *Washington Post* quoted her as saying, "If black people kill black people every day, why not have a week and kill white people?" (Mills B1). The quotation was obviously confrontational, but it allowed then candidate Bill Clinton to demonstrate his credentials as someone who was tough on crime by criticizing Souljah in the harshest terms. Significantly, Clinton's war of words with Souljah also functioned as a censure of hip-hop music and culture, as Sister Souljah had recently joined the rap group Public Enemy, known for its political and black nationalist message. Thus, although she was a well-traveled college graduate from Rutgers, Souljah was positioned as a voice of the streets and of ordinary black folks. From the get-go, she entered American and African American popular culture as a dissenting voice challenging white supremacy. Perhaps even more important, she deployed the language, symbols, and metaphors not of the middle class but of black urban America.

Souljah released a solo rap record and an autobiography before publishing her first novel, *The Coldest Winter Ever*, in 1999. Unlike *The Boondocks,* Sister Souljah's novel offered a literary representation of the life that hip-hop and its many fans idolized—and by which many were horrified. Drawing on the models of 1970s black pulp writers such as Iceberg Slim and Donald Goines, *The Coldest Winter Ever* helped create, along with books by Teri Woods and Vickie Stringer among others, a new genre of writing known as "street lit" or urban fiction. But these writers did not enjoy the relatively unprecedented distribution deal received by Aaron McGruder; these women started by selling their novels out of their automobile trunks and any other way they could. Today, however, street literature is ubiquitous and can be found in online stores and major bookstores, while *The Boondocks* is no longer published in daily newspapers.

Clearly *The Boondocks* and *The Coldest Winter Ever* have taken different routes through American and African American culture. As a result, they found overlapping but distinct audiences. While McGruder sought and found a national distribution deal through major urban newspapers, Sister Souljah's book found its audience in a more decentralized manner: readers recommended *The Coldest Winter Ever* to their friends, and it gained credibility from the bottom up. The distinctive journeys of these two texts through black popular culture are a product, in part, of how the two authors go about representing and criticizing African American culture. Souljah's novel captures the sights, sounds, and "reality" of urban America that could not be found elsewhere. Unlike more recent entries into street lit, it neither overly criticizes nor glamorizes its protagonist's choices, enabling an effective connection with her audience of young urban African Americans. It is this ambiguous authorial perspective, however, that confused the students in my class. McGruder, on the other hand, reiterates familiar criticisms of hip-hop and urban culture, especially in handling the character of Riley, which was a position that my students found familiar.

Why did the students eventually find common ground with *The Boondocks* but not *The Coldest Winter Ever?* The concept of black cultural traffic helps explain how the production, distribution, publication, and reception of texts is crucial for shaping how audiences—and students—respond and how texts come to gain a social meaning. When there is a traffic jam, like my attempt to teach *The Coldest Winter Ever*, it signals social and cultural conflict. In retrospect, it makes complete sense that white middle-class kids from largely conservative and rural backgrounds would struggle to find common ground with Winter Santiaga but be able to connect at some level with middle-class suburban kids like Riley and Huey. In her seminal essay "Mapping the Margins," Kimberle Crenshaw argues that social policy has relied too much on sets of overbroad binaries that do not capture fully or effectively how identity works (1242). While Crenshaw is writing about the failure of legal institutions to remedy sexism and racism, I would argue that her insight applies to the college literature classroom as well. My experience has taught me that students can overcome one or two social differences, but encountering too many social differences at one time can and will interfere (i.e., create a traffic jam) with the ability of readers to relate to characters and ultimately connect with a popular text.

When I came up with the idea to assign *The Boondocks* to the white students in my African American Literature and Culture class, I thought it would be the perfect way to introduce the main course themes, since I had enjoyed it myself and believed at least some of my students would be regular readers. But to my surprise, none of the students had ever heard of Aaron McGruder or *The Boondocks*. Immediately, then, my purpose in choosing a popular text to engage my students was frustrated. This is not to suggest that they did not enjoy reading a comic strip for homework; they did. However, the text, much of its subject matter, and its allusions were just as new and foreign to them as beginning the course with a slave narrative would have been. Actually, the situation was more difficult because many of them knew less about the civil rights movement and post–civil rights era politics than they knew about the Civil War, which they were trained to treat as worthy of intense study and careful reading. A comic strip, they told me, was just fun, not something to be read systematically or analyzed. I also think that these particular students had concluded, perhaps unconsciously, that education was supposed to address only the "best" of what has been thought and written, and that it should not necessarily engage students in contemporary political, moral, and existential conflict.

I quickly found that rather than using a popular text to engage students by having them look at "their" beliefs, values, and practices as articulated by McGruder, decoding and explaining the comic strip become the focus of class discussions. For example, when I asked them to discuss how a particular strip criticized some aspect of contemporary race relations, they frequently responded that they did not know the issue being discussed, did not understand the political reference, and certainly did not see what was funny about the strip. After picking my jaw up off the proverbial floor, I would then work through the situation, explaining how the strip was a metaphor for the experiences of many African Americans, identifying the people, events, or texts it discussed, and finally trying to illuminate the joke at the heart of the strip. Sometimes, the humor remained after it had been fully discussed; sometimes not. Once I gave the class a homework assignment to research an especially funny strip and try to figure out why it was funny; I even allowed them to ask up to three people for their insight. But even that strategy did not work because they mostly asked their white rural friends and families, who also did not understand the strip's cultural context. I now realize that our conversations rarely focused on the text's journey through popular culture, traffic jams, or the life cycle of texts from creation and publication to distribution and reception.

By now, the paradox of my teaching should be obvious: how to teach white students about African American culture through texts that have been a part of black cultural traffic yet continue to circulate within and between varied social and cultural groups. I frame this as a paradox because, as Jackson argues, black texts can travel in multiple directions and end up in different places as they make their way through culture. While most texts journey between and within social groups, black texts travel in complex ways, especially after the civil rights movement and the Black Arts movement, when black writers are frequently encouraged to integrate within dominant culture yet maintain a distinctive black aesthetic. Moreover, reading and consuming black texts has also become a marker of "enlightened" racial attitudes for many nonblack readers today. Rarely, however, can a single black text meet all these expectations and all these audiences. So, while certain texts may be popular, their popularity is highly specific: *The Boondocks* and *The Coldest Winter Ever* were popular for those who bought them and read them *initially*. *The Boondocks* straddled black and white audiences with its middle-class sensibility and its ironic attitude toward black cultural politics, whereas *The Coldest Winter Ever* embraced the politics of authenticity, shared by hip-hop and the Black Arts movement. Rather than use class time to explicate passages, it would have been more effective to focus conversation on how these texts travel through American culture to various groups.

In a perspicacious essay on Paul Laurence Dunbar, who tried to reach a similar large range of black and white audiences as McGruder and Souljah, the poet Kevin Young contrasts dialect and vernacular language and provides a road map of sorts to trace the terrain of black popular culture. For Young, dialect is a literary shortcut or stereotype that "is a fiction posing as the real thing" (99). Vernacular, by contrast, constitutes a more accurate representation of how ordinary people talk. Dunbar's genius, according to Young, is his ability to see both dialect and modernist poetics as "artificial languages that mirror yet mask actual speech" (115). The goal of "African American Vernacular English," Young asserts, is often "to confuse as much as communicate; it is 'untranslatable' because it does not want to be. Rather, it seeks to divide: black from white, young from old, hip from square" (129). Significantly, Dunbar actually wrote poetry both in dialect and in "standard" English. While it is the latter poetry, especially his "We Wear the Mask," that is most frequently anthologized today, black and white audiences of his day gravitated to the dialect poetry. Indeed, it constituted the "popular" black poetry of his day, so much so that Alain Locke and the members of the Harlem Renaissance created an artistic program, the "New Negro" movement, to challenge this popular conception of African Americans. Young's discussion of the shifting way Dunbar's poetry has been read and valued helps illuminate the concept of black cultural traffic. First, Young's analysis reveals how a given text can gain or lose popular acclaim as shifting patterns of receptions respond to specific textual elements. Second, Young shows how a text's starting point can affect and shape its journey through American culture. Third, it suggests that some authors resist the general flow of cultural traffic and certain destinations for their work.

While neither McGruder nor Souljah explicitly engage or explain their use of dialect and vernacular language, they have used language, metaphors, and symbols to affect their texts' journeys through American culture. McGruder's strip and Souljah's novel go out of their way to offend and exclude readers who do not share their perspective and values. McGruder has gone so far as to print reader criticisms of the strip on the back covers of his books. One collection, for example, quotes a disgruntled reader: "I think it's horrible ... I glance at it, and sometimes I read it, and afterwards I think 'Why did I do that?'" (2001). Another quotes Robert Johnson, then the owner of the Black Entertainment Network (BET): "The most appalling of McGruder's reckless charges was that BET 'does not serve the interest of Black people.' Our response to this slanderous assertion is that the 500-plus dedicated employees of BET do more in one day to serve the interest of African Americans than this young man has done in his entire life" (2000). These criticisms are offset by supporting comments from hipper fans, from the documentary filmmaker Michael Moore and Public Enemy's "Media Assassin" Harry Allen to the satirical newspaper and website *The Onion*. Hence McGruder seems to embrace conflict and even hostility, reveling in how his social, political, and cultural criticisms hit their targets and produce a certain amount of controversy. Echoing Stuart Hall, McGruder realizes that a popular culture text is not describing a "way of life" but is engaged in a hegemonic struggle with white America. In oversimplified terms, *The Boondocks* is journeying from black America to attack white America in its most vulnerable spot, the suburbs.

Sister Souljah has a different point of departure in mind for her writing. For Souljah, *The Coldest Winter Ever* represents a firm stand against the nihilistic and degrading elements that have taken over hip-hop culture and urban America. She explains her motives in writing the novel: "I knew I wanted to be part of stopping the cycle of stupidity in our community. I knew that to do so, I had to write something that kids and adults could take home and devour, learn from, and share, and pass on" (305). She also describes how after the novel was published she was invited to women's groups, schools, and even prisons. Those trips caused her to realize the potentially liberatory effects of the novel and how it "could become responsible for thousands of teenagers, women, and men, staying out of prison" (292). In other words, Souljah created a text that would circulate primarily within the black community in order to criticize its potentially destructive elements.

Critics have been ambivalent about urban lit texts like Souljah's and their potential effects. On the positive side, Almah Lavon Rice claims that "urban fiction has been credited for converting an entire generation [of African American teens] into readers." On the other hand, however, Rice observes that the novels represent only a portion of black America, a highly sensationalized version at that. She ultimately concludes that novels such as *The Coldest Winter Ever* leave African Americans both "highly visible and still seldom seen." Sean Elder is a bit more critical: "[M]ost of the characters are one dimensional, and the occasional bits of speechifying, while impassioned, complement the crime novel about as well as spinach goes with cherry pie." Nick Chiles is particularly damning of street lit. He asks, "[H]ow are we going to explain ourselves to the next generation of writers and readers who will wonder why they have so little to read of import and value produced in the 21st century, why their founts of inspiration are so parched?" From the perspective of Jackson's theory of black cultural traffic, the resistance to *The Coldest Winter Ever* is a key part of the text's contemporary meaning and value.

The vitriol aimed at McGruder, Sister Souljah, and the writers of street or urban literature follows from the tremendous stakes for African American writing and cultural forms. Since the freedom narrative, African American writers have been forced to balance the burdens of positive representations of African American intellect and culture, political advocacy for improving African American lives, and demonstrating self and group worth via artistic production. Texts, such as McGruder's and Souljah's, that represent aspects of African American life in order to criticize them seem to "air dirty laundry." Because the journeys of these texts cannot be regulated in advance, there is a persistent fear that the wrong people will read these books and get the wrong message. To be sure, there are signs that these burdens are lessening in the twenty-first century as Henry Louis Gates and Touré (among others) argue that there are as many ways to be black as there are African Americans; they have been trying to liberate African American writers from the strictures that have bound earlier generations (Touré 5). Nonetheless, contemporary black writers lament that publishers accept and publish books that provide a fairly narrow representation of black life. In a 2007 *New York Times Sunday Book Review* essay, Martha Southgate, a contemporary author of several post–civil rights era novels, writes:

It saddens me to think of the dreams that have been ditched, the stories that haven't been told because of racism, because of fear and economic insecurity, because that first novel didn't move enough copies. I hope to see the day when there are more of us at the party (and the parties), when the work of African-Americans who tell our part of the American story well receives the celebration, and the sales, it deserves. ("Writers")

Focusing on cultural traffic and the observations of Southgate can help students understand that texts do not simply appear in the classroom, ready to be analyzed and accompanied with writing prompts. Rather, the texts professors choose to teach bear the marks of the publishing industry, the academy, and even the institutions of popular culture. Understanding and evaluating the text should also mean exploring how the text flowed or didn't flow through these sites.

In the context of African American literature, the boundary between elite and popular texts is riddled with anxieties about how African American writers *should* write differently for black and nonblack audiences. Like many popular texts (not just those within African American literature), *The Boondocks* and *The Coldest Winter Ever* reinforce and further cultural and linguistic boundaries. Souljah and McGruder realize that their texts, images, and characters are located quite specifically in terms of social class, race, and gender, and that their stories may not be universally accessible. The texts demand that readers adopt a critical tone or perspective about how whiteness, gender, place, sexuality, and social class shape contemporary social relations. Winter Santiaga of *The Coldest Winter Ever*, along with Huey and Riley from *The Boondocks*, make more sense if viewed through the perspective of intersectionality. If these characters offend, intimidate, or annoy their readers, this only enhances their status as realistic representations or asserts their underlying truth. Of course, this truth is a partial one, at best, and potentially counterproductive at worst because Winter, Huey, and Riley are caricatures, not fully developed characters. Their predicaments and commentary are rooted in today's racial realities, but they emphasize more extreme points of view in order to make their case. As a result, even when my students considered the text's journeys through popular culture, the texts seemed threatening to them primarily because the texts asked their readers to look at contemporary race and social relations from different points of view.

Perhaps contemporary texts such as *The Boondocks* and *The Coldest Winter Ever* become what James Baldwin derisively termed "protest novels" when introduced into the college classroom. Reading popular texts in the classroom asks students to reflect on contemporary issues and highlights social problems that may have been invisible to them. Assigning these texts transforms reading from being mere entertainment to demanding that students take a position on inequality and injustice. For Baldwin, no matter its merits in galvanizing or shaping public opinion, the protest novel lacks aesthetic refinement or depth and fails to represent its characters and conflicts adequately. Baldwin writes:

> The avowed aim of the protest novel is to bring about greater freedom to the oppressed. They are forgiven, on the strength of their good intentions, whatever violence they do to language, whatever excessive demands they make of credulity. It is indeed, considered the sign of a frivolity so intense as to approach decadence to suggest that these books are both badly written and wildly improbable. (14)

Baldwin criticizes the protest novel because it tends to be poorly written. The characters tend to become mere caricature and the plots get reduced to romance or melodrama. In Baldwin's words, "they [protest novels] emerge for what they are: a mirror of our confusion, dishonesty, panic, trapped and immobilized in the sunlit prison of the American dream" (14). I think this quotation presciently summarizes the worlds in which Winter, Huey, and Riley reside and the truths these texts reveal about how readers—whether black or not—accept or reject these characters and the critical vision about contemporary America articulated by these writers.

While Baldwin used the term "protest novel" to criticize Richard Wright and diminish the significance of his work in the pantheon of African American writing, the concept of the "protest novel" may help students take texts like *The Boondocks* and *The Coldest Winter Ever* and their criticisms of American culture more seriously. By viewing popular texts as "protest novels," it requires readers to contemplate what they are protesting and what kind of solutions the writers are offering. *The Boondocks* is more overtly political than *The Coldest Winter Ever*, frequently criticizing political leaders, popular figures, and cultural texts.

The main characters, Huey and Riley, represent competing strategies for responding to remnants of racism and an ongoing racialized society and culture. The humor of the strip and show follows from Huey and Riley's efforts to criticize and/or adopt the representations of blackness offered by American culture. For my students, the *Boondocks* constitutes an alternative public sphere in which they can learn how American culture looks from another point of view. It is an open question, however, whether the strip and later television show reinforces the predictable caricatures of black life offered by dominant culture—for example, blacks as radicals or wannabe street thugs, the ambivalence surrounding multiracial families—or provides an alternative vision.

By contrast, Sister Souljah is much more consciously didactic as she offers Winter as a cautionary tale of what happens when a young girl embraces the stereotypes presented by hip-hop culture. Rather than becoming the hustler and player she imagines, Winter's life falls apart. Not too surprisingly, it is Winter's dramatic descent into a putative hell that resonates with young urban audiences and made the book into a best seller. Souljah intended to use Winter's story to instruct her readers on how to live a better, more moral life. For my students, the lessons fell flat mostly because they could not relate (or would not do so publicly) to Winter's being seduced into the urban drug trade as a young teenager. The other challenge with this novel was the students seemingly being bothered by Winter's sexual escapades. Framing the novel as a protest novel would have helped my students see the book not as a celebration of drugs, sex, and gang life but as a wake-up call for those heading down the wrong path. If I had focused classroom discussion more on whether cautionary tales and protest novels are effective, I could have moved my students away from expressing their feelings about Winter and toward exploring the social value of novels and whether popular culture texts can play a positive role in changing society and culture. Moreover, the question for the protest novel may not be what is it about, but what the journey it takes is and where it ends up.

A Right to Be Hostile

When I initially decided to incorporate contemporary black popular culture texts into my classes, I wanted to build on the excitement of the 1980s and 1990s cultural studies movement. My hypothesis was that these materials would help my students enter into the debates about the ethics and politics of African American literature and race relations as a prelude to sustained critical reading of canonical texts later in the semester. To my surprise, the texts I chose did not instantaneously engage students. Rather, my students were baffled because they either did not understand the references or were angered by them because their preconceptions had not been matched. I recoiled from this conflict and initially viewed my experiment with *The Coldest Winter Ever* as a failure.

Now that I have had some time to reflect on the experience, what I have learned, I think, is that engagement is the wrong way to view the pedagogical value of popular materials. Too often the turn to popular texts seeks to activate notions of "cool" and to find new ways to energize class discussions. But hostility, not cool, is what we need to be exploring with our students. The popular is and has frequently been a place for marginalized groups to challenge hegemony, and we ought to approach it as such when we bring it into the classroom. Even more interesting is how these texts travel or don't travel within and between communities. Kennell Jackson's metaphor of black cultural traffic demands that we attend to the putative departure points of these texts and the routes they travel, especially if they are texts by minority groups. This focus on traffic helps to emphasize blockages—i.e., locations where the texts find hostility—and helps keep the underlying structures of popular culture, from the publishing industry to how texts circulate, as subjects for inquiry. It is the anger and adversarial positioning that makes these texts challenging for students as well as pedagogically productive. What these texts offer are not ready-made issues to debate, like domestic violence, employment discrimination, black crime, or race in the media, but an opportunity to explore how the very debates around these issues are overdetermined by what we think we know about race in America. Black popular texts can help reveal how popular culture structures limit what we know and the kinds of voices we get to hear.

Jackson's approach to black popular traffic is rooted in contemporary theoretical concerns, such as performance theory and the global turn in cultural studies, but I have found that his work has also pushed me backward to James Baldwin's critique of the protest novel. Baldwin's concept of the protest novel explores the ability of literature to speak truth to power and challenge social relations, potentially at the cost of full characterization or by oversimplifying the nature of contemporary black life. If popular cultural materials circulate, in part, as a form of protest and to engage in a struggle against dominant values, their pedagogic value ought to be in their ability to elicit strong emotional responses in students. Asking what is this text protesting and whose views does it seek to change, extend, or challenge is a provocative way to make the text relevant to students. It also highlights the journey the text took to arrive in the classroom. As Aaron McGruder frames it, African Americans have a "right to be hostile," and we do a disservice to our students if we fail to present, explore, and analyze this hostility. Moreover, recognizing this "right to be hostile" authorizes students to challenge—within certain limits—the constraints that popular writing faces. As I think about continuing my forays into using African American popular fiction in my classes, the question for me is how to engage the latent hostility around race and racial representation to help my students become better and more critical readers of the popular imagery that surrounds them.

Gothic, Then and Now

"By showing students how [Lady Gaga] adapts ideas similar to Poe's in new media, I . . . motivat[e] students to look again at Poe's literature as applicable to twenty-first-century discourse surrounding gender in politics and culture."—DEREK MCGRATH, "Teaching *Bad Romance*: Poe's Women, the Gothic, and Lady Gaga"

"With his myriad of literary references, [Stephen] King's work is ideal for bringing the canonical and the contemporary into dialogue with one another."—ALISSA BURGER, "Crossing the Barrier: An Active-Text Approach to Teaching *Pet Sematary*"

Teaching *Bad Romance*

Poe's Women, the Gothic, and Lady Gaga

DEREK MCGRATH

∽

WHEN TEACHING my undergraduate course on the works of Edgar Allan Poe, I strive to capitalize efficiently on student interests and knowledge in order both to teach the major movements in the author's poems, stories, and criticism and to help students hone their analytical and rhetorical skills through close reading. In designing and teaching this course, I practice an approach similar to one outlined by Christine A. Jackson in her studies of Poe and popular culture. That is, I trace Poe's continued influence on popular culture—in film, television, new media, and especially recent music. Albums incorporated into the course range from Lou Reed's spoken-word rock album *The Raven*, to the Gorillaz's pop-electronic album *Plastic Beach*, and finally to Ke$ha's dance-electric pop album *Animal*. Examples from popular culture spice up classroom discussions and draw in quieter students, who are asked first to respond to a set of more recent works of popular culture inspired by Poe that they already know, then to apply those same reading skills to those works of Poe that are less well known. As Richard Keller Simon argues, "[m]any of the differences between trash culture and high culture" revolve around how "storytelling adapts to changing economic, social, and political conditions" (2). This argument guides my approach to teaching in order to motivate myself to update course content each year and stay engaged with the texts that I teach.

I also strive in my class to identify how Poe's frustrating yet varied portrayals of women emerge within the context of the time when he writes, and how the nineteenth century continues to inform twenty-first-century representations of gender. Although my syllabus includes works by Poe's female contemporaries—as well as Poe's own reviews of their works—such as Elizabeth Barrett Browning, Frances Sargent Osgood, and Sarah Josepha Hale, my most successful lessons actually come from tracing Poe's gothic tropes forward into the music of Lady Gaga, alias Stefani Germanotta. In her songs and music videos, Lady Gaga approaches tropes found also in Poe's overall body of work in tales, poetry, and criticism, including the idealized death of beautiful women, heightened representations of domestic violence directed against women, and the mixing of a conventionally feminine sentimentalism with conventionally masculinized images of horror. By showing students how a female artist adapts ideas similar to Poe's in new media, I expand the range of topics and texts available to students in our course for their research, while motivating students to look again at Poe's literature as applicable to twenty-first-century discourse surrounding gender in politics and culture.

Lady Gaga's music video *Bad Romance* appropriates gothic imagery to portray feminine empowerment by using Poe's very tropes, changing the deceased lover from female to male. Lady Gaga's performance suggests how a female protagonist might reenact his violent stories, focusing our class discussions around debates about gender assumptions. Furthermore, although Lady Gaga's use of the word *romance* speaks largely to a sexual relationship, as is often the case in Poe's literature, the word also prompts the class to reconsider the issues of the romance as a dominant literary genre in the nineteenth century. In this essay, I wish to relate some of the opportunities that have resulted from teaching Lady Gaga alongside Poe, the nature of which allows for a more nuanced conversation about Poe's own professional relationship with women, the genre of the romance, and the ways the gothic lineage still persists in modern media.

Although this course's objectives include introducing students to advanced studies of literature and exploring Poe's influence on twenty-first-century popular culture, discussions in our class frequently turn to the author's representations of women. Poe has an affinity for killing off the female characters in works such as "The Black Cat," "Ligeia," and "The Oblong Box"; these characters serve as devices to motivate the plot of his murder mysteries. In addition, his representations of women as idealized objects of beauty (as summarized in his essay "The Philosophy of Composition" and as portrayed in "The Raven") have compromised the potential feminism that scholars such as Leland Person and Nina Baym have attempted to locate in his overall body of literature. These scholars focus primarily on the critical praise that Poe gave to many of his female editors and fellow writers in a number of journals. However, these arguments must be kept in context with images of women in his literature; often, these female characters serve as idealized images of beauty, or as what has become known in online vernacular as "the lost Lenore," placeholders whose loss motivates the plot but who are otherwise silenced characters lacking depth. To guide undergraduate students through the large body of criticism regarding how Poe worked alongside women writers and how he portrayed female characters, I ask them to identify shortcomings that they have seen in twenty-first-century popular culture when it comes to representations of women—and students are highly aware of such discourse, whether in the Bechdel test, the "stuffed in the fridge" trope, the Madonna-whore binary, or how the number of male characters (and male writers) in film and television far outweighs the number of their female counterparts. Students' responses to the representations of women in recent films, music, and television suggest that Poe is part of a larger history of negative representations of women in literature, and his work, which alternatively undermines or celebrates women, provides an excellent opportunity to debate how gender operates throughout a long literary history. Similarly, the violent imagery in Lady Gaga's music videos can potentially undermine the feminism of her body of work.

"All Relationships Are Power Struggles": Love and the American Romance

The song *Bad Romance*, written by Lady Gaga and Nadir "RedOne" Khayat, is about finding a lover to share a relationship that includes the best and worst aspects: Lady Gaga sings that she wants "your love" but also "your ugly," "your disease" (lines 13, 11). In the music video, directed by Francis Lawrence, Lady Gaga's character has been brought forcibly into a futuristic bordello, where her body and mind are slowly altered to make her the perfect female companion for potential male clients. The location is appropriately gothic, with clawing women emerging from above-ground coffins to latch upon their newest test subject, Lady Gaga. Initially resisting the attempts by the bordello's employees to strip her and force her to drink, she seemingly falls under the sway of this tech-nocratic sex-house, dancing for male clients at auction as the bordello's numerous computers track bids. She has been brainwashed, emphasized by how her bodily appearance changes as much as her outfits: her arms and legs twitch and her pupils dilate. Yet the indoctrination does not take for Lady Gaga's character. The video climaxes (so to speak) in the bedroom, where she sets her male client's heart afire—literally, somehow making him burst into flames before ever initiating services. The last image presented is femme fatale Lady Gaga lighting a cigarette off the man's remains, reduced to a smoldering skeleton.

From just its lyrics, *Bad Romance* emphasizes points we raise throughout the semester about the major literary styles Poe uses—and allows us to make use of our university's online subscription to the *Oxford English Dictionary*. The deeply carnal desire that Lady Gaga expresses in her song—"I want . . . the touch of your hand, / I want your leather studded kiss in the sand" (lines 15–16)—allows the class to reflect more deeply on one of Poe's key words, which appears in Lady Gaga's subsequent lyric: "I want your horror" (line 33). *Horror* draws upon an etymology engrained in the body; its most literal definition is "roughness" (def 1a), but, most apt when reading Poe's works, it is also "[a] shuddering or shivering," fear felt on the skin itself (def 2a). The class also considers how Lady Gaga uses the word *romance*. Referring to an intense (traditionally heteroerotic) relationship, this most su-perficial definition likely emerged around 1858, just when Poe's career was concluding (*Selected Writings* 160 n3; def A.I.5.b). In one of its most literary uses, *romance* may also refer to the fantastic, appealing to almost mythological images. Earlier definitions of the word also referred to literature that appealed to lay audiences, as such works were written in vernacular Romance languages rather than the more refined Latin. (Significantly, in her song Lady Gaga translates lyrics back and forth between English and that well-known Romance language, French.) Much later, in part thanks to Poe's contemporary Nathaniel Hawthorne, the word *romance* referred to literature less indebted to actuality, instead more exotic or supernatural in nature, engaging with the imagination to present "the truth of the human heart" (def A.I.5.a; *Selected Writings* 160; Hawthorne 3). Lady Gaga's word choice—titling her song *Bad Romance*—hence invites speculation as to whether she is deliberately drawing on this larger literary history. Although certainly the song refers to problems in sexual relationships, the almost mystical quality to Lady Gaga's video suggests that she is developing a twenty-first-century analog to the nineteenth-century literary genre of the romance. The title *Bad Romance* therefore helps to establish course objectives and invites students to think more deeply about the wider range of definitions associated with particular literary genres: romance need not be a love story but could be much more fantastical.

In addition to this etymological overlap, the music video *Bad Romance* includes visual markers that adapt tropes related to Poe's works. *Bad Romance* visualizes *decadence* and the *grotesque* as described in Poe's works, the former in the evident wealth of the well-dressed men sipping on expensive alcohol while visiting the electronically enhanced bordello, the latter in the physical torture experienced by Lady Gaga as she is transformed into the most suitable product to be auctioned. Both ideas as well correspond with *horror*, which emphasizes the physical transformations experienced by this persona and the ultimate immolation of her would-be suitor. *Decadent*, for example, takes on a double meaning for those men who would purchase her: the word refers as much to richness (like that of the expensive setting for this bordello) as it does decay (like the smoldering corpse of Lady Gaga's murdered client). Numerous appearances of the word *monster* in the video point to the grotesque, a concept whose name derives from *grotto*, as in the locations in Rome where historians during the Renaissance discovered paintings of the kind of exaggerated, hence monstrous bodies that Poe and Lady Gaga present in their works (def A1; *Selected Writings* 78). Most relevant, such grotesque figures emerge in Poe's female characters, whether the horrific transformation of Rowena into Ligeia—a point that I will stress in a moment—or the sickening mutilation of the two women in "The Murders of the Rue Morgue." (Not coincidentally, Lady Gaga's bodily modifications in *Bad Romance* coincide with her mental deterioration, all taking place within her opulent bordello prison.)

Ironically, and according to Poe's own oft-cited philosophy, the death of these women should be elevating. Simply put, as he argues in "The Philosophy of Composition," death is the inevitable movement to a higher state of being, hence the most perfect instance of beauty, which should be the goal of all poetry. In his essay, Poe contrasts beauty with that basest emotion, passion, which possesses "a homeliness (the truly passionate will comprehend me), absolutely antagonistic to that beauty." In contrast, beauty stems not from the stimulus of the heart but "the excitement or pleasurable elevation of the soul" (*Selected Writings* 678). Poe goes on to blame passion as the narrator's flaw in his poem "The Raven," "whose solution he has passionately at heart, [. . .] half in superstition and half in that species of despair which delights in self-torture" over the lost Lenore, an idealized object (*Selected Writings* 680). Significantly, a woman of the same name appeared in Poe's early poem, simply titled "Lenore," who was "the most lovely dead / that ever died so young!" Although the narrator of "The Raven," who felt merely passion, mourns the loss of his lover, her demise in "Lenore" is for the better, "her sweet soul" risen from this "damned earth" to rest "[b]eside the King of Heaven" (lines 7–8, 50, 54, 58).

Lady Gaga, however, revels in brutal demise—albeit, in her music video, happening to an aggressive male sex client, not a young, beautiful woman. Scholars have identified hauntingly beautiful images in her other works, "a beautiful construction of the monstrous body [as] Gaga transforms the dead body signifying the unknown, the hopeless, lifelessness, and death itself into an object of beauty" (Gray 126). In contrast, students in my classes identify how Lady Gaga draws upon Poe's tenuous boundary in distinguishing beauty from mere passion. Students notice how, in *Bad Romance*, Lady Gaga actually strips much of the beauty from any violence or death that is otherwise sentimentalized or etherealized when put into poetry by Poe. Judith Butler, included in our course readings, argues that desire, defined in itself as dependent upon a lack, "is never fulfilled," for to acquire the desired object—in Poe's case, a woman—is to "dissolve the very subject which is the condition of desire itself," and thus no longer to want what is now possessed (381). Poe's solution, then, is the death of a beautiful woman: dead, she possesses no agency to return any love, while the man can go on loving her, continuing to possess her—"Annabel Lee" being a prime example. However, this eternalizing of the female figure is not without some advantage to women placed into seemingly subservient positions to male characters and even a male author such as Poe. These women possess a posthumous power over these men to frighten (as in the case of Poe's Ligeia and Lenore) and destroy (as in the case of Lady Gaga) their male suitors.

To trace how beauty, passion, and love/desire facilitate the appearance of the grotesque in Poe's literature, students seize upon the mystical elements of his texts, echoed in the confusing ending of Lady Gaga's video. Poe's stories (excluding his detective stories) tend to avoid explaining how outcomes arise: building suspense is more important than potentially mundane explanations, such as how the narrator dismembered and hid the body in "The Tell-Tale Heart," how the titular building actually collapsed in "The Fall of the House of Usher," or how Berlifitzing's vengeful spirit returns in the form of a fearsome horse in "Metzengerstein." (Poe's lengthy, and singular, explanation for how a raven learns to speak—it involves a shipwrecked sailor—only made my students chuckle.) What really matters, as Poe himself argues in "The Philosophy of Composition," are not realistic explanations but the effects produced in literary works. Similarly, the ending of *Bad Romance* never explains how or why the client bursts into flames; Lady Gaga, however, presents something new to understanding Poe's portrayals of women. Just as Bonita Rhoads has argued that the murders of women in Poe's stories can be read as the expulsion of female influence from dominant literary movements in his time, Lady Gaga's violent dismissal of her client quickly, effectively dispatches any threat. As her persona was brainwashed to become a sex slave, Lady Gaga's almost-rape-revenge narrative concludes with her as the hero, but without a backstory, without any justification or presumed motivation.

Poe and Lady Gaga therefore both use the mystical to accomplish different ends: where the desired effect Poe describes in "The Philosophy of Composition" is to elevate the soul in sympathy for the dead beautiful woman, Lady Gaga's use of the mystical element serves to highlight the death and bodily disintegration of the male client. Lady Gaga's employment of mystery results not so much in a spiritualized punishment but in a more secular presentation of how this woman's superior, dominant sexuality ultimately kills this man debased by his burning passion.Who or what might be elevated in *Bad Romance* is left unclear, yet the difference in approaches between Poe and Lady Gaga highlights differences in the contexts of the works' productions and receptions. Although Poe's works tend to (but not always) only kill off female characters, Lady Gaga produces content in a time period in which the revenge narrative favors women's acts of violence in retaliation against physical abuse. Yet in her appeal to mystical allusions in *Bad Romance*, Lady Gaga makes the ending so abstruse that the mystery to it mirrors the more bizarre occurrences in Poe's works that receive little logical explanation for how they can happen. Although both Poe and Lady Gaga emphasize the mystical in their works, her works tend to be more sensationalistic, thanks to the visual media she uses through music videos, whereas his attention to torture and murder is filtered through the written word, hence dependent more on individual readers' varying levels of imagination.

Despite different results from similar methods, Poe's and Lady Gaga's works speak to each other based on how students take control of those texts in directing their own critical arguments in classroom discussions and in their seminar papers. Students' responses tend to focus on *Bad Romance*'s similarity to Poe's short story "Ligeia," assigned the same day we watch Lady Gaga's video. The parallels are indeed striking. Because this narrator introduces himself as ignorant of how he met Ligeia, a lover from his past, students are quick to assume he is another of Poe's drug-addled characters, like the narrator of "The Fall of the House of Usher," who imagines his surroundings as "the after-dream of the reveler upon opium" (*Selected Writings* 199). And Ligeia's suitor does himself no favor by admitting his own "opium dreams (for I was habitually fettered in the shackles of the drug)" (169). In true gothic fashion, his story is predicated upon both moral and physical decay: "believ[ing] that [he] met her first and most frequently in some large, old, decaying city near the Rhine" (159), he is left alone when Ligeia dies from disease. However, he felt alone even when with her, because Ligeia was so superior that she was intellectually and emotionally distant—partly symbolized when the narrator knows her only by one name, ignorant of his supposedly beloved Ligeia's "paternal name" (159). And yet he needs her: "sufficiently aware of her infinite supremacy," the narrator "resign[s]" himself "with a child-like confidence" to "her guidance through the chaotic world of metaphysical investigation" (163). Following Ligeia's death, he is desperate enough to kill his new wife, Rowena, and then, using occult magic, to resurrect Ligeia, having her soul occupy Rowena's corpse. But Ligeia comes back wrong, not as a lover but as a monstrous figure who continues to stand over the narrator.

One student reflected on how Rowena/Ligeia comes to mirror Lady Gaga's monstrous appearance in *Bad Romance*: like a vampire or a succubus possessing the woman's body, the Rowena/Ligeia hybrid appears at story's end, initially "[s]hrinking from [the narrator's] touch." He wonders, "*[H]ad she then grown taller since her malady?*" because he fails to realize who—or what—now "stood before [him]." He concludes: "Here then, at least, can I never—can I never be mistaken—these are the full, and the black, and the wild eyes—of my lost love—of the lady—of the LADY LIGEIA!" Her arrival signals just what Lady Gaga means by a bad romance: the female figure, no longer kept in that idealized state of beautiful death, now brought back as something horrifying, "huge masses of long and disshevelled hair, [...] *blacker than the raven wings of the midnight!*" (*Selected Writings* 173; all emphasis in the original). Although blonde Lady Gaga contrasts with Poe's dark-haired woman, she shares with Ligeia (and even accentuates with contact lenses in *Bad Romance*) the dark eyes referred to in the story as "Houri" (*Selected Writings* 161)—in Islam, benevolent women waiting upon the deceased in Heaven.

As in "Ligeia," Lady Gaga's video documents a man and a woman unable to have a romantic relationship: this "bad romance" is a destructive sexual contract, abusing the mind and body of the woman and resulting (if only potentially in Poe's story) in the murder of the man. But as one student identified, the violence is also implicit in the dissonance between the lyrics and the images: a seemingly innocuous dance song about couples simply failing to see eye to eye becomes, in visual terms, a fierce struggle. Similar dissonances arise in the process of reading Poe's literature, as darker insights emerge from reading his love poems through the lens of his gothic tales. Moreover, the manipulation of Lady Gaga's mind and body parallels the corruption of Rowena: where Poe's narrator used occult magic to place Ligeia's soul in Rowena's corpse, the bordello uses cybernetics to effect the mental changes to Lady Gaga in order to make her a more marketable product for consumption. This difference motivates classroom discussions about Lady Gaga's attention to potential dangers in both technology and mass consumerism. By juxtaposing images of the online auction for her sexual services with more traditional gothic images—the coffins, the dancers' twisting limbs, even the bearskin train attached to Lady Gaga's dress—*Bad Romance* mystifies these tools in ways that make them almost magical and hence as fearsome as the occult that Poe presents in his literature. In reading Poe's works alongside Lady Gaga's video, students see how the gothic is employed as rhetorical shorthand to persuade viewers by playing on their emotions through powerful visual elements.

Most interesting is the simple but provocative point typically reached by students: in the words of one, "All relationships are power struggles." I push the question: What appears in Poe's works that makes you see the link to Lady Gaga in terms of power? One student pointed to the violent relationship between Lady Gaga and her male client, as she rests next to his still smoldering corpse. This violence mirrors the kind done to women in Poe's other works—buried alive like Madeline Usher in "The Fall of the House of Usher," mystically defiled like Rowena in "Ligeia," or stuffed behind the house's wall like the unnamed wife in "The Black Cat." That student concluded, "When are two people in one of Poe's works ever happy together?" This student identified a challenge in teaching Poe's literature, namely that a teacher must balance Poe's tendency to idealize images of beauty and love, especially in his poetry, with the brutality apparent in the more frenetic quality of relationships between lovers in his short stories: for every ode to Annabel Lee, Helen, and Lenore, there are victims of lovers' brutality in "The Black Cat," "Ligeia," and as concerns the supposedly incestuous siblings, "The Fall of the House of Usher." This student's remark serves as a helpful model when teaching the complexity of Poe's literature, as it is easy to overlook the density of his overall oeuvre and thus reduce him to either a master of horror or an overly sentimental writer of love poetry. These two archetypal models have equal hold in defining Poe's career, but they must be considered jointly for a fuller understanding of his entire literary production.

"The Most Poetical Topic": Women in Poe's Literature

Dominant strains in literary scholarship regarding Poe's portrayals of women tend to follow three paths. First, scholars consider how Poe's works idealize women as merely objects of beauty, as in the "To Helen" poems. Second, scholars discuss Poe's tendency to kill off female characters, interpreting whether Poe merely objectifies such characters, as in "The Philosophy of Composition" (where they are "the most poetical topic in the world" [*Selected Writings* 680]), or uses such characters to advance the plot, as in "The Fall of the House of Usher" or "The Murders in the Rue Morgue." Third, scholars explore Poe's representations of women as inferior artists (e.g., the humorously named Signora Psyche Zenobia in "How to Write a Blackwood Article"). However, not all scholarly attention to women in Poe's works has been negative. Some scholars identify the bidirectional stylistic influence Poe had with Frances Sargent Osgood, Sarah Helen Whitman, and other women writers, especially as Poe incorporated into his poems and tales literary tropes inherent to genres traditionally thought of as feminine. Even the structure of the detective story, a genre developed in part by Poe, draws heavily upon women's domestic literature.[1]

Of course, Poe has been the subject of numerous studies demonstrating his works' relation to larger trends in gothic literature in the nineteenth-century United States. But it is his ability to appeal to women publishers, editors, writers, and readers that motivates significant discussion with my students. For instance, students are interested in how some of Poe's darkest gothic tales (e.g., "The Assignation," "The Cask of Amontillado") premiered in leading women's journals. Yet many of Poe's works effectively silence their female characters—limiting women to roles as the victims of murder who cannot identify their murderers or as idealized objects of beauty to be spoken of by their admirers but not for themselves—and are difficult to read alongside the close attention he gives to women writers, judging their works on their merits and flaws with little chauvinistic posturing and no patronizing. Especially for twenty-first-century readers, it is a challenge to recognize the potential misogyny in his fiction and poetry while noting his simultaneous appreciation of the works of women.

Studies of nineteenth-century United States culture have long emphasized important contributions by writers such as Harriet Beecher Stowe, Rebecca Harding Davis, and Louisa May Alcott in developing early American gothic literature, especially in slave narratives.[2] Significantly, some of these women used similar tropes and styles as Poe and addressed similar topics, which Elaine Showalter reads as feminist ideals: "the Gothic suggested independence, adventure, narrative boldness, and self-reliance" (130). Indeed, Poe at one point approached colleague Frances Sargent Osgood to write a poem for him that he could present as his own, claiming her style and his were so similar (Richards, *Gender and the Poetics of Reception* 1). These women writers provided the audience for his gothic literature, as well as editorial guidance: "The Assignation," "The Cask of Amontillado," and "The Oblong Box" were just some of the tales of murder and mystery to appear in *Godey's Lady's Book*, a journal whose audience was imagined by its editor, Sarah Josepha Hale, to be made up of middle-class white women who strove to supply a Christian, highly moralistic education to their children and spouses. That Poe's darker tales were directed to women readers identifies the tension between the sentimental and the gothic as it plays out throughout his oeuvre.

Students entering this course, however, which is primarily an introduction to higher-level literary analysis, may not be familiar with women authors' development of the gothic genre in the eighteenth and nineteenth centuries, and the inclusion of Poe's transatlantic predecessors and near-contemporaries such as Elizabeth Browning, Jane Austen, and Rebecca Davis can become overwhelming. Moreover, although students quickly note the intense focus on women in Poe's works, they also occasionally fall into the trap of reading his life more than the literature he produced: they are prone to scholastic scavenger hunts about the identity of the real Annabel Lee, or about whether

Poe really did romance Osgood. It is essential, then, to introduce how women writers in Poe's time contributed to the production of content portraying them. Rather than reading his texts only in their moments of production, I insist that students also read his works in various moments of reception, including their own: this strategy allows them both to trace a continuing historical legacy, from Rufus Wilmot Griswold to F. O. Matthiessen to Leland Person to Nina Baym, but also to take ownership of his works and pursue their own avenues of investigation within them based on the ideas that already interest them.

For example, students' attentiveness to the life of Poe allows me to pivot in class discussions toward considering how scholarship remains preoccupied with the author's life in ways not dissimilar from today's attention to the private lives of celebrities—a helpful transition when our course discussions move toward Poe's influence on popular culture. Lady Gaga's outlandish appearance and demeanor, in addition to her Poe-like content, allows for productive cross-references that underscore connections among fame, decadence, and the gothic as cemented by Poe in his life and works.

"Little Monsters" and "Freaks": Pop Singers' Appropriation of the Gothic

Although decadence as a literary motif developed especially in late nineteenth-century European literature, it has its roots in the works of earlier gothic artists on both sides of the Atlantic, including Poe. Baudelaire's translations of Poe's works into French make much of the decadent setting of drugs, madness, sensuality, and death—ideas not too dissimilar from much of what can be found in the works of Lady Gaga. She catapulted to fame with her own party song, 2008's "Just Dance," which provides an ironic romanticization of the party-girl culture. Halberstam notes that, unlike prevalent readings of sexually active women as monstrous, especially in Poe's time, pop performers such as Lady Gaga are firmly "in charge of their mass media images" as they "use sex boldly in their music, [and] also flaunt their bodies" (7). Lady Gaga herself refers to the potential objectification of her body onstage as actually "incredibly liberating": "I have no problem with my sexuality, and any woman who wants to get more confident about her body should try stripping" (Lester 23). Lady Gaga's argument is admittedly problematic: ownership of one's sexuality and pride in one's physical appearance can still be co-opted by the male gaze. Nevertheless, she re-purposes potentially problematic representations of women—stripped bare onstage—as an act independent of voyeurs' own desires and one of her own empowerment through decadence. When referring to her fans as "Little Monsters," Lady Gaga identifies their varying appearances through the lens of the grotesque as a democratizing redefinition of beauty, such that "every monster is sexy and is allowed to feel that way too, in part because of Gaga's dismissal of traditional notions of feminine (and masculine) sex appeal" (Gray 25). Lady Gaga's gender-confounding performances have other implications as well. Thanks to not only songs such as "Born This Way" but also her philanthropic work, she has built herself into an icon for the larger GLBTQIA community. Hence her role as celebrity and advocate affords a unique counterpoint to the more conservative portrayals of gender and sexuality in Poe's time. Her music videos—surprisingly developed from the same tropes Poe uses—show how these older works continue to resonate but also evolve into new formulations, in this case extending but also challenging Poe's gender portrayals.

Lady Gaga's immediate significance in recent popular culture is made evident by her financial success and number of fans. Her 2008 album *The Fame* made her the first musician with at least four number-one hits in a debut album, and up to this point in her career she has sold more than 16.5 million albums and 29.5 million digital singles. This success owes especially to her adept deployment of both traditional and new media; for example, she has attracted more than 7 million followers on Twitter (Corona 725; Click et al. 360). This fame comes with criticism: debates persist as to whether her music is overshadowed by her exaggerated visual appearance and at times larger-than-life personality. Although this mixed image provides a helpful entry point in discussing celebrity identity in Poe's own time—since Poe similarly was surrounded by both admirers and detractors, and much of his legacy relates less to his writings than to his personal life and related rumors of murder, addiction, and sexual depravity—Lady Gaga's comments and actions nonetheless create tensions. On the one hand, she is a committed activist on behalf of women, members of the GLBTQIA community, and those contending with bullies: she has partnered with Harvard University to fund the Born This Way Foundation to "foster a more accepting society, where differences are embraced and individuality is celebrated" (Dumenico). On the other hand, some of her actions may compromise her activism: her reluctance to be labeled a feminist, her access to white privilege while engaging in cultural appropriation, her seeming defilement of Christian motifs, and her apparent fetishization of violence as commodity.[3] The difficulty defining Lady Gaga and the meaning of her works is apparent especially in her music videos, as she appears to both celebrate and repudiate the violence in these fictionalized cinematic presentations. For example, her collaboration with R. Kelly for the song "Do What U Want" has been criticized, given his reduction of women into sexual objects (Katie) and draws attention to how her own ownership of her sexuality risks celebrating the male gaze, constructing women as hypersexualized objects for voyeuristic pleasure (Lynch 48). Her attitudes toward men also come off as contradictory. She has been hesitant to refer to herself as a feminist, claiming, "I hail men, I love men" (N. Williams)—as if in her conception feminism inherently refers to hating men (Gray 221). Yet in videos such as *Bad Romance*, *Telephone*, and *Paparazzi*, graphic portrayals of men's murders seem inconsistent with her expressed celebration of men and her objection to violence against any person. Whereas camp and parody are instrumental to Lady Gaga's persona (Gray 85–106), the violence against men within these videos can also be read along a meta-structure: the tension in reading her becomes embodied in the power struggles inherent in the gendered relationships portrayed in her videos, especially *Bad Romance*. This brings us back to Poe, whose works embody similar tensions concerning violence and women. The domestic violence inherent in Poe's tales, whether he is excoriating that brutality or merely sensationalizing it, is put into greater relief upon being restaged in current media. Twenty-first-century popular music and new media—*Bad Romance* having longevity thanks to dissemination through its video's release online—makes that violence in Poe's work more visual and potentially more apparent, providing another avenue through which students may continue to analyze Poe.

"Two Hearts":
Poe and Lady Gaga's Public and Private Personas

Despite Lady Gaga's provocative nature—whether wearing a dress of meat, presenting sadomasochistic Catholic iconography in her video *Alejandro* (which aligns well with Poe's "The Pit and the Pendulum"), or teaming up with Beyoncé to commit mass murder in *Telephone*—she balances that public, often fictionalized persona against a sentimental-ized autobiographical presentation. When discussed in class, this aspect of Lady Gaga's performance allows us to consider the complexities of the culture of celebrity, since Poe, too, was followed in the popular press of his time; indeed, the sensationalist aspects of his life make it nearly impossible for readers, past or present, to consider his works without reference to his biography.

In his own time, the subject matter of many of Poe's writings was decried as exploitative. One critic accused him of using the death of his young bride, Virginia, whom he married when she was thirteen, as literary fodder, "hurrying her to a premature grave, that he might write 'Annabel Lee' and 'The Raven'!" (Gilfillan 154). The sentimentalism in-herent in Poe's biography owes in part to the way he fashioned himself, in his fictional writing and in his public persona. This argument follows from Jonathan Elmer's reading of sentimentalism and an almost gothic sensationalism—inherent in the description of horrific and terrifying violence—as happening simultaneously not only in nineteenth-century US publishing at large but within individual works. In other words, sentimentalism and sensationalism serve as "complementary modes, dependent on each other for their own proper functioning," which is, according to Elmer, "the moral discourse defining the death of the female hero (as just, as tragic but necessary, as beautiful, and so forth)" (94, 100). Poe had little chance to defend how he used (or abused) sentimental tropes in his gothic literature, especially those more auto-biographical texts; upon his early death around age forty, Rufus Wilmot Griswold published a memoir that thoroughly discredited him, partic-ularly emphasizing his alleged drug use.

Lady Gaga, too, has garnered negative media attention, although she plays off such fascination as merely another bad romance in her song

"Paparazzi." Also, whereas Poe would have to rely, posthumously, upon his literary colleagues John Ingram and Sarah Helen Whitman to defend him against Griswold's accusations (Richards, "Women's Place" 11), Lady Gaga is still alive to respond to her critics—albeit at times cryptically. Significantly, she draws upon the decadent culture surrounding pop music and her own lyrics as a defense for her songs; like Poe's depressed artist Roderick Usher, she identifies a messy pseudo-romance between art and drugs: "[M]y music also heals me. So is it heroin, and I need the fix to feel better? [. . .] You have to commit yourself to this struggle and commit yourself to the pain. And I commit myself to my heartbreak wholeheartedly. [. . .] As artists we are eternally heartbroken" (Strauss 61). To defend herself further, Lady Gaga has drawn upon those grotesque yet sentimental portrayals of the death of a beautiful woman that are also deployed by Poe. She cites as artistic inspiration Joanne Germanotta, her late aunt, who died when only nineteen years old. As Poe writes in "The Philosophy of Composition" in defense of his poetic portrayals of deceased women, Lady Gaga, too, capitalizes upon the image of a dead, pure woman to elicit pathos from her audience: "I really believe I have two hearts. I think I actually carry two souls in my body, and that I'm living out the rest of her life and her goodness—she died a virgin, she died never having experienced all these things that we all get to love and experience in our lives" (Naughton and Born).

Lady Gaga portrays her relationship with her departed aunt as a sisterly bond, much more so than the fetishistic admiration that, say, Poe's Roderick Usher has for his sister, Madeline. And yet Lady Gaga bears a tattoo of the date of Joanne's death, making the memory embodied. Much as Ligeia comes to occupy Rowena's body, so, too, does Lady Gaga see herself as embodying the soul of more than one woman. Thus she comes to represent those idealized arguments that Poe puts forward in his transcendental treatises such as *Eureka*: the brutal violence against the body is in service to a shedding of physical form for ascension to a more perfect spiritual elevation, which, as Poe defines in "The Philosophy of Literature," is the goal for a poet. Both Poe and Lady Gaga blur the distinction between sentimentalism and gothicism to the point that images of physical violence become both horrific and hauntingly beautiful.

In my classes, I caution students to relate any autobiographical material back to the context of what we are reading. The analysis of authors' lives is not to read intention into their works but to recognize strategies for applying literary analytical techniques to other studies. Celebrity culture, whether in studies of the nineteenth or twenty-first century, provides an opportunity to examine the larger cultural issue of performance, which relates closely to gender. Although celebrity status is sometimes thought to depend on artificiality rather than necessarily legitimate talent (Hollander 151), the production of celebrity is like the production of art or even gender: it is an act in progress, a performance that is subject to methods of interpretation analogous to how students engage with literature and regardless of intention by that celebrity.

This attention to celebrity culture expands options for the range of texts available for students to analyze, moving beyond a lowbrow versus highbrow binary so as to teach a range of middlebrow texts that may be overlooked for being seemingly artless. Such texts are important to teach so that students may trace how mass culture, especially popular music, defines acceptable gender performances.[4] It is not necessarily that popular music limits gender performances, but as indicative in Lady Gaga's ability to take ownership of both her gender and sexuality, popular music may provide a wider range of gender models for persons who feel constrained by heteronormative guidelines. This work is important, as celebrity culture functions within parts of larger economic systems of exchange (Davisson 4), an idea allegorized by Lady Gaga herself in *Bad Romance* when the music video presents a fictionalized bidding war to claim ownership of her body—before she turns the tables and torches anyone who would possess her. Lady Gaga's actions on- and offstage have made indistinguishable the line between authentic self and performed self, complicating the distinction between private and public spaces and exposing how sex appeal can be used by or against persons, depending on how they embrace themselves (Gray 36). In her analysis of Lady Gaga's engagement with celebrity culture, Amber L. Davisson identifies how Lady Gaga "owns the fact that the public is almost always watching" (6). Davisson productively reads this public-private disruption as analogous to what she refers to as a celebrity-monster confusion. Even as she celebrates her fans as Little Monsters, "[w]hen Lady Gaga appears as physically both the celebrity and the monster, she seems to be warning society of what happens when celebrity is achieved while also questioning the terrible consequences of becoming a monster" (12–14). Her performance therefore exposes the boundaries set up by society, then destroys them, giving rise to a grotesque, hence gothic, view of gender and culture.

Poe and Lady Gaga have been made into icons of decadence, not necessarily through their own agency but in how their art defies clean categories in terms of genre but also gender. This critical instability can be frustrating, however: although Poe's critical essays bring attention to underrepresented women authors, his short stories operate on the basis of limited representations of women, and although Lady Gaga's music and activism bring attention to the challenges faced by women and members of the GLBTQIA community, her lyrics and music videos appropriate images of murder and torture that risk fetishizing the same sexualized images of violence that she ostensibly decries. The frustrations that Poe and Lady Gaga promote in my students—and in me—nevertheless open opportunities for future discussion. The focus is less about finding permanent solutions than treating our studies as works in progress, as feminism and gender studies are constantly evolving and improving.

"Everywhere and Nowhere": Future Course Improvements

This course on the works of Edgar Allan Poe has succeeded in incorporating popular culture as a means of reading not only gender but also the gothic and the culture of celebrity in literary and historical context. Future instances of this course will benefit from incorporating even more works from the past, from those women who inspired Poe and wrote alongside him, as they will help to broaden the context for understanding the performative preoccupations of Lady Gaga and other twenty-first-century artists. It would be especially useful if more women writers from Poe's era could be used for comparative purposes. "Women are everywhere and nowhere in Poe studies," Eliza Richards argues ("Women's Place" 10), and a course like this can address that problem. By reading Poe's works through the lens of Lady Gaga, students can recognize strategies in which they can claim ownership over his tropes and consider new ways of keeping his literature relevant to future audiences.

In the violence and gender-bending of her performances, Lady Gaga disrupts the feminism that she articulates in her lyrics, performances, and activism, in a manner similar to how, in his criticism, Poe disrupts the implicit misogyny of his fiction and poetry. This disturbance results because the gothic is itself a "return of the repressed," represented in art and literature through uncanny physical manifestations, often upon the human body, to bring forward that which "threatens the established order" but "must be acknowledged" (Clemens 4). This upending of traditional ways is a productive avenue of exploration for both literary and gender studies, and taking popular culture seriously lends further dimension to both. Lady Gaga's fictionalized self-destructive love, not only a "bad romance" but also a frightful, gothic one, redefines Poe's texts, echoing the same appeal of his literature that today makes Gaga sing, "I want your horror" (line 33).

Crossing the Barrier

An Active-Text Approach to Teaching Pet Sematary

ALISSA BURGER

IN TEACHING popular literature, we often have to make the case—to colleagues, students, or both—for its critical validity and place within the classroom. The question of whether Stephen King has a rightful place in literary circles has long been debated. King's win of the National Book Foundation Award in 2003 for Distinguished Contribution to American Letters made headway in establishing his legitimacy, though some critics remain unconvinced of his place within the literary canon.[1] Stephen King has been slowly making his way into the high school and college classroom over the past decade, and according to a lesson plan developed by Penguin Publishers for their Signet editions of King's short story collections, "Recent surveys of high school and college students indicate that the fiction of Stephen King is highly read" (Weiss 2). Given students' frequent familiarity with King and the fact that students are often enthusiastic about reading popular literature, we can foster heightened critical engagement by positioning King's works within the paradigm of the active text—as one that has been inspired by earlier works and has inspired later works, as one piece of a larger and ongoing conversation. This theory of the active text, or the intertexually engaged text, is particularly useful in engaging with the gothic literature genre. As John Sears explains, "The Gothic mode is notoriously predicated on varieties of repetition, on the recycling of narratives and forms, on revisiting older, preexistent texts, on labyrinthine texts and spaces, and on the seemingly endless resurrection of an apparently dead, outmoded tradition" (2).

In my upper-level literature course on King,[2] I regularly use this approach, capitalizing on students' willingness to read popular horror fiction to encourage them to engage with this larger tradition and gain a more expansive perspective of King's work and the genre of which he is such a significant part. This can be effectively achieved through a three-part approach to teaching King's fiction. First, I provide students with background on the gothic and horror genres. Second, I pair King's novels with classic works from which King drew narratively specific and thematic inspiration. Finally, turning to popular culture representations of King's novels highlights some of the ways in which King's work has influenced its surrounding culture. No matter what type of literature we bring into the classroom, whether classical or contemporary, we can productively engage students with the text by positioning it within relevant historical and genre-based contexts. While this contextualization within the larger discourse of classic literature acquaints students with cultural and historical realities far afield from their own experiences, a similar approach to contemporary literature encourages students to bring the same critically engaged perspective to more recent eras and their own personal frames of reference.

One of King's novels that works especially well with this approach is *Pet Sematary*. Even before its publication, *Pet Sematary* had a terrifying reputation, as a novel King himself "deemed . . . too gruesome to be published" (Vincent 75), and after he'd read through the manuscript following its completion in 1979, he tucked it into a desk drawer, "where he intended for it to stay forever" (ibid.).[3] However, *Pet Sematary* was eventually published and soon became one of King's best-known works. It also serves as a productive entry for students to King and the larger horror genre, specifically because *Pet Sematary* is considered such iconic King and because many students have at least a passing, generally popular culture–based familiarity with the novel even if they've never read it (or any King, for that matter).

The first step in the active text discussion surrounding *Pet Sematary* is establishing the context of supernatural horror that informs the novel. This is completed early in the course, or if the course is organized by different thematic approaches, at the beginning of the supernatural horror section of the course.[4] After these introductory discussions of genre and the backstory of *Pet Sematary*'s writing and publication, we move on to the reading of the novel itself. As we read *Pet Sematary*, we pair it with W. W. Jacobs's "The Monkey's Paw," with its themes of disastrous wish fulfillment, and excerpts from Mary Shelley's *Frankenstein*, as the archetypal reanimated monster; both of these works also highlight the theme of hubris, which has tragic consequences in all three works. The Jacobs and Shelley works are inserted in our reading and discussion at narratively significant points in the novel, engaging with Kelly Chandler's argument that "the membrane between high culture and popular culture is, in many cases, a permeable one" (113) and exploring the influence of these classic texts upon King's work. Finally, after we have finished discussing the novel, we move on to *Pet Sematary* in popular culture, with the 1989 film adaptation and the Ramones' *Pet Sematary* music video. This three-part approach both highlights the dynamically engaged and active position of *Pet Sematary* within the larger gothic tradition and enables students to gain a more in-depth, multitextual understanding of the novel itself.

This engagement between classic and contemporary texts brings us back to the debate surrounding the literary canon. While classics remain an essential foundation for any well-read student, as Collings points out, with these canonical works, "students may not understand the language, the authors' concerns, the social and cultural heritages which elicited the stories. And without those backgrounds, much of the value of the book may be overlooked, ignored, or lost" (123). M. Jerry Weiss echoes Collings's perspective, underscoring the potential pedagogical advantages of pairing classic and contemporary literature when he argues that King's works "can be excellent springboards to the work of the classic novelists" (2).[5] Obviously, getting our students to engage with these influences and the deeper meanings of literature are our main goals in the classroom, and popular literature can be an excellent bridge in achieving that aim. With his myriad of literary references, King's work is ideal for bringing the canonical and the contemporary into critical dialogue with one another. As Burton Hatlen argues of King's frequent incorporation of literary allusions and epigraphs,

How many people would write a novel like King does and include all those epigraphs from literature? He's a key mediating figure between mass culture and traditional culture. That split between high and mass culture can be debilitating. We can't just have high culture. But if all we have is a media culture, then we're impoverished. He has allowed us another possibility: to get these two perspectives into dialogue. (qtd. in Chandler 105).

Through these engagements, King shows himself to be knowledgeable of and critically engaged with the canon of literature that has preceded him, establishing himself as one voice within a much larger conversation, responding and adding to that dialogue.

Through reading King's work, especially with an emphasis on the canonical—and popular—literary references within, we can simultaneously address these dual perspectives to which Hatlen refers, engaging with contemporary issues, popular fiction, and classic literature in a multitextual and dynamically interactive discussion. This active text approach, in putting the genre conventions and themes of classic and contemporary literature into conversation with one another, allows students to build an appreciation for classics of the gothic and horror genres, while also more concretely and critically contextualizing the content and literary merit of contemporary fiction, such as King's.

Contextualizing the Gothic Genre

Early in the semester, it is essential to establish the characteristics of the gothic and horror genres that inform King's writing. We begin with a definition of gothic literature, a genre of writing that became popular in the late eighteenth and early nineteenth centuries, with emphasis on the dark, horrific, and grotesque. Beginning with a general description of these key characteristics of the gothic, we then move on to a more nuanced definition, establishing "a sense of the gothic which more fully develops the idea of gothic as a 'tendency' in human thought, feelings, and modes of expression, rather than one limited to particular places or times. Here, there is the clear suggestion that the gothic transcends history, or at least permeates all history" (Stevens 31), one that revolves around the unchanging reality that, as H. P. Lovecraft has argued, "[t]he oldest and strongest emotion of mankind is fear, and the oldest and strongest kind of fear is fear of the unknown" (25). This negotiable definition of the gothic lays the groundwork for the rest of the class, over the course of which we explore key gothic themes, both classic and contemporary, within King's works. Contemporary horror contains many key elements of the traditional gothic genre, though much like gothic in its own period, horror is often considered lacking in literary merit as a result of the violence, gore, and contrived plot lines frequently associated with its current incarnation; as we begin establishing and employing these definitions early in the semester, we develop a somewhat hybrid approach to exploring King and horror, one which includes the familiar tropes of the classic gothic genre, as well as the more visceral and terrifying hallmarks of contemporary horror.

We also discuss the impact of horror literature on readers and the goal of creating fear and terror. As King argues in *Danse Macabre*, his critical consideration of the genre, effective works of horror "always do their work on two levels" (4). The first of these is the "gross-out," the blood and gore that make up the visual hallmarks of the genre, the scare achieved through shock and physical, visceral horror (4). However, according to King, "on another, more potent level, the work of horror really is a dance—a moving, rhythmic search. And what it's looking for is the place where you, the viewer or the reader, live at your most primitive level" (4). Going back to Lovecraft's "oldest and strongest emotion" (25), this second type of horror demolishes the boundaries between the façade of predictable and safe everyday life, violently upending these expectations and underscoring the fact that no one and nowhere are ever safe from the horror that lies just on the other side of our own world, whether in the realistic horror of random violence or the supernatural horror of haunting, telekinesis, or the reanimated dead.

Beyond the visceral and primitive experiences of horror, we can critically approach the gothic genre from a symbolic perspective as well. Moving from the individual to the larger social and cultural context, Susan Allen Ford explains that the gothic is ideally suited for "mapping the psychic, emotional, and cultural labyrinths of our world, our selves" (177). Within this larger, symbolic discourse, horror provides not just the momentary thrill of a serial killer jumping out from the darkness or a zombie munching on brains; horror gives readers and viewers the opportunity to work through and negotiate real-life terrors, from mental illness and psychological turmoil to larger cultural issues such as racism, class discrimination, and gender violence.[6] There are no shortages of real-life horrors in our day-to-day, twenty-first-century lives; as Michael R. Collings argues, "Horror writers are an intrinsic and essential part of late 20th-century American culture . . . [who engage with contemporary] issues through the metaphor of the monstrous and horrific, because AIDS, molestation, homelessness, physical and psychological abuse, racism, sexism, and other frightening *-isms* of various sorts are indeed monstrous and horrific" (121; emphasis in the original). For example, in the contemporary moment where there is great anxiety about terrorism, infection, and in the horrifying combination of the two, bioterrorism, horror engages with this tension in both classic and contemporary guises, from the newfangled vampires of Chuck Hogan and Guillermo del Toro's *The Strain* trilogy, to the technology-gone-wrong zombies of *Resident Evil* (in all its varied film, video game, and popular culture permutations), to box office medical thrillers like Steven Soderbergh's *Contagion* (2011).[7] While horror fiction and films do not solve these problems, they provide their readers and viewers with a safe space in which to face their own powerlessness, consider the worst possible scenario, and then cathartically release the tension of that fear, if only for a moment.

With this diverse and multifaceted framework of critical approaches to horror established, as we move forward in our reading and discussion of King's short stories and novels, we can connect back to the larger context of gothic literature and the horror genre, drawing on the traditions and tropes that have informed King's work.

Text Pairing

Moving on to a focused reading and discussion of *Pet Sematary*, we then pair narratively specific texts with the novel to illuminate key moments of resonance and inspiration. Two classic gothic literature texts that pair well with *Pet Sematary* are W. W. Jacobs's "The Monkey's Paw" and Mary Shelley's *Frankenstein*. Jacobs's short story is read in its entirety, while with the limited time available, Shelley's novel is incorporated through the use of excerpts.[8] The central conflict of *Pet Sematary* is man's temptation to control the powers of life and death, to challenge the very laws of nature and emerge victorious. Both Jacobs's and Shelley's works tackle the theme of individual hubris with tragic consequences, though each also moves beyond that theme of hubris to more specific gothic tropes that King employs in *Pet Sematary*.

Jacobs's short story "The Monkey's Paw" explores many of the same themes of death and reanimation, though in this case it does so through magical rather than medical means. The active text pairing of "The Monkey's Paw" with *Pet Sematary* engages students in drawing connections between these works on several levels, including key themes of grief and monstrous wish fulfillment, the characterization and motivation of grieving parents in each, and the stylistic traits of seen versus unseen horror. As "The Monkey's Paw" is a significantly less well-known text than Shelley's *Frankenstein*, it may be helpful to begin with a brief summary of the story itself: The tale centers on a dried monkey's paw with the power to grant the user three wishes, "a sophisticated tale in the lengthy tradition of wish fulfillment stories" (Buchanan 408). A friend of the White family, Sergeant-Major Morris, shows up on a typically gothic dark and stormy night, regaling his hosts with tales of his exotic travels, including his acquisition of the mystical monkey's paw. As Morris explains, the paw "had a spell put on it by an old fakir, a very holy man. . . . He wanted to show that fate ruled people's lives, and that those who interfered with it did so to their sorrow" (Jacobs 181). The reader never learns exactly what happened to give Morris such a disillusioned point of view or what came of his own three wishes, "but he does reveal that the man who possessed the monkey's paw before him used his last wish to ask for death" (Vincent 78). Despite these cautionary signs, Mr. White still wants the paw and his wishes. Mr. White's first wish is for the money to pay off his family's house. He gets the money, but in the most unexpected and horrific of ways: his son is killed in a factory accident and the settlement offered by the factory owners is the exact amount required for the remaining mortgage.[9] The monkey's paw is temporarily forgotten in the Whites' grief and Mr. White's feelings of guilt over how his wish played out. However, it isn't long before Mrs. White realizes that a macabre solution is well within their reach, and it is this exchange which King includes as an epigraph to part 3 of *Pet Sematary*:

"I only just thought of it," she said hysterically. "Why didn't I think of it before? Why didn't *you* think of it?"

"Think of what?" he questioned.

"The other two wishes," she replied rapidly. "We've only had one."

"Was that not enough?" he demanded fiercely.

"No," she cried triumphantly: "we'll have one more. Go down and get it quickly, and wish our boy alive again." (Jacobs 186–87; emphasis in the original)

Mr. White is resistant, but driven by love, grief, and outrage, Mrs. White makes the wish. As a knock falls on their door, Mr. White makes the third and final wish: to return his son to his grave. As Jacobs hauntingly concludes the story, "the knocking ceased suddenly, although the echoes of it were still in the house.... The street lamp flickering opposite shone on a quiet and deserted road" (189).

Reading Jacobs's "The Monkey's Paw" with *Pet Sematary* highlights the theme of fate and the consequences of defying fate, even in the face of tremendous loss and grief. Carl J. Buchanan argues that in "The Monkey's Paw" "the journey toward the inevitable, Death, is filled with many paths, re-windings and turnings—labyrinthine" (415). However, the end point is inescapable. Both Mrs. White and Louis Creed fight against this fate, drawing on a power they cannot understand to fulfill the dearest wishes of their hearts, and in both cases those dreams turn into nightmares with the resounding reaffirmation of fate and the horrors that await those who fight it.[10] Students commented that pairing these two works helped them get a better and more comprehensive understanding of the themes of resurrection and the potentially destructive nature of wishes. For example, one student said in her reflection on these pairings that "I enjoyed the concept of the story ['The Monkey's Paw'] itself. I found the idea of having a darker side to being granted any wishes you want very realistic, and frightening in its simplicity in reflecting karma." Another student made a similar remark concerning the sense of inevitability set up in both "The Monkey's Paw" and *Pet Sematary*, saying that "in both stories [there was a feeling of] knowing that something bad will happen . . . but continuing to do what you shouldn't."[11] As these student responses show, the theme of fate in these two tales of horror create a powerful sense of suspense, of knowing things won't end well for the characters no matter what they do or how hard they fight the losses they must face. While this active text pairing highlights the resonance of themes between these two works, it also engages students with the larger psychological traditions of grief and individuals' responses to it, which in turn gives them further insight into Louis Creed and why he makes the choices he makes, in the full knowledge that those choices are monstrous and destructive.

In *Danse Macabre*, King argues that for readers, oftentimes the un-seen has its own unique horror impact, at times proving even more effective than the blood and guts of more explicit, visual horror. As he points out, in "The Monkey's Paw" "we actually *see* nothing outright nasty. . . . It's what the mind sees that makes these stories quintessential tales of terror. It is the unpleasant speculation called to mind when the knocking on the door begins . . . and the grief-stricken old woman rushes to answer it" (22; emphasis in the original). As she fumbles with the lock, suspense builds, the terrified anticipation growing in the mind of the reader of the horrifying possibilities that lay just on the other side of the door, while the story itself pauses in a kind of narrative holding pattern, giving the imaginary terror room to stretch its legs, insinuate itself further into the mind of the reader. As King continues, "nothing is there but the wind when she finally throws the door open . . . but what, the mind wonders, *might* have been there if her husband had been a little slower on the draw with that third wish?" (22; emphasis in the original).

In many ways, *Pet Sematary* takes that "what if" King raises and lets it play out, embracing both the nuanced, psychological horror of "The Monkey's Paw" and the more visceral "gross-out" King discusses in *Danse Macabre* (4). The Creeds moved from Chicago to Maine so that Louis could take a job running a student medical center; the first day students return to campus is marred when student Victor Pascow[12] is hit by a car and brought into the medical center, though his injuries are so catastrophic that Louis can do nothing to help him. King terrifies readers with imaginary, unseen horrors, like the footsteps of Pascow returning from the dead and climbing the stairs in the Creed family's house before Louis wishes him away (144), echoing the old man's final wish in "The Monkey's Paw." Pascow haunts Louis after his death, appearing to Louis as a full-body apparition and leading him up through the Pet Sematary, admonishing Louis not to go beyond the barrier of the deadfall. However, as Louis ignores Pascow's cautions, Pascow becomes more ephemeral, passing from the seen horror (both in his dying on the medical center floor and Louis's dream of their night walk) to an unseen horror. As Louis lies in bed after burying his daughter's cat Church, "it seemed to him that he heard bare feet slowly climbing the stairs and he thought, *Let me alone, Pascow, let me alone, what's done is done and what's dead is dead*—and the steps faded away" (144; emphasis in the original). However, as Louis is drawn ever further into the dark magic of the Micmac burial ground, it turns out that "what's dead" does not necessarily stay dead, and the unseen horrors that Louis fears press ever closer upon reality, threatening to breach the barrier between the real and the horrifically fantastical, the living and the dead.

However, King also does not shy from the physical horror, balancing the seen and the unseen, the psychological and the "gross-out," as he shows readers the broken bodies of Pascow and Gage at each level of terror, both in their deaths and their reanimation, foregrounding the grotesque elements of the gothic tradition. The moment Louis looks at Pascow, he knows that no matter what he does, "the young man was going to die" (72). King then goes on to give readers the "gross-out" through an extended and detailed description of the physical destruction of Pascow's body: "[H]alf of his head was crushed. His neck had been broken. One collarbone jutted from his swelled and twisted right shoulder. From his head, blood and a yellow, pussy fluid seeped sluggishly into the carpet. Louis could see the man's brain, whitish-gray and pulsing through a shattered section of skull" (ibid.). Both Louis and the readers alike are horrified by the fact of Pascow's death, as well as by the visceral, gory description of the trauma of his broken body. When Pascow comes to Louis in his dream, it is in this same shattered form rather than a sanitized embodiment of a soul that has shed its earthly shell: "[H]e stood there with his head bashed in behind the left temple. The blood had dried on his face in maroon stripes like Indian warpaint. His collarbone jutted whitely" (83). Pascow's presence and physical appearance provide an excellent example for addressing the key concept of the liminal in gothic and horror literature, the inexplicable areas of in-betweenness, in this case with the corporeal and the supernatural coming together to highlight the permeability of the boundary between the living and the dead, one that as a doctor, Louis has always believed to be unbreakable.

Engaging with the stylistic balance of seen versus unseen horror and building upon the intimacy of the family that is one of the central themes of *Pet Sematary*, the descriptions of Gage's ruptured, destroyed body are even more horrifying than Pascow's, despite the fact that the level of detail is significantly less developed, reflecting Louis's refusal to clearly see and understand the severity of Gage's physical injuries and accept the finality of his son's death. When Louis goes to the cemetery and digs Gage up, he has to face the horrifying reality of Gage's broken body, no matter how little he wants to. In addition to the unremitting march of death and decay that have begun to claim Gage, Louis is also faced with the compromised state of his son's body itself. Louis thinks that "looking at his son was like looking at a badly made doll. Gage's head bulged in strange directions. His eyes had sunken deep behind closed lids" (342). Gage's body, dead or alive, is clearly damaged beyond repair, a "gross-out" reality of which Louis, as a doctor, should be objectively aware, as he was with Pascow. However, blinded by his love and grief, he refuses to see the reality of Gage's body, closing his eyes to the external horror to chase his internal dream of being reunited with his son and reclaiming his family. This grotesqueness is underscored after Gage's return. As Gage attacks Jud, the old man notices that "one eye had gone to the wall; it stared off into space with terrible concentration" (381). Later, when Gage is reunited with Rachel, his mother's surprise and joy are tinged with horror as well, as she notices that "his face was . . . dirty, smeared with blood. And it was swollen, as if he had been terribly hurt and then put back together again by crude, uncaring hands" (388). These descriptions of Gage underscore a horror that continues beyond death, the body remaining while the spirit departs, highlighting the significant difference between the reanimation of the body and the resurrection of the soul.

In considering the motivation and shifting characterization of

Louis Creed, Mary Shelley's *Frankenstein* is very effective in this active text-pairing approach, with its own doctor, Victor Frankenstein.[13] King's work is informed by and engages with the classics of gothic and horror literature, and in *Danse Macabre* King identifies *Frankenstein* as one of these predominant texts,[14] and one which resonates especially well with *Pet Sematary*, demarcating a clear connection between past and present horrors. As previously discussed, students often struggle to dynamically engage with classic literature, whether as a result of the hurdles of unfamiliar language or lack of relevant contexts (i.e., social, cultural, historical). Connecting King's *Pet Sematary* to Mary Shelley's *Frankenstein* achieves several interconnected pedagogical aims: (1) it positions *Pet Sematary* within the larger tradition and themes of the gothic, in this case, of the reanimated dead; (2) it provides students with a more contemporary frame of reference through which to approach and interpret Shelley's *Frankenstein*; and (3) it illustrates the dynamic ways in which King's work has been influenced by his predecessors, critically contextualizing and enriching students' understanding of and engagement with King's work as a whole, as well as creating a context of cultural recognition, where they can take pleasure from recognizing and critically interpreting the textual allusions within the novel.

Given the limited amount of time in this course, I use *Frankenstein* in excerpt, though this partial reading doesn't present much of a hurdle, given the popular culture pervasiveness of the *Frankenstein* story. As King mentions in *Danse Macabre*, *Frankenstein* "became caught in a kind of cultural echo chamber, amplifying through the years" (55), until its cast of characters and themes of scientific horror and man's desire to overcome death have become instantly recognizable.[15] In incorporating Shelley's *Frankenstein*, chapters 3–5 are ideal for excerpting: this takes us through the death of Victor's mother, his grief and anger at her loss, his growing obsession with building his Creature, the Creature's animation, and Victor fleeing his home (and his responsibility for his creation) in horror. This brief set of chapters highlights details of Victor's characterization and motivation that productively inform our reading, discussion, and understanding of Louis Creed. In addition, these doctors are united by a common theme: as Heidi Strengell explains, "[D]espite the difference in background and personal experience, Louis

Creed's and Victor Frankenstein's individual lives culminate in a similar disaster for the same reason: hubris" (58). This shared character flaw is at the root of the choices each man makes, as well as the repercussions of those destructive actions.

First, the pairing of these two works engages with the themes of hubris, the reanimated dead, and—much as with "The Monkey's Paw"—the complex characterization and motivation that drive their doctor protagonists, centering around timeless, existential conflicts of love, loss, and grief. Victor Frankenstein is an obsessive man, whose refusal of death and his own hubris destroy him and those he loves; Louis Creed is a contemporary version of this antihero, following the same familiar path and ending the same way as Victor Frankenstein, horrifically punished for his abuse of a power that was never rightfully his to claim in the first place. But like Louis, Victor does not start out this way, making his downfall and degeneration a particularly powerful part of the novel's central action. As Mary Ferguson Pharr points out, before the death of Victor's mother in *Frankenstein*, "the domestic circle is perfect, inclusive, untouched" (117). In *Pet Sematary*, the Creeds are similarly depicted as a quite ideal family, loving and happy. The death of Victor's mother breaches the wall of "the domestic circle" Pharr discusses, and Church's death similarly shatters Louis's belief in the special, protected nature of his own family. As Louis thinks to himself, "Church wasn't supposed to get killed because he was inside the magic circle of the family" (121). Like Victor, Louis's realization that even with his medical authority, his family is not safe from death, is earth shattering, regardless of how objectively he has accepted this truth. In fact, it is Louis's medical background that draws him to the power of the Micmac burial ground. As Tony Magistrale argues in *Hollywood's Stephen King*, Louis "attempts to usurp the role of God when he learns the ultimate secret associated with his occupation as a physician—control over life and death. Once he's in a position to access this power, he cannot help but use it" (102). For both doctors, this initial death separates them from their former selves, their grief and rejection creating a schism between the largely rational men they were and ushering them into obsessive rejecters of death and a dark claiming of the power of life itself, or at least an undead facsimile of it.

155

Both men feel they are entitled to this power, as doctors and as patriarchal heads of their respective families. As Victor reflects in the creation of his Monster, "[L]ife and death appeared to me ideal bounds, which I should first break through" (Shelley 58), a power that he believes should be within his grasp and which he should be able to rightfully wield. Louis goes a step further, seeing himself as fighting one on one with death and keeping score, which often comes out in Louis's favor. Ministering at Norma Crandall's side when she collapses on Halloween night, Louis thinks to himself "*won one tonight, Lou*" (*Pet Sematary* 110; emphasis in the original), and he has a nearly identical thought later, when he treats a group of drunken tobogganers at the university's medical center, when "his laughter was partly relief, but it was partly triumph too—won one today, Louis" (185). Taking this adversarial stance against death, when it touches their lives, Victor and Louis are unable to accept it, grieve, and move on in a healthy way. Instead, they push back, invalidating death's claim on those they love and wrongfully seizing the power of life.

For both doctors, this power turns out to be more curse than blessing. As Pharr explains of Victor's Creature, "[T]he dream made flesh, then, is inevitably a nightmare, taking the dreamer not to divinity but to infamy, even insanity" (119). On the night Victor bestows his Creature with life, he says, "I saw the dull yellow eye of the creature open; it breathed hard, and a convulsive motion agitated its limbs" (Shelley 60). However, rather than the triumph he has expected to feel, instead for Victor "the beauty of the dream vanished, and breathless horror and disgust filled my heart" (61). Propelled by this horror, Victor abandons his creation, a rejection that puts the destructive events of the novel into motion as the Creature demands Victor's acknowledgment of his progeny. Like Victor, Louis is horrified by what returns after he and Jud bury Church and, later, after he buries Gage. In addition to a bad smell, Church's personality is fundamentally changed: "Church was swaying slowly back and forth as if drunk. . . . Church had never looked like this—had never *swayed*, like a snake trying to hypnotize its prey" (*Pet Sematary* 152; emphasis in the original). Church has become sinister, if not actively malevolent, but this is nothing compared to the debased, inhuman reanimation of Gage. The Gage-thing that returns to Jud's house is driven by vengeance and retribution, the burial ground spirits' punishment for Jud attempting to interfere with its predation on Louis. Further debasing the body that once was Gage's, the creature that has returned from the burial ground is cannibalistic, feasting on Jud and on his own mother, "his mouth smeared with blood, his chin dripping, his lips pulled back in a hellish grin" (401). None of these facsimiles of life fulfill the dreams of their makers but are instead repellant and sickening nightmares.

Finally, Victor and Louis both remain largely unrepentant. As Pharr writes of *Frankenstein*, "[T]he darkest part of this nightmare is that Victor never really gives up on his original vision" (119). On his death-bed, some of Victor's final words to Captain Walton are not a warning against repeating his own mistakes or learning from his destruction but, instead, his reflection that "I have myself been blasted in these hopes, yet another may succeed" (Shelley 185). The possibility that once done, Victor's unnatural experiment could be repeated remains open at the close of Shelley's novel.[16] Louis's addiction to the reanimating power of the Micmac burial ground is even more self-destructive and circuitous, a self-perpetuating cycle of degeneration and personal annihilation. Louis knows, from both his emotional and medical perspectives, that Church and Gage came back from the dead fundamentally changed, no longer themselves, animated instead by a demonic presence. However, he still cannot prevent himself from attempting the experiment again, when he finds Rachel's body after she's been murdered by Gage. As Louis madly attempts to explain, "I waited too long with Gage. . . . Something got into him because I waited too long. But it will be different with Rachel" (408). Both are broken men, driven to insanity and, in Victor's case, to death, but each remains unremitting in his obsession, his sense of rightness in claiming and using his power over death.[17]

The text pairing of Shelley's *Frankenstein* directs students' attention to the shifting characterization and motivation that unite these doctors over nearly two centuries of gothic literature. As one of my students explained, "Dr. Frankenstein is much like Louis in the example of trying to play god." Looking more specifically at character motivation, another student said that the pairing helped her understand Louis's shifting characterization and that exploring "Frankenstein['s] relationship to

Louis gave me a better understanding of why he [Louis] acts and reacts to certain things." Finally, a third student explored the more comprehensive perspective of these text pairings, reflecting that "it helped me gain a more well-rounded literary and historical point of view when regarding the horror of reincarnation." Combining these texts with *Pet Sematary* helps create a larger context of the gothic tradition, as well as facilitating a more in-depth and multitextual understanding of the novel.

Popular Culture

Chronologically, the active text extends its discussion both back to the past and into the future, taking inspiration from its predecessors and inviting reimagining of its own. In the case of *Pet Sematary*, these popular culture engagements include the 1989 film adaptation of the same name and the *Pet Sematary* music video by the iconic punk rock group the Ramones, who are also referenced repeatedly throughout King's book, creating a uniquely symbiotic relationship between the novel and the music video.

King himself wrote the screenplay for the film adaptation of *Pet Sematary*,[18] and in Linda Costanzo Cahir's film adaptation terminology, *Pet Sematary* is a "traditional translation," a film "which maintains the overall traits of the book (its plot, settings, and stylistic conventions) but revamps particular details in those particular ways the filmmakers see as necessary and fitting" (16–17). In this case, the changes are relatively minor, which means we don't have to spend much time in class talking about adaptation theory or conducting an extended comparison and contrast between the novel and the film, as is necessary with many other King adaptations.[19] Given the limited class time available, we only screen the film's trailer and a handful of relevant clips, such as Louis and Jud's journey into the forest and the reanimation of Church and Gage. These excerpts are thematically focused and give us plenty to talk about in exploring and discussing how filmmakers visualized the story, though it has been my experience that many of my students have seen the film, either as a complement to their reading for our class[20] or in their own earlier, extracurricular viewing, often allowing us to expand our discussion beyond the clips screened in class. I raise a couple of questions to the class: In what ways was the visual experience of seeing events play out on screen a different narrative experience than that of reading? In what ways does this viewing contribute to students' understanding or give them a different perspective on what we've read and discussed? Several students commented that these screenings gave them a chance to visualize and more clearly imagine the characters and the action of the novel; as one student wrote, "The film trailer helped put actual faces to the characters I was reading about." In addition, students learn in a wide variety of different ways, and for students who perhaps struggle with reading and comprehension, screening the film trailer and clips provides a new perspective and approach to the material that can prove very effective in engaging visual learners, as well as providing students with a multitude of perspectives and approaches, regardless of their dominant learning style.

Finally, we conclude our popular culture discussion of *Pet Sematary* with a viewing of the "Pet Sematary" music video by the Ramones, who get multiple mentions in King's novel.[21] One of the epigraphs of part 2 of *Pet Sematary* includes lyrics from the Ramones' "Blitzkrieg Bop" (227), and when Louis checks into a local Howard Johnson's to wait for darkness to fall so he can go liberate Gage's body from the cemetery, he does so under the name Dee Dee Ramone (309). In addition, as David E. Thigpen has noted, "the group's music crops up regularly in film versions of [King's] books" (75). In addition to underscoring some of the extended themes of King's novel, the music video provides a culminating popular culture pastiche to conclude our discussion, intercutting footage of the group singing in a cemetery—and even at times from within open coffins and graves themselves—with clips of the film adaptation. The music video also functions as a kind of parody, defusing the traditional horror of the gothic, which allows us to consider those characteristics and the ways in which they are challenged, for example, by the band singing from within open graves and coffins with no real threat or danger. Ending with the Ramones' music video also dynamically underscores the active—and interactive—nature of these popular cultural texts: King was inspired by the Ramones; Hollywood has embraced King and transformed *Pet Sematary* into a film; finally, the Ramones were inspired by the novel and film, bringing the chain of inspiration back to where we began, with King's incorporation of the Ramones' lyrics and allusions. As this demonstrates, the text is not a concrete artifact that is read and shelved but rather a work that impacts the world around it, responding to that larger context and eliciting responses from it in kind.

This popular culture engagement has proven to be an excellent way of getting students to think about and critically discuss the ways in which the active text gets appropriated and actively negotiated by the filmmakers and the Ramones, who make something new and different from it, as well as taking us back to the novel itself and the Ramones references we find there, bringing our discussion of engagement and the active text full circle.

Learning Outcomes

Having students read popular fiction, such as Stephen King, is an excellent way to get them engaged with literature. However, popular fiction can present its own unique set of challenges as well, including encouraging students to look beyond the immediate fun and seemingly uncomplicated accessibility of the fiction itself. Combining the reading of King's *Pet Sematary* with a larger genre context, narratively specific text-pairing readings, and popular culture interpretations allows the students to perceive the novel as one piece of a larger conversation, as well as exposing them to gothic literature precedents and the impact of the text itself on its surrounding culture. In addition to this larger perspective, the text-pairing discussions focus students' attention on individual literary elements, such as the themes of fate and seen versus unseen horror in Jacobs's "The Monkey's Paw," the characterization of the flawed doctor in Shelley's *Frankenstein*, and the echoes of both of these in King's *Pet Sematary*. Finally, emphasizing the active text approach as a productive way of reading and critically understanding King's fiction reiterates the idea of the literary text as an ever-changing and constantly negotiated entity, giving students a new perspective on the written word that will hopefully follow them long after the class has ended.

Teaching the Popular through Visual Culture

"My students don't want literature. . . . [T]hey want at least 'reality,' the pleasure of the quickened pulse, the shock that what they read in the classroom might actually speak the same pop vernacular as the music they listen to, the movies they watch. Where does that leave us teachers of nineteenth-century American literature? In a pretty good place, actually."—MICHAEL DEVINE, "The Literature of Attractions: Teaching the Popular Fiction of the 1890s through Early Cinema"

"Dime novels expose current entertainment narratives' roots in American imperialism."—LISA LONG, "Thomas Chalmers Harbaugh's Dime Novel Westerns and Video Game Narratives"

The Literature of Attractions

Teaching the Popular Fiction of the 1890s through Early Cinema

MICHAEL DEVINE

"'Murder and sudden death,' say you? Yes, . . . it's reality, it's the thing that counts. We don't want literature, we want life. [. . .] The tales are here. The public is here." —FRANK NORRIS, in 1897, on why San Francisco offered "Great Opportunities for Fiction Writers"

"In just a moment, a cataclysmic moment, my friends . . . you will see this train take life in a marvelous and most astounding manner. It will rush towards you, belching smoke and fire from its monstrous iron throat." —EARLY CINEMA EXHIBITOR preparing audience for a screening of *Black Diamond Express* in the 1890s

FRANK NORRIS WAS RIGHT. My students don't want literature. If not tales of "murder and sudden death" exactly (although, in a fix, that'll do), they want at least "reality," the pleasure of the quickened pulse, the shock that what they read in the classroom might actually speak the same pop vernacular as the music they listen to, the movies they watch. Where does that leave us teachers of late-nineteenth-century American literature? In a pretty good place, actually. If, as Nancy Bentley argues, Americans in those years discovered "the thrill of watching forms implode"—big screen crashes, mostly, but also the conventions of genteel literature blown to bits—as teachers we might do well to consider ourselves more like the early cinema operators of my second epigraph: not guardians of high literary culture, but exhibitors of truly pop tales.[1] In this chapter, I show how works by Norris, William Dean Howells, and Kate Chopin regain their status as popular fiction (what they originally were) once we reestablish their profound continuities with the "marvelous and most astounding" technology of their age: the cinema. Teaching in light of this popular cultural form, it turns out, reveals something essential about tainted lit: how it registers the tastes of a dynamic public and the emerging media shaping those tastes. The public of the 1890s demanded "life" itself, which was thought to "rush towards you" like the Black Diamond Express. Norris's public is not so different from the one sitting in our classrooms. What they wanted then is what they want now—what I call the "literature of attractions."

What is the "literature of attractions" and how does one teach it? In the spirit of an early cinema exhibitor, let me demonstrate. I introduce my students to this period with a bit of showmanship. First, a question: "What happened on Twenty-third Street?" The question refers to the Edison film *What Happened on Twenty-third Street, New York City* (1901). Rather than simply screen the one-shot, minute-and-a-half film, however, I keep its urban sidewalk scene paused before the classroom; that is to say, I keep it suspended ("In just a moment, a cataclysmic moment . . ."), a simple yet defamiliarizing move borrowed from those early exhibitors to confront students with the qualities of a medium they too often take for granted. Then I field guesses: they usually range from the canned ("Someone falls in love") to the criminal ("A pickpocket"), from the ecstatic ("A political rally!") to the existential ("Nothing happens"). What, in fact, happens? A man and woman emerge from the mess of ordinary details, walk toward the camera and over a steam shaft. Suddenly, her swirling dress transforms her into a Salome of sorts, while her companion looks on. End of film—but one in which seemingly unremarkable actuality footage introduces some of the core concepts of cinematic study as well as of late-nineteenth-century American literature. Moving in the direction of storytelling but brimming with what Tom Gunning calls the sudden, exhibitionistic, outward energy of the "cinema of attractions," the film revels in its brief, titillating moment to invoke us and involve us in the world of the street ("Astonishment" 116). It is a world of rupture and contingency, transformation, chaos, and sexual energy churning beneath the everyday. It is, in short, the world of early cinema that posed its own rather difficult question to the literary establishment of its era: Was there any room in "the domain of aesthetic expression and convention," as Bentley phrases it, for this disruptive, anarchic, popular energy (1)? Or, to put it another, more direct way: was there a "literature of attractions"?

What Happened on Twenty-third Street, New York City (1901). Library of Congress, Motion Picture, Broadcasting, and Recorded Sound Division.

"Was there a literature of attractions?" In fact, that question was put to me by a student. It was less a question, really, than a startling observation, the result of having watched *What Happened* shortly before tackling Frank Norris's *McTeague* (1899). Shock and brevity are obviously not the first things that come to mind when students sit down to read. Nevertheless, the question emerged, driven by the sense that even this imposing naturalist tome, a Zolaesque tale about the demise of a hulking dentist in San Francisco, that this, too, was participating in—and what's more, was made legible by—the culture of the attraction. Legible, perhaps, because putting the pop back into such stories reinvests them with a primitive energy that students just don't expect to find in the literature classroom.

Precisely that energy is what Norris wanted to capture, evident in my first epigraph, where he exhorts young writers to subvert the protocols of high art and literary decorum. In that pop manifesto of sorts (it's titled like a classified ad: "Great Opportunities!"), the young author sounds like someone shooting actuality footage for Edison, attuned as Norris is to a cityscape temporally punctured by radical contingency: "Think of the short stories that are *happening every hour of the time*. Get hold of them, younger writers, grip fast upon the life of them. It's the life that we want . . . not the curious weaving of words and the polish of literary finish" (249; emphasis mine). And it's precisely this energy that shocked critics who thought they had seen the last of the realism wars by the end of the century. One reviewer had even claimed victory in 1899, comforted by "the sudden on-rush of works of ideality and romance, which arose like a fresh, sweet wind to clear the literary atmosphere." *McTeague*, at that late date in the century, brought with it the street and the smell of the gutter: Norris was "searching out the degraded side of humanity," one critic lamented, telling just "about the most unpleasant American story that anybody has ventured to write," concluded another. Far from fresh and sweet, one of the more infamous dirty scenes in the book happens at a vaudeville theater movie screening, where a young boy loses control of his bladder, giving genteel reviewers the delicate task of not sullying themselves in their condemnation: "[Norris] descends to descriptions of incidents which have no place in print; to comment upon or even suggest them is vulgar to the last degree." Norris's work was indeed tainted, a foul wind amidst "ideality and romance" that, nevertheless, proved to one progressive reviewer a welcome change in weather patterns: *McTeague*, for William Dean Howells, completed the shift "from the romantic to the realistic temperament . . . suddenly, and with the overwhelming effect of a blizzard."[2] Life, real life, comes at you like a blizzard. Or like a train.

While scholars have been busy arguing for a "pop modernism" that bound together the nation's arts, literature, and audiences from 1910 to 1960, it's important to remember, as film historian Charles Musser does, the late nineteenth century was an age of "active viewers" expert at traversing the "different media" exploding around them.[3] To this audience, even Howells's metaphor for the excessive, unpredictable nature of Norris's work would have situated it instantly among pop cultural forms celebrating sudden transformation and disaster—disasters participated in bodily, more often than not, through the pleasurable shock of the screen. Indeed, even a blizzard could become a cinematic attraction in films like *In the Grip of the Blizzard* (1899), an "actuality" survey of New York City shut down—and at play—because of sudden weather. In the following pages, I show how *McTeague* and works by Howells and Chopin all explore the ramifications of this period's emerging media:

the newspapers, but especially the cinema. This exploration left them tainted, their fitting symbol, perhaps, the incontinent moviegoer that scandalized *McTeague*'s early reviewers (more on him later). By channeling the energy of the screen and the street, this taint helped to reconfigure the very notion of the literary, "the domain of aesthetic expression and convention" that Bentley writes of. This reconfiguration is at the heart of why we teach popular literature, and why what has become "canonical" from this period must be recovered first and foremost as the "literature of attractions." This means reading the stories of the 1890s as stories of their hours, and the shocking convulsions an hour—or a moment—can bring.

"Y ought t'have seen": Norris's Street Cinema

McTeague is a work about sliding social classes and the regulatory pincer jaws standardizing modern life. Mac, as he's known, will be forced to shutter his dental parlors because he lacks a license, the first step in a dark journey toward madness and murder. It is a work about the body, its impulses, and its war with convention: the dentist kisses a patient while she is under ether and immediately asks for her hand in marriage when she awakes (spoiler alert: she vomits). However, as my student pointed out after her first foray into the work, the opening chapter makes clear that it's most simply about what happens, and what can suddenly happen, on the street. It begins there, in a space of leisure ("It was Sunday," begins the text), with McTeague behind his window "looking down into the street. The street never failed to interest him."[4] What interests, or really, reassures him is the reliable order of Polk Street, its well-worn routine of "day laborers" hurrying at eight o'clock in the morning, with "clerks and shop girls" following after, and finally the grand ladies "from the great avenue a block above . . . promenading the sidewalks leisurely, deliberately" at eleven (8). The street reflects an order particularly gratifying to the dentist, who counts himself lucky no longer to be among the sweating classes (as a child he worked in the mines, we learn early on). Everything is in its place, with McTeague safely ensconced behind his window, as Norris turns to the visual culture to reinforce the point: "Day after day, McTeague saw the same panorama unroll itself. The bay window of his 'Dental Parlors' was for him a point of vantage from which he watched the world go past" (9). The panorama, as Angela Miller points out, was enjoying its last boom as a mass visual spectacle in the final decades of the nineteenth century; around since 1789, the circular or stationary panorama "satisfied the nineteenth-century craving for visual—and by extension physical and political—control over a rapidly expanding world."[5] It is a carefully chosen image through which the street initially assumes the dimensions of a secure narrative space. Like spectators watching panoramas of epic battle scenes in those years, from McTeague's perch above the street he, too, is afforded what Miller calls "the illusion of mastery over random, distant, or otherwise incomprehensible events" (36).

When introduced to the novel with a film like *What Happened*, students are quick to note just how intent Norris is on rupturing this "illusion of mastery." If the sweeping scope of Norris's work promises to reproduce the panorama in some form, it is a panorama now inflected and punctured by the culture of the attraction at every turn. *McTeague*, in other words, is the panorama in the age of early cinema. Upon turning from his bay window, the dentist meets his neighbor, Marcus Schouler, who breathlessly recounts what happened to him on the street, among other places:

> In recounting a certain dispute with an awkward bicyclist, in which it appeared he had become involved, Marcus quivered with rage. "'Say that again,' says I to um. 'Just say that once more, and'"—here a rolling explosion of oaths—"'you'll go back to the city in the Morgue wagon. Ain't I got a right to cross a street even, I'd like to know, without being run down—what?' I say it's outrageous. I'd a knifed him in another minute. It was an outrage. I say it was an *outrage*."
>
> "Sure it was," McTeague hastened to reply. "Sure, sure."
>
> "Oh, and we had an accident," shouted the other, suddenly off on another tack. "It was awful. Trina was in the swing there—that's my cousin Trina, you know who I mean—and she fell out. By damn! I thought she'd killed herself; struck her face on a rock and knocked out a front tooth. It's a wonder she didn't kill herself. It *is* a wonder; it is, for a fact. Ain't it, now? Huh? Ain't it? Y'ought t'have seen." (10–11; emphasis in the original)

What is remarkable about Marcus's entrance is not simply the foreshadowing involved—he'll attempt to knife McTeague soon enough; rather, in light of the coherent view Norris carefully establishes from the outset, there is a sense of exposure here to the defiantly nonnarrative order of the street, a space of violent contingency where bodies and rights are crashing into one another, undoing the complacent belief in progress and social order the novel initially unrolls and lulls its reader into accepting.

With Marcus's dangerous and digressive entry, we get our first glance at the culture of the attraction, or to put it more historically, what Ben Singer considers the "radically altered public sphere" of the late nineteenth century, which threatened "traditional conception[s] of safety, continuity, and self-controlled destiny."[6] On the one hand, Marcus brings with him into the novel the popular culture of sensation and screaming headlines that first gave Norris the outline of his story ("Twenty-nine Fatal Wounds" was the title of one of the 1893 *San Francisco Examiner* stories that inspired *McTeague*, detailing the vicious murder of a wife by her husband in the kindergarten where she worked).[7] Like the media and media consumer of his day (and every day), Marcus has a penchant for getting "very excited over trivial details. Marcus could not talk without getting excited" (10). On the other hand, Norris choreographs Marcus's entrance into the novel as an explicitly visual turn away from the bay-window view of the world, and the secure, extended vision it promises. Like the early cinematic visions of elephants being electrocuted or oncoming trains, Marcus invites McTeague and the reader to attend to an "accident" that is both "awful" and a "wonder"—invites him, that is, to attend to an attraction, which "ought" to be "seen" not in spite of its threat to bodily safety and social decorum but precisely because of that threat.

Perhaps it is too much to say that the novel that proceeds from this accident is simply one (long) attraction that repeats this initial one: Trina at the mercy of accidents—winning the lottery, poisoned by lead paint, losing her fingers, and murdered, finally, at the hands of her now husband, McTeague. By positioning the attraction against the panorama early on, however, Norris does foreground his novel's pop logic, its exposure to the street, its exhibitionism, and its taste for contingency; it is a willingness to go, like Marcus, "suddenly off on another tack" in its effort, like the cinema of attractions, to solicit readerly attention. And thus we have wrestling matches (with separated shoulders), men swallowing (and nearly choking on) pool balls, and what Norris originally conceived of as the main attraction: Trina's graphic murder, which did not make it into the final published novel. In that scene, not surprisingly, Norris had choreographed Trina's end as yet another strange performance at once kinetic, uncontrollable, and astonishing: "At every moment she dodged and ducked, panting for breath, spinning around, jumping from side to side. No acrobat ever went through such wild gymnastics, such contortions, such furious gambols. The frail body bounded about from wall to wall of the room with the vigor and elasticity of a rubber ball. . . . It was astonishing how long Trina lasted under [his blows]."[8] Compared to contemporary news accounts of the actual crime that dwelt almost exclusively on the murderer's actions—"The broom fell from her hand and a scream was strangled in her throat" is all we get of the passive victim—it is evident that the showman in Norris, like Marcus, was not going to squander this "awful wonder" that really ought to be seen.[9] Obviously drawing on more than just the lurid daily news, Norris here taints his text by sampling the period's vernacular visual culture, a world of vaudeville performers and kinetoscope loops. Indeed, the kinetoscope, the cinema's earliest peephole form, seemed expressly designed for glimpses of "wild gymnastics," bodies contorting in short film loops—sneezing, flexing, dancing—without apparent beginning or end. Like Trina, who turns into a "rubber ball," the kinetoscopic body was a body confined, convulsed, and transformed into an attraction.

Ironically, leaving the murder offstage and out of the published text makes Trina's death even more of an attraction. Shuttered in the kindergarten cloakroom away from the delicate eyes of the reader, it erupts before the eyes of another unsuspecting audience: schoolchildren. "McTeague going out," Norris carefully notes, "had shut the door of the cloakroom, but had left the street door open; so when the children arrived in the morning, they entered as usual" (208). Taking pains to stress the "usual" routines of the children, and how they went "across to the cloakroom to hang up their hats and coats as they had been taught," Norris makes it clear that no one and nowhere is safe in the culture of the attraction, when even a kindergarten cloakroom is the stage for an audience spectacle: not one child witnesses it, but "they all ran in," the scene grimly concludes (208).

The school scene is but one of many moments in a novel that focuses on "the spectacles of spectatorship,"[10] to use Paul Young's apt phrase, the most significant of which occurs when McTeague takes Trina and her family to a vaudeville show, featuring "the crowning scientific achievement of the nineteenth century, the kinetoscope," a film screening (not the peephole technology) of urban actualities that "fairly took their breaths away":

"What will they do next?" observed Trina, in amazement. "Ain't that wonderful, Mac?"

McTeague was awe-struck.

"Look at that horse move his head," he cried excitedly, quite carried away. "Look at that cable car coming—and the man going across the street. See, here comes a truck. Well, I never in all my life! What would Marcus say to this?"

"It's all a drick!" exclaimed Mrs. Sieppe, with sudden conviction. "I ain't no fool; dot's nothun but a drick."

"Well, of course, mamma," exclaimed Trina, "it's—"

But Mrs. Sieppe put her head in the air.

"I'm too old to be fooled," she persisted. "It's a drick." Nothing more could be got out of her than this. (62–63)

For Gunning, this scene shows that, far "from confusing the film image with reality," early spectators received even actuality footage as a kind of spectacle or visual illusion—a kind of "drick."[11] But perhaps most striking about this scene in light of *McTeague* is how far removed it is from the bay-window view of the world, even though the subject—street life—is the same. For there is something about the cinema, Norris senses, that changes the spectator, and here Mac is expressive in a way that is rare in the novel: he is reactive, excited, even digressive as the screen ("Look at that horse," "Look at that cable car"). Indeed, we hardly need to wonder what Marcus would say to all of this, because Mac the moviegoer has done a fairly good turn as his excitable friend.

The novel shows, then, how even actualities participated in the direct, bodily address of the attraction, often offering a "point of vantage" literally on the street, no longer where one can comfortably watch "the world go past." As Mary Ann Doane demonstrates in *The Emergence of Cinematic Time*, and films like *Corner Madison and State Streets, Chicago* (1897) make clear, the early screen could be an awfully crowded, illegible space, due in part to the technology's hyperindexicality; film's ability to capture every movement of an unfolding world made "contingency itself . . . a display."[12] Defining the outward energy of the attractions, this sense of display addressed the viewer in a visceral way—thus, the early fears that conflated watching film with hypnosis and hysteria.[13] The moviegoer's body was a pop body, a permeable body, one open to influence, not totally in control. This offers some context for appreciating the infamous "dreadful accident"—in a book rife with accidents—that befalls Trina's brother, young "Owgooste," who wets his pants at the theater, the scene that early reviewers found scandalous and Norris was pressured to change (63).

Corner Madison and State Streets, Chicago (1897). Library of Congress, Motion Picture, Broadcasting, and Recorded Sound Division.

It should be clear that if Norris's work can be thought of as a kind of "literature of attractions," it is not simply on account of its explicit engagement with early cinema; rather, the visual traces are a measure of the work's pop permeability, the way it channels and remediates the age's sensations and street life, leaving both characters and readers newly exposed, vulnerable, even awestruck like McTeague before the screen. Early cinema, I have found, is an easy way to invite students to reconsider their rather complacent ideas about the dynamism of popular culture and the ways texts popularize themselves by participating in that culture. Far from an object for passive consumption, the popular culture of the late nineteenth and early twentieth centuries was an invitation to step outside—to return to one's body and the street, to rediscover madness, maybe even solidarity, by all manner of accidents. The invitation can be found, if one looks for it, in any number of artifacts from the period. Take the women from the world of Ashcan painters like John Sloan, for example: they stare confidently back at us, the viewers, and through the closed space of the canvas in the same way that attractions ruptured the screen. On the screen, of course, are works like Lumière's *The Arrival of a Train at La Ciotat Station* (1895). If it is true that the earliest viewers of that film did not actually flee from the screen, as Gunning has long maintained, the myth is a handy one, regardless, if only we think of those spectators running for the exit signs and into the street. In structuring a class around the tainted texts of early cinema, Chopin's "The Story of an Hour" (1894) is the most obvious choice, a brief work haunted by a shocking media specter. But the attraction is even at the heart of a text much less frequently taught, Howells's *A Hazard of New Fortunes* (1890). Next, I want to suggest a few ways these two works can be illuminated by the flicker of early cinema.

The Arrival of a Train at La Ciotat Station (1895). www.criticalcommons.org.

"Safe Distance": Pop Lit's Proximity to Attractions

Hazard is a work that has long been considered an emblem of the chang-ing, increasingly pop-minded literary world of the late nineteenth cen-tury. Howells's own departure from heading Boston's *Atlantic Monthly* for New York's *Harper's New Monthly Magazine* finds its counterpart in the novel, which begins with Basil March's move to New York to edit the new literary undertaking *Every Other Week*. From the drawing rooms of New England to the streets of New York, from Old to New World, from high to low culture, *Hazard* also meditates on the political implications of opening a narrative space to engage with the attraction, namely, a riotous street car strike that gives the novel its climax. A small selection from the novel is enough to get students thinking about the complex relationship between the literature of this period and the street, that is to say, the politics of a truly popular literature.

Like *McTeague*, *Hazard* is a novel about the street; unlike *McTeague*, it is the story of a writer's effort to grasp what happens, as Basil is com-missioned to write literary "sketches . . . about life in every part of New York."[14] As a result, the novel's sense of exposure to the street is inter-estingly mediated; in fact, Howells takes for his subject the high cost of this literary distance—from the popular culture, the popular press, and the political turmoil of the day. To get a sense of this distance, one need only observe what happens on the way to Twenty-third Street: "March professed himself vulgarized by a want of style in the people they met in their walk to Twenty-third Street" (301). Fittingly, it is only behind another window—not a bay window this time, but rather the elevated train's—that the street is escaped and everything put into place:

> [Isabel, March's wife] declared [the elevated train] the most ideal way of getting about in the world. . . . She now said that the night transit was even more interesting than the day, and that the fleet-ing intimacy you formed with people in second and third floor interiors, while all the usual street life went on underneath, had a domestic intensity mixed with a perfect repose that was the last effect of good society with all its security and exclusiveness. He said it was better than the theatre, of which it reminded him, to see those people through their windows: a family party of work-

folk at a late tea, some of the men in their shirt-sleeves; a woman sewing by a lamp; a mother laying her child in its cradle; a man with his head fallen on his hands upon a table; a girl and her lover leaning over the window-sill together. What suggestion! what drama! what infinite interest! (76)

Students are quick to see this passage in cinematic terms, and I have often presented it alongside kinetoscope films to emphasize the closed, repetitive nature of that early technology. And yet, what's most striking here is the distance from the street in literal and symbolic terms, as this moving technology enables not the culture of the attraction but its exact opposite: "repose," "security," and "exclusiveness" (unlike, for example, the "wild gymnastics" of Trina's death scene). What March wants, and what this window-watching technology affords, are nothing less than urban still lifes deprived of their vitality, symbols of a harmonious social order and the writer's legible, panoramic, disembodied literary view.

Like Norris, Howells undermines this vision by pushing the novel closer to the street, where a streetcar labor strike, a site of violence and contingency, will ultimately demand to be noticed. "And yet," as Christopher Raczkowski points out, "when the strike erupts in *Hazard*, March and the editorial staff of *Every Other Week* are at a loss as to how to represent—or, for that matter, 'to see'—the strike."[15] Howells frames this blindness as a measure of the gap between the (engaged) popular press and the (removed) literary artist:

While March watched them at a safe distance, a car laden with policemen came down the track, but none of the strikers offered to molest it. In their simple Sunday best, March thought them very quiet, decent-looking people, and he could well believe that they had nothing to do with the riotous outbreaks in other parts of the city. He could hardly believe that there were any such outbreaks; he began more and more to think them *mere newspaper exaggerations* in the absence of any disturbance, or the disposition to it, that he could see. (411; emphasis mine)

Ultimately, it is "safe distance" that Howells refuses to grant March and the reader in producing his own "literature of attractions." Likewise, "safe distance" in the culture of attractions is also at the thematic center of Kate Chopin's classroom-friendly short story, "The Story of an Hour."

On the one hand, the story is about the failure to distance Mrs. Mallard from the news of the train accident in which her husband is supposed to have died—a "newspaper exaggeration" of sorts, one might generously say (he's alive). Oddly enough, the genteel effort to break the news to her softly—and quickly—which begins the story, only reinforces the shock of living in an age in which temporal delays have been erased. The story is about the age of the media, in this sense, opening as it does with Richards, her husband's friend, outpacing the news by bringing word of the death directly from "the newspaper office."[16] On the other hand, it is the husband's own safe distance from "the railroad disaster," the age's attraction par excellence, that gives the story its dramatic conclusion. As in *McTeague* and *Hazard*, such "safe distance" signifies unawareness or insensitivity to the new age of upheaval and liberation heralded by the story: "He had been far from the scene of accident, and did not even know there had been one" (200).

The irony, of course, is that the wife's proximity to the culture of the attraction—the media, and through it the violence and contingency of industrialized modernity—reconnects her with "life," visually connected in the story, not surprisingly, with an "open window": "She could see in the open square before her house the tops of trees. . . . In the street below a peddler was crying his wares. The notes of a distant song which someone was singing reached her faintly" (198). Like those first spectators of Lumière's train, she is addressed bodily through this "open square" in a scene that Chopin frames as a primitive visual encounter: she had a "dull stare in her eyes. . . . It was not a glance of reflection, but rather indicated a suspension of intelligent thought. There was something coming to her and she was waiting for it, fearfully" (199). The something outside—of traditional narrative limits, gender roles, and social decorum—is the culture of contingency, shock, and violence. But it is also one of liberation and transformation: it's what happens on the street, "outrage" in *McTeague* and "outbreak" in *Hazard*, which soon enough will be what happens in the home. It is, in short, the "awful wonder" of the attraction that here becomes the "monstrous joy" of the liberated woman (199).

As a truly popular fiction, "The Story of an Hour" is a work of multiple attractions, a literary effort with a window open to the street. Chopin's work allows in, among other noises, the sensational energies of the daily newspapers, with their almost giddy coverage of railroad accidents featuring lists of the "Killed" and "Wounded." Through her minimalist, time-stamped approach, Chopin clearly inscribes her work into this age of the popular press and popular reading habits. But, ultimately, it is the attraction of the liberated woman that aligns the text with the newborn cinematic technology. In the very same year as "The Story of an Hour," the kinetoscope was revealing to a scandalized public looped visions of liberated bodies, both strong men and serpentine dancers, Samsons and Salomes. With no real beginning or end, these early visions were attractions of abandonment, ones that defied narrative containment, like the liberated body of Mrs. Mallard, who had "abandoned herself" and now "carried herself unwittingly like a goddess of Victory" (200). In her own sudden turn, Chopin kills off her heroine on her way out the door, and gives the doctors the last solemn word to explain what happened. This is an author, students quickly realize, having some fun with authority, especially the authority of narrative. As readers, we know what happened, just like what happened on Twenty-third Street was nothing less than a transformation. This transformation—into pop lit, through pop forms—is what we mean by the "literature of attractions."

"'Murder and sudden death,' say you? Yes." Mallard's sudden death returns us in its own looping way to where we started, Norris's call for young novelists to pay close attention to what the public wanted. "The tales are here": Norris's advice is as applicable today for teachers who want to connect their public, their students, with popular writing that forever altered a nation's attitudes about what could be considered "literary" material. Indeed, for teachers of late-nineteenth-century American literature, the tales are here; however, because these works have become canonical, it is easy to overlook their pop culture provenance, the way that, by interacting with the culture of the attraction, they reimagined readers as embodied, active participants rather than detached narrative spectators of what happens on the street. With a vast early film archive now available to us online, the films are here, too: it is easier than ever to bring this period's visual culture to our students and start teaching the "literature of attractions." This means, above all, bringing a bit of drama to our classroom, by reintroducing students to a cinematic medium that has become all but invisible to them, as well as to writing that threatens to become just as invisible—or worse, merely "classic." Done right, you might even feel like you are back in the 1890s, one of those early cinema exhibitors, but now with an updated pitch: "In just a moment, a cataclysmic moment, my friends . . . you will see this book take life in a most marvelous and astounding manner."

Thomas Chalmers Harbaugh's Dime Novel Westerns and Video Game Narratives

LISA LONG

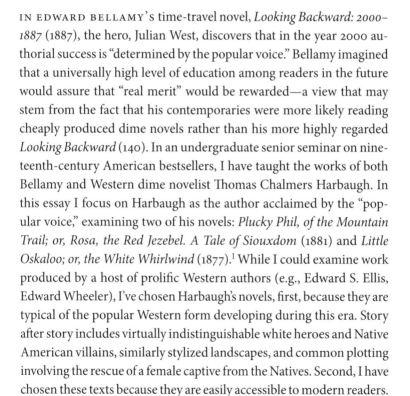

IN EDWARD BELLAMY's time-travel novel, *Looking Backward: 2000–1887* (1887), the hero, Julian West, discovers that in the year 2000 authorial success is "determined by the popular voice." Bellamy imagined that a universally high level of education among readers in the future would assure that "real merit" would be rewarded—a view that may stem from the fact that his contemporaries were more likely reading cheaply produced dime novels rather than his more highly regarded *Looking Backward* (140). In an undergraduate senior seminar on nineteenth-century American bestsellers, I have taught the works of both Bellamy and Western dime novelist Thomas Chalmers Harbaugh. In this essay I focus on Harbaugh as the author acclaimed by the "popular voice," examining two of his novels: *Plucky Phil, of the Mountain Trail; or, Rosa, the Red Jezebel. A Tale of Siouxdom* (1881) and *Little Oskaloo; or, the White Whirlwind* (1877).[1] While I could examine work produced by a host of prolific Western authors (e.g., Edward S. Ellis, Edward Wheeler), I've chosen Harbaugh's novels, first, because they are typical of the popular Western form developing during this era. Story after story includes virtually indistinguishable white heroes and Native American villains, similarly stylized landscapes, and common plotting involving the rescue of a female captive from the Natives. Second, I have chosen these texts because they are easily accessible to modern readers. While the vast majority of dime novels are available only in archives,

Harbaugh's *Plucky Phil* is included in Paul C. Gutjahr's fine anthology, *Popular American Literature of the 19th Century*, and *Little Oskaloo* is available online for free through Project Gutenberg.

Finally, I focus on Harbaugh's novels because of the many features they share in common with contemporary forms of popular entertainment—commonalities that have proven crucial to my ability to teach dime novels effectively. While one might argue that the wooden characters and quick-paced plots of Harbaugh's novels, which posed no impediment to his popularity in his own time, would make them easier for modern students to digest than more complex texts from the era, I find that students struggle mightily with the work of Harbaugh and other dime novelists, scornful of their "poor" writing and unsure about what to do with these texts. Specifically, they are annoyed by Harbaugh's dialect work, but they are frustrated even more by his disjointed narratives, caused by a lack of connective tissue; timelines that move in fits and starts; shallow, unstable characters; and unbelievable plot twists. In modern pedagogical praxis, we tend to teach our students to read in a particular way: for "round," complex characters; metaphorical and symbolic complexity; well-developed and original plots; and ambiguity. And when students try to apply these reading strategies to novels like Harbaugh's, they yield very little. While we may believe that we are training our students to be sophisticated readers with refined literary tastes, especially when it comes to pre-twentieth-century American literature, I suggest that we may be training them a bit narrowly and not providing them with an array of interpretive strategies that will allow them to navigate a variety of texts—not just those accorded the highest literary merit.

Thus I found that I needed to help students see the continued relevance of dime novels, and to recognize that these texts, which might seem at first to be the detritus of simpler times, are more potent than they think. When I suggested to my students that we read dime novel Westerns through video game narratives, they perked up considerably. They noticed immediately that the quick changes from one disjointed scene to another are reminiscent of video game play. Also, they were able to make sense of the odd places where solitary characters speak aloud, presumably to forward the plot, labeling these "cutscenes" (in video game terminology, a scripted break from the flow of the game to forward or enhance the narrative). Read in this way, the underdeveloped characters leave space for imagined projections, much as video game avatars do. Harbaugh's landscapes, like video game landscapes, are also highly stylized, in his case craggy or overgrown, dramatic and segmented; the characters cannot see before and behind them and are "trapped" in discrete spaces where they must solve some sort of problem before they can move on to the next scene/space. And winning at "this mountain game" is the motivation for all of the characters—something that makes much more sense within the context of video game narrative. Surprisingly, while one might expect a deeply Christian ethos in these texts, given the conventions of nineteenth-century literature, the terrain in these novels is amoral and only (p)luck determines the outcome of the story. Indeed, the language of fate, gambling, and gaming more generally suffuses Harbaugh's texts.

Finally, Harbaugh's Westerns are rife with violence, particularly against anonymous ethnic others. In *Plucky Phil* the famous Lakota (Sioux) leader, Sitting Bull, is a main character and Custer's last stand, which took place in the Black Hills in 1874, is a featured plot point. And in *Little Oskaloo* Harbaugh situates us in the Ohio River Valley in 1794 as the Shawnees, Delewars, and Wayndots gear up to face General "Mad" Anthony Wayne in the Northwest Indian War, which resulted in a treaty where the Native American confederacy "gave" Ohio to the United States. Both texts include masses of often nameless, indistinguishable foes—"real red athletes, with great breadth of chest, and strong arms"—who are mowed down by white heroes (*Little Oskaloo*). This trend is still evident in the neo-Western video game, *Red Dead Redemption* (sequel to *Red Dead Revolver*, both set in 1911 after most Native Americans were forced onto reservations), but it is also a significant subtext to phenomenally popular first-person shooter series such as *Call of Duty* and *Halo*, which stigmatize more contemporary ethnic threats from terrorists and other "aliens."

Helping students to see the continuities between popular American entertainment narratives of the nineteenth through the twenty-first centuries is significant work. I contend that students' eager and easy dismissal of dime novels reflects their desire not to look too closely at their own immersion in video game narratives and other modern diversions (e.g., sporting culture). Their initial distaste for dimes signals both college students' still tenuous grasp of canonical literature and their deep discomfort with the ethnically inflected violence that has permeated and distinguished American culture. Dime novels expose current entertainment narratives' roots in American imperialism. Like the dimes before them, video game narratives reflect the masculinist cultures and concerns of the times. While scheming, violent Indians have been replaced by bloodthirsty warriors, aliens, and ethnic criminals, the games are still distinguished by imperialist impulses and characterized by extreme physical violence against anonymous "others." The preservation of symbolic white womanhood that is imperiled during combat also drives these narratives, though white women, too, become more brutal. Indeed, given our own culture's discomfort with the violence at the heart of these games, it should come as no surprise that dime novels were named as the "actual cause of the crime" at several murder trials in nineteenth-century America, signaling, as Bill Brown notes, that our precursors, too, saw violent behaviors as stemming from "some sort of mass-cultural contamination" (3).

Thus I ask students to take these seemingly innocuous, almost laughable texts seriously because their influence is so profound and ubiquitous: millions of readers and gamers throughout American history have immersed themselves in these blood-and-thunder stories—just for fun. In this way, students learn to see seemingly simple entertainments as complex, to recognize the ways that such narratives act upon them, and then to expand the scope of their interpretive capabilities. These are crucial, twenty-first-century skills, inculcating in students of literature the sort of broad-minded discernment that transfers into any number of contexts.

The Business of Popular Narratives

Thomas Chalmers Harbaugh was a remarkably prolific author, publishing over three hundred paper stories throughout his career (many, under militaristic, alliterative pseudonyms such as "Captain Howard Holmes" and "Major S. S. Scott") in addition to three volumes of sentimental poetry and several juvenile novels, with a healthy dose of political journalism thrown in. Born in Maryland, Harbaugh's family moved to Casstown, Ohio, when he was still a baby, and he lived his whole life there. His education did not extend beyond the common schools in Casstown, yet Harbaugh's literary proclivities were soon apparent; he published his first story in 1867 at the age of sixteen. A. F. Broomhall (a Dayton-area lawyer), writing of Harbaugh's poetic achievements in 1889, remarks that "he has not been surrounded by stirring scenes, nor has he lived among people of literary tastes" (155). While his education was limited, his imagination was prodigious, as he never traveled further west than Ohio, yet set so many of his Westerns in vividly drawn frontier landscapes. Biographical sketches depict a man far removed from his adventurous, rugged heroes. Broomhall notes, "He is slender, short of stature, and afflicted with a stoppage in his speech" (155). A second local biographer, a self-described friend, adds that Harbaugh is

> as modest as a girl, and unassuming in every respect. He is a small man with light hair and blue eyes, and if ever he had a love affair it has been kept a profound secret. He spends the greater part of his time in his library; sometimes he will be found along the banks of Lost creek or the Miami river with rod and minnow bucket, but he fishes more for quiet thought than for bass or perch.
> ("Thomas Harbaugh")

Broomhall's revelation of Harbaugh's stutter (which, apparently, disappeared when he read his poetry) provides some insight into his isolation; nothing definitive can be discerned about the confirmed bachelor's love life from this scanty biographical material, though Harbaugh emerges as somewhat effete and introverted. Elsewhere in the article, Harbaugh's anonymous local biographer praises Harbaugh's earnest and humorous work as a political journalist with Republican interests and lauds his poetry, which treats "the realm of true patriotism" and the "sweeter, gentler plane of home and love."

And as for the dime novels? After the publication in 1878 of another Western, Harbaugh's hometown newspaper, *The Saturday Journal*, reported that

> T. C. Harbaugh has published another cheap novel entitled "Dandy Jack; or, The Outlaw of the Oregon Trail." We are proud

of "T.C.H." as a poet of our own, but regret exceedingly that he should add in any wise to the already overloaded market of cheap, trashy literature. It is ruining our boys and girls. (Johanssen)

Harbaugh accepted the critique with grace, penning a good-natured but pointed poem called "My Pen and I," where he says to his pen: "We'll not write any more today / On madrigal or story; / But let the critics have their way / And starve to death on glory" (Johanssen). His local biographer emphasizes that unlike other local authors, Harbaugh had been able to support himself as a writer; his dime novels allowed him to avoid the "hard grind of other occupations" that can crush one's literary ambitions. Harbaugh is "adept in situations and scenes of thrilling interest," the biographer notes, and the demand for this popular work has allowed him "not only a good living," but also the means to "lay by a nice little sum for old age" ("Thomas Harbaugh"). As Christine Bold emphasizes, though writers like Harbaugh were labeled "hacks" because of their willingness to churn out formulaic work, they were also, as another Beadle and Adams author put it, the only men able to make a living by "pure literary labor" simply by writing books "for the largest possible market in this country" (qtd. in Bold 29). Harbaugh earned between $100 and $150 per story from Beadle and Adams (Johanssen); during the years he published *Plucky Phil* and *Little Oskaloo*, that would be around $3,500 per story in modern currency.[2]

The creators of modern video games also do not generally receive the respect reserved for literary artists. Yet they design for the masses of our own time, similarly living at the cutting edge of entertainment technologies and the bounds of decency. According to the Entertainment Software Association, in 2012 sales of video game software generated $6.7 billion and sales of consoles and related accessories generated another $5.9 billion. Late nineteenth-century mass culture begat our own, in that new forms of entertainment were spawned by quickly evolving technological innovations. One might think immediately of obvious turn-of-the-twentieth-century technologies like moving pictures and sound recordings, of course. However, for my purposes, other nineteenth-century technologies—such as the Linotype mechanized typesetting machine and case-making, booking-binding machines; the production of cheap paper from wood pulp; advances in transportation (e.g., freight trains) and distribution models (e.g., subscription sales); even the spread of electric light and the availability of eyeglasses—all allowed for the mass production, distribution, and consumption of paperbacks, magazines, and papers that even the laboring classes could afford.[3] "Respectable" literature often remained more retrograde in its printing and distribution strategies (although older works were pirated in cheap editions or sold through new subscription structures), while "trashy" fiction took advantage of new modes of production and distribution. This is the case in our own time, too. Video game technologies and distribution modes are constantly evolving (e.g., from cartoonish 2D to photorealistic 3D environments, game cartridges to downloadable apps), and games proliferate to feed the popular desire for more "realistic," sensational, and novel play.

The Allure of Popular Narratives

While the technologies driving the development and distribution of dime novels and video games are dramatically different, of course, I believe that the narratives at the heart of each form work on audiences similarly and that popular appetites have also remained relatively constant. Over the past quarter century, academic debate has raged over whether or not one can use narrative theories to analyze the stories at the center of modern video games. Jan Simons has done a fine job of summarizing the conflict between narratologists—those who have adapted narratological theories to the new computer media—and ludologists—those who believe such maneuvers constitute academic imperialism and call for a "new paradigm" to appropriately theorize video games by focusing more on the mechanics of game play (Simons).[4] This heated debate lost some of its steam by the mid 2000s, Simon claims. Though I heed Henry Jenkins's warning that we must be "attentive to the particularity of games as a medium, specifically what distinguishes them from other narrative traditions," for the purposes of this paper I choose to focus on the continuities between these two popular forms and rely on Marie-Laure Ryan's discussion of the issues at hand. She argues that "narrative is a sign with a signifier (discourse) and a signified (story, mental image, semantic representation)." And since "the narrativity of a text is located on the level of the signified," considerations of it can be "medium free." Ryan also asserts that some written forms (e.g., popular literature) lend themselves to "narrative interpretation" more readily than others (e.g., postmodern novels). I add that some video games— in this case, phenomenally popular action-adventure games such as *Grand Theft Auto*, *Halo*, and *Mortal Kombat*—also lend themselves to narratological interpretation more easily than, say, a popular building game like *Minecraft*. However, while there are not specific goals in *Minecraft*'s "creative" mode where the focus is on building elaborate environments, those who choose to play in "survival" or "adventure" modes face challenges and pursue goals, much as they would in other action-adventure games. Interestingly, the demand for narrative-driven play has grown along with the game's popularity, attesting to the continued allure of the narrative form.

The key difference between video game and dime novel narratives, of course, is that video games render an actual physical space that is navigated by gamers who are active participants in shaping an evolving story line. The emphasis on visual culture and the story's seemingly infinite possibilities are surely distinctive, and I make no claim here that dime novel and video game narrative are completely commensurate. Yet, ironically, one could also emphasize how both forms are invested in the proliferation of a fundamentally static form. In the case of dime novels, serialization offered variations on a theme—not immediate interactivity, of course, but an apparently engaging and comfortably familiar script played out in different versions. Harbaugh's Westerns deploy the same narrative arcs and character types: an inexperienced but brave young man, accompanied by an older and more experienced guide, seeks to protect or rescue white settlers from the clutches of savage Native Americans. A pure, young white woman who is particularly prized by the Natives is the focus of this mission. The search is complicated by a number of factors: the ethnic crossing of the white characters as they pass as Indians; the "nobility" of some of the Natives; and the machinations of a powerful and avaricious white man who also seeks to possess the white woman and, in many ways, is more brutal than the Native Americans. The stories seem virtually indistinguishable. Brown counters that dime novels are not wholly interchangeable, pointing out that their "escalating violence" can be interpreted as "an effort to compensate for the regularity of the serial system" (6). Yet, while "every traversal yields a new story"—whether through ever gorier options within a narrative or between different texts—the authors of dime novels and video game designers build "the virtual world by selecting objects and actions from a fixed set of system-internal possibilities" (Ryan).

Though the rate of production for successful video games is much slower than that for dime novels, given the complexities of design and programming, they, too, continue to multiply familiar narrative forms. All of the most popular action-adventure games have been serialized, producing new game scenarios based on the basics of the original game. Sometimes they are "authored" by different designers, much as dime series were, and evolve into corporate-owned franchises. Granted, even within one discrete interactive game, there may be potential for infinite variety within the details of the story, as the plot will change depending on which path is chosen, but "the stories themselves are not radically different from traditional narrative patterns" (Ryan). While players still have control over the routes taken through the game, game designers "make sure that the player's options will remain within a certain range, so that the overall destiny will not deviate from the general line of the master plot." Thus the fundamentals of these narrative options remain constant, as well.

Moreover, audience participation arguably enhances the likelihood that stories will draw on acknowledged conventions. Publishing serially allows writers and editors to adjust their text's development based on reader response. Bold even argues that pulp magazine editors in the early twentieth century solicited letters from readers and eventually became "servant[s] to [their] audience, adapting characters and inventing incidents according to suggestions printed on the Letters page" (41). Thus readers became increasingly invested in popular reading forms, and the forms responded by becoming more interactive and allowing readers to help shape narrative—a dynamic that leads to video game play. Even today, gamers seem content with the tried-and-true narrative formulas that have dominated popular entertainment. Instead, they seek authenticity in the visual realm—valuing characters that are less cartoonish, and more lifelike violence and sexuality. In a recent piece about how contemporary, American wars are routed through video game narratives, Chris Suellentrop writes, "Video-game designers and players like to brag about how 'realistic' the games are, but when gamers talk about verisimilitude, they're usually talking about graphical fidelity, about how lifelike the characters and environments are in an otherwise fantastical world—and not about how the medium reflects anything else about the actual world in which we live."

The specific narrative techniques designed during the era of the dimes to both physically and emotionally arouse readers and then nurture compulsive textual consumption have persisted into video game design, as well. For example, the "cliffhanger" technique was used to pique reader interest at the same time that it repeated plotting within each installment. Ending chapters by leaving main characters in peril simulates a number of small endings within the larger narrative—potential losses that are reversed by the conclusion of the text, if not by the very first lines of the subsequent chapter. At the end of chapter 4 in *Plucky Phil*, for example, the rope which the white villain, Goldboots, has been using to descend down a steep cliff wall is severed by Rosa, the Red Jezebel. Grasping a protruding stone floor, Goldboots "hung between life and death by the frail hold of a pair of almost nerveless hands," while Rosa "was leaning over the cliff with uplifted hatchet" ready to hurl it at him (1005). The suspense of this literal cliffhanger is broken quickly in the very next chapter. As Bold notes, the conventions of dime novel Westerns "derive not from the influence of literary genre, but from the pressures of the market-place" (43). Like contemporaneous critics of Harbaugh's work, modern students trained in creative writing curricula that emphasize creativity, self-expression, and writing "what you know," can be appalled by the imperatives for compulsive, "empty" reading promoted by the cliffhanger and other formulaic devices. Yet placing main characters in serialized peril is a technique taken up and magnified by video game designers.

Thus narrative is still highly relevant in today's gaming culture as the games' fantasies entice players to enter and stay within the game world. Narrative is also the means of conveying one's exploits in the game. As Ryan writes, "[I]f narrativity were totally irrelevant to the enjoyment of games . . . why would the task of the player be presented as fighting terrorists or saving the earth from invasion by evil creatures from outer space rather than as 'gathering points by hitting moving targets with a cursor controlled by a joystick'?" (Ryan). However, though narrative works as a lure to draw the player into the game world, and then provides a means of recounting one's progress, the play is not necessarily experienced as the creation of a story to be recounted. It is primarily problem driven. Dime novel narratives are driven by similar goals. Their disposable heroes and plots—indeed, the flimsy nature of their physical forms, which were not meant to last—suggest that dime novels were not meant to be retained as texts worthy of being reread for the value of their language or plotting. They, too, were a cheap vehicle for providing readers with "distraction and sensation": engaging readers in a fictional game world, solving problems, and moving on (Brown 20). Narrative tidiness, or even basic coherence, is sacrificed in the name of visceral engagement. The addictive factor in both texts involves getting the protagonist to the end, relatively unscathed. Indeed, their narratives are so convoluted and repetitive as to be unrecountable. Like a gaming experience, the dime novel experience is designed to be ephemeral and not necessarily reproducible.

Getting into Character

While the character types deployed in the dime Westerns—young hero, pure heroine, wise guide, debauched villain, noble savage, and bloodthirsty warrior—are relatively stable, individual characters in Harbaugh's work often have multiple names and identities, which make them both unstable and empty at the core and contribute to each text's indeterminacy. Like the video game avatars into which players must be able to slip in order to reach their goals, dime novels provide conventional yet baggy character types with which a wide range of readers can easily identify and which authors could craftily maneuver ideologically. Most of the critics who have written on the dime Westerns are interested in the mobile performances these shifting names, coupled with frequent disguises, allow—of gender, of race and ethnicity, of class. Daniel Worden argues that dime novels promulgate a performative masculinity unmoored from particular bodies and available to men and women alike—a masculinity that could, then, be used for rebellion as well as conformity and oppression. Indeed, though gender fluidity is not the focus of this paper, it is worth noting that Harbaugh's female characters, both white and Native, are often brave, canny, and even violent. Worden continues that "dime novel Westerns are an important part of the history of alternative masculinities, often characterized in the twentieth century by appropriations of working-class bodies and fashions" (52). These tactics underscore the characters' symbolic function, or as Michael Denning explains it, their utility as allegorical sites of cultural contestation (77).

For example, in *Plucky Phil* our young hero's proper name is Phil Steele, but he is called "Plucky Phil." When his confidence flags, he buoys himself up and the narrator tells us "he still had a right to be called Plucky Phil" (875). Thus his name is behavioral, not familial or intrinsic. The traitorous white villain in *Plucky Phil* is called Captain Montana or 'Tana or Goldboots or The Nabob, depending on the context in which he has been known—as military man, ruthless capitalist, professional gambler, or San Francisco social climber. Hence characters are gauged by action and disposition. Like Plucky Phil, Policy Pete's name becomes an epithet, as he is a guide who frames all narrative conflicts in "policy" terms: "[P]olicy is policy at all times" and it is the "best policy" that wins, he explains (*Plucky* 972). Harbaugh's character types are archetypal, writ large, and easily recognizable.

However, as in video games, where players can assume identities that do not align with their gender, ethnicity, character, or even species as they perform them in their daily lives, dime novel characters' looks can be deceiving. Most mobile in Harbaugh's work is one's ethnic identity, though that does not seem the case, at first glance. Skin color is part of nearly every character description. In some cases, these colors are meant to reify racist discourse. Phil's "white fingers" tighten on his gun at one point, and his "pale white face" is the first thing seen by captive Nora Dalton when he arrives to save her (*Plucky* 980, 994). Nora is named "the white flower" by her captors, and her small white hands are often noted. Indeed, Harbaugh repeats the color of Phil's and Nora's hands, almost always describing them as white. Jefferson D. Slagle insists that dime Westerns and shows used so many pseudonyms to emphasize that the body always speaks truth to readers able to decipher its signs correctly (32–33). In *Little Oskaloo*, Areotha, also known as White Moccasin, has been held captive by the Indians for many years, yet her "true" ethnic identity is never in doubt either, as she possesses "a pretty face, oval and faultlessly formed. The skin was not so dark as a warrior's, and the eyes were soft and full of depth." She also has "tiny, almost fairy-like" feet (*Little Oskaloo*); like Nora Dalton's small white hands, they mark her as a white woman physically unfit for harsh labors. These captive women also serve as the object of "game play" in these novels. Possession of the "white" women propels Harbaugh's plots, and threats to their womanhood justify imperialist and racist violence.[5] Read through the racist discourse of the times, ethnicity seems intransigent.

Indeed, Toni Morrison's theory of the Africanist presence helps to explain the deep-seated, insurmountable black-white racism at the core of Harbaugh's Native characterizations.[6] While the nameless masses of Natives are casually called "red niggers" (*Plucky* 968), the "Ape" or "Red Dwarf" who guards Nora most overtly represents this Darwinian discourse, where African American "science" was overlaid on Native American stereotypes. Half man, half monster, the Ape is a deformed, monkey-like being who is summoned by a "queer whistle" (78). He can see at night and has claws and sharp teeth. On just one page he is described as having a head that is both "snaky" and "ogreish" and as inhabiting "the den of a monster" (980). The Ape possesses no modern firearms, and like a true savage he inhabits a cave and lurks in the mountains, like an early Donkey Kong, throwing rocks at his pursuers. He is abhorrent yet easily vanquished by the white characters. The death of this inhuman Other is almost farcical and accustoms readers to the desired deaths of barbaric animals who seek to defile white women while ghosting the craggy landscape. He evokes both the Caliban of the past and the King Kong of the future, and his fate augurs turn-of-the-century lynching culture.

While Harbaugh's racism is, thus, undeniable, his depictions of many other characters reveal anxiety about the stability of his racial categories and of American identities more generally. In this way his novels gesture toward the virtual transformations and individual fluidities with which we are familiar in our own culture—even the real, physical transformations to which we are becoming accustomed as extensive cosmetic surgery becomes even more ubiquitous. No characters in *Little Oskaloo* are as devolved as the Ape; in fact, the most barbaric character is a white man, James Girty, who possesses "almost supernatural strength" and bears a "repulsive face [that] surmounted an ungainly body" (*Little Oskaloo*). He is the eponymous "White Whirlwind," a British agent sent to stir up Native hatred toward the new Americans. While not represented as irredeemable, his betrayal of white characters and of American interests makes him bestial. While eloquent and persuasive, he is also physically imposing: "his massive arms folded upon his giant chest" with a "face, almost brutish in anatomy, [which] denoted the glutton" (*Little Oskaloo*). He lives in a cabin that "looked like the lair of a beast, for there were cleanly-picked bones before the door, beside which a fresh wolf skin had been nailed" (*Little Oskaloo*). These descriptions turn him into the beast of European fairy tale, rather than the savage of modern lore. Like other characters, however, Girty crosses ethnic boundaries, here using a tomahawk to murder a young brave who tries to expose his exploitation of the Native Americans. Indeed, the young hero Harvey Catlett claims, "Jim Girty has caused more anguish in this part of the world than the tomahawks and fire brands of a whole red nation," and Girty himself admits, "I *am* a bad man, the worst perhaps in these parts. The Indian is my companion, and when he can't invent new deviltry, he comes to me" (*Little Oskaloo*). He describes himself as "virtually an Indian," paralleling our modern ability to "virtually" enter unsavory types through game play. Apparently, a white man who turns his considerable strengths against his own people—here a traitor to the United States who stoops to working with Native Americans—is far worse than Native Americans who, though animalistic, are justified in their fight.

Even "good" white characters and "bad" Native Americans become morally ambiguous upon further inspection, allowing readers to step into any characters' shoes without impunity. While in *Plucky Phil* Nora notes Phil's white face, she also says that "sun and adventure had given [it] a hue which she had never known it to possess" (994). Indeed, the line between white and red (and black), civilized and savage, is often permeable in these novels. Though marked by dialect, Sitting Bull seated astride "the back of a magnificent steed was an Indian whose garments were more than half civilized." His status as a "chieftan" and ability to admire Phil, whom he proclaims "brave as a bear," also suggest that Sitting Bull is not wholly devolved. Harbaugh humanizes Sitting Bull by treating him as an individual and "not an assemblage of tribal traits" (Berkhofer 106). On the other hand, Policy Pete, whose Indian moniker is Aggawam, is easily a passable-looking Indian, a "tall, slim red-skin" who is "playing the role for policy's sake"; "mountain air and mountain suns had more than bronzed [his skin]. In the moonlight, it looked almost black" (*Plucky* 972, 997). As in modern American enter-tainment culture, we find "traditional" (read: racist) values and moral absolutism residing alongside moral relativism and cultural empathy here, creating a dissonance for readers asked to be attentive to such textual incongruities.

Characters track similarly through ethnic identity in *Little Oskaloo*. Here the experienced guide, Wolf Cap, and young Harvey are disguised as Native Americans so they can move through the forest without being detected by Indians. When the young men of the white settlers' party determine to kill the first "redskins" they see as sport, Wolf Cap and Catlett are almost murdered. "Their skin proclaimed them savages; but they seemed to be washing—a thing which no Indian warrior ever does," the two trigger-happy white men think. Just in time, "water had metamorphosed [Catlett] into his true character," though he and Wolf Cap remain interesting hybrids, "with white hands and faces, but with shoulders copper-colored like the Indians" (*Little Oskaloo*). As Coyote, a spineless character in *Plucky Phil* claims, "We've all got red-skin handles, you know" (975). Disguise is ubiquitous, and the ability to "slip in" to someone else's skin and then act savagely or interact with one's environment in new ways is alluring to white characters. While inhabiting computer-generated avatars and making decisions that affect the fictional environment is not exactly the same, of course, there are significant similarities between the two "gaming" experiences.

The blurring of ethnic boundaries is more than skin deep, however. Further along in *Little Oskaloo*, two of the young white men become blood brothers with their Native American captors who "cut the sign of the banded brotherhood on [their] breast[s]." "You are one of us now and forever," the white men are told. And though the captive, Little Moccasin, in *Little Oskaloo* is clearly "white," she has forgotten her white roots, embraced her Native mother, and assimilated into Native culture. Indeed, white characters do more than "play Indian" for sport or survival. In *Plucky Phil* both the evil Coyote and noble Plucky Phil are described as having "wolfish" eyes in their desire to possess Nora Dalton (980, 982). The experienced scout in *Little Oskaloo* is named both Abner Stark and Wolf Cap, signifying both his puritanical character and his ruthless tracking capabilities. Most interestingly, being a "wolf" links Wolf Cap to the Shawnees, who fall like a "pack of wolves" upon his Kentucky home, burning it to the ground. In running the "wolf" imagery through both novels and allying it with burning emotion—desire, ambition, murder—Harbaugh not only destabilizes his characters but also erases the distinctions among them.

On the one hand, in depicting so many whites disguised as Natives, kidnapped and assimilated, or even bonded by blood to Native Americans, Harbaugh expresses great anxiety about white Americans' similarities to people who were being brutally killed, displaced, or assimilated by white culture during this era. Of course the appeal of "playing Indian," which entails the appropriation of desirable and distinctively "American" attributes, has a long history in the United States, as Phillip Deloria reminds us.[7] The current fascination with [Italian] mobsters, [African American] gangbangers, and [Middle Eastern] terrorists evident in popular media extends this tradition. At the same time, Harbaugh empties out characters, stripping them of distinctive individuality and allowing fundamental contradictions to reside in almost all: they are both civilized and savage, criminal and lawful, white and "colored." The ubiquity of disguises further makes characters flat and pliable. This technique allows readers to identify with a number of characters and enter a sometimes amoral landscape where good and evil are slippery. In this way, Harbaugh's novels prefigure the dangerous, quickly shifting landscapes of modern video games that also nurture moral ambiguity. Indeed, they initiate the ascendancy of the antihero and the romanticization of the villain that dominates modern media.[8]

Simulating the West

Slagle argues that Western character types "look nearly exactly alike, as indeed they must in order to signal their authenticity" (26). Heroes, villains, and female love interests become virtually indistinguishable from book to book. Thus our young heroes Plucky Phil and Harry Catlett are described very similarly. Phil is simply "handsome, athletic, and of course determined"—a list of admirable attributes that could just as easily be assigned to Catlett (*Plucky* 963). À la Baudrillard, Slagle explains that the "simulacral" nature of dime novel Westerns and the compulsive repetition of identical Western scenes responded to post-bellum readers' insistence on "authenticity," or "how well a western or westerner fits notions of what westerns and westerners should be, based on previous westerns and westerners that have been judged authentic" (21). Like Western characters, Western backdrops are both predetermined and hollow at the core. Though the settings of the two Harbaugh novels I discuss here are separated in time by nearly a hundred years, there is virtually no distinction between the two in terms of dress, speech, mannerism, or any other details an author might use to situate his or her text in time. Particularly striking is the interchangeability of the "Indians"; as Berkhofer reminds us, "the original inhabitants of the Western hemisphere neither called themselves by a single term nor understood themselves as a collectivity" (3). The West and its native residents are somehow outside of time, mythological, unreal, even as the genre laid claim to historical fidelity. As Daniel Worden writes, and we have already observed, dime novels "were not quite realistic novels" and were, rather, wedged between emerging realism and "popular culture centered on folk tales and theater" (38–39). Harbaugh does not create cartoon characters; granted some emotional fullness and a tenuous connection to history, they are recognizably human. Like modern video games, dimes were valued for their realistic qualities, as well as their aesthetic and entertainment value. However, given that the characters and settings are so flat, derivative, and ahistorical, and the plots are full of cartoonish violence, they are also not quite real. Something niggles at the edges of contemporary readers' consciousnesses.

But one might argue that this superficiality is precisely the reason that dime novels appealed broadly and that their most salient features persist into video game forms. Ryan argues that as readers we toggle between first-person and third-person perspectives: "We simulate mentally the inner life of characters, we transport ourselves in imagination in their minds, but we remain at the same time conscious of being external observers." She continues "that only selected types of emotional experiences, and consequently selected types of plots will lend themselves to first-person perspective," to the type of full immersion possible in virtual environments. Consequently, while as readers we may derive pleasure from temporarily entering the lives of canonical literary characters such as Anna Karenina or Hamlet, we don't want to *be* those characters in a video game. We don't want to actually feel vulnerable, ill, suicidal: tragedy is not fun. Instead, gamers prefer adventures with "a rather flat character whose involvement in the plot is not emotional, but rather a matter of exploring a world, solving problems, performing actions, competing against enemies, and above all dealing with interesting objects in a concrete environment." In such texts, readers/protagonists feel that they have more control over their destinies. As Ryan continues of these types of popular narratives, "this kind of involvement is much closer to playing a computer game than to living a Victorian novel or a Shakespearean drama." And yet teaching students to navigate Victorian novels and Shakespearean dramas is fundamental to most literature curricula. We train students to be empathetic, to appreciate the psychological realities of tragic characters and the ironic complexities of tragic plots, and hence they struggle when a text offers them stock characters, pragmatic problem-solvers who inhabit action adventures.

Of course, though the plots and characterization of the archetypal "hero quest" are common to both dimes and video games, both Ryan and Henry Jenkins remind us that game designers are "narrative architects" who "design worlds and sculpt spaces" in addition to telling stories (Jenkins).[9] Jenkins agrees with Ryan that games fit the "older tradition of spatial stories" such as "hero's odysseys, quest myths, or travel narratives"; however, game designers do not "draw story elements" from canonical texts but, rather, from the "out borders of literature": those who write "fantasy, adventure, science fiction, horror, war" are the "most invested in world-making and spatial storytelling." Westerns obviously qualify as well. Still, game designers move beyond these popular generic conventions to "respond to alternative aesthetic principles," namely the creation of rich environments for exploration rather than the development of coherent plots or characters.

While dime novelists certainly do not invent "spatial stories" in this modern sense—the visual splendor of a video landscape was unthinkable at the time—they do foreground setting in ways that gesture toward our current video game ethos. Harbaugh spends a great deal of time creating detailed, concrete environments for his novels—highly stylized in some cases, and central to his plots. Figurations of the West are critical to his ability to write in this way, as it is an ideology as much as a material fact, a blank canvas for American thinkers and dreamers and an uncharted space waiting for colonial imprint. Jenkins posits that the "core narratives" of many video games also center "around the struggle to explore, map, and master contested spaces." The western frontier and all it represents has merely moved, one might argue, into these virtual spaces.

Harbaugh's rich, detailed environments are integral to his storytelling and suggest clear parallels to video game architecture. "The Trail" is the central motif of *Plucky Phil* and *Little Oskaloo* and also their literal, geographical spine. Ostensibly, "the Trail" is the path our white heroes forge, respectively, to save the "white flower," Nora Dalton, and to protect the vulnerable Merriweather family, especially daughter Kate, from Indian captivity. But as readers discover, "Indians were constantly leaving the trail," and it becomes a stand-in for one's engagement in the game/plot or, conversely, one's withdrawal from the action. For example, in *Little Oskaloo*, the young scout, Catlett, veers off the trail and out of the action. The narrator tells readers that we will soon return to Catlett, who is "confident that he would soon be enabled to strike the trail." In fact, once we rejoin Catlett we follow him to spots we have already been as he "catches up" to the plot, examining the aftermath of actions readers have already witnessed. Furthermore, there are various, individualized trails that diverge and intersect. For example, in *Plucky Phil*, Rosa is eventually set on "the trail of vengeance" (1019). And in *Little Oskaloo* the "trail" to bring the Merriweathers safely into military custody is soon joined by a second "trail" they need to forge to rescue Kate when she is abducted.

And on each "trail" are discrete spaces where our main characters engage in physical battles and discover clues that direct their actions. For example, as Phil starts on his journey he finds himself in a canyon where "far above him towered the bush-covered sides." Once within its confines he discovers the spot where Sitting Bull's braves had attacked the wagon train and murdered almost all of its members. In addition to unearthing some skeletons and a soldier's bayonet, "a lot of mountain creepers met his eye, but putting out his hand he brushed them aside to utter a cry of discovery" as he finds a message carved in the wall of the canyon—a clue that sets him "West—toward the unknown lands of the Sioux" (966). Similarly, in *Little Oskaloo*, tracker Wolf Cap and Catlett spy in a great tree trunk "about six feet from the ground [. . .] a hole large enough to admit a medium sized hand" in which messages are left to forward the plot.

An even clearer analog to the video game progression is Harbaugh's canny use of discrete and distinct spaces that are inhabited for a brief time by significant characters, who must solve some problem or vanquish a foe before moving on to the next discrete space. One of the most distinctive "game spaces" or trail stops in *Plucky Phil* is the site where the Ape keeps Nora Dalton imprisoned in a "cavern about five-and-twenty feet below the top of the wall" that towers above the valley trail (989). Phil must manufacture a rope to scale the walls of the cliff while the Ape throws rocks at him. He then comes face to face with Sitting Bull and engages in combat with the Ape before entering the cave and exploring its dark interior to find an exit. Once he successfully navigates the dangers of this site, he moves on to the next stop on the trail, the next set of challenges. At times the setting itself advances the plot, as in Echo Gulch, where the echoes reveal the presence of other characters entering the scene (985). At other times, that same environment is part of the challenge. In *Plucky Phil* the South Dakota landscape is full of crevasses, caves, and valleys that make it impossible for one to see behind or in front on the trail: once a character leaves a valley or gulch a "bend in the mountain trail hid it from his sight" (922). While *Plucky Phil* is set in

South Dakota, in *Little Oskaloo* we mainly move from densely forested encampment to encampment along glittering Ohio rivers, with some exciting time in the rapids and a fair amount of portaging in between. Yet here, too, actions are set in discrete spaces shut off from view: "As the woods were not very clear of underbrush, the progress was of necessity quite slow, and at nightfall the party halted in a picturesque ravine . . . wild, luxuriant grass covered the bed of the place," and "the mouth of the ravine was hidden by a fallen tree." The isolation of this spot, again, contributes to the challenge that must be met there. In addition, much of the action in both novels takes place at twilight or after dark. In *Little Oskaloo* "the gloom of impenetrable darkness" also impedes the scouts' abilities to see the action. The narrator tells us that "danger lurked along the shadowed banks" of the river, when what appears to be a rolling log in the dark is, in reality, a traitor leaving their night camp. All of these environmental factors thwart our heroes' efforts to find and escort the Merriweather family from their home to the military camp—to move from point A to point B, just as one would do in a video game.

The disjointed narrative created by these compartmentalized spaces is sometimes mitigated by cutscenes—what Henry Jenkins calls "mechanical exposition." Ironically, in video games, the cutscenes' "poor" production values and substandard acting have a kitsch appeal for many. But perhaps the cutscene's charm derives from its roots in dime novels. Bold notices that early dime novelists spend a great deal of time commenting upon the composition of the text, "often pausing to indicate that [they are] about to close one chapter and open another" (33). Harbaugh is of his time in this respect: for example, at the beginning of chapter 3 of *Little Oskaloo*, the narrator directs, "Leaving the characters of our story already mentioned for a brief time, let us turn our attention to the devoted little band of fugitives who were flying through the gauntlet of death to Wayne's protecting guns." Later, leaving Kate Merriweather in the hands of her unknown abductor, and another minor character a captive in some warriors' canoe, the narrator directs, "Let us return to two characters of whom, for a while, we have lost sight." Here, Harbaugh uses metaphors of sight to reinforce the circuitous, visual logic of the exposition. While this sort of commentary does not constitute a cutscene in the strictest sense of the term, it does draw us out of the flow of the game for a moment, providing an extremely efficient but rather awkward mode of turning the plot.

Bold sees the writer working as an editor in these moments, foregrounding the "formalized devices" that are central to the production of these texts and exposing the rules of the dime novel marketplace to readers (36). I extend Bold's point to argue that it is apparently important for Harbaugh to expose the seams of his work, so to speak, the machinations behind the fictional façade. In more conventional cutscene mode, he has characters both enact and comment upon the plot. For example, *Plucky Phil* begins with Phil's desertion by his military comrades and an extended spoken monologue by Phil as he embarks upon the trail: "I can explore the pass now," he said, starting off. "It will be a further advance into Sitting Bull's country, but what do I care? I am here to find or to die!" (945). Since he is completely alone in the wilderness at this point, there is no need for him to speak aloud, no one for whom he must maintain his bravado; in having him speak in this manner, Harbaugh arrests a more natural or realistic unfolding of the plot, having Phil pause to address his readers and supply exposition, motivation, and character. During Phil's monologue, background information is supplied concisely and the perils of this life-and-death game emphasized.

Finally, gaming metaphors are central to Harbaugh's dime Westerns and cement the connections between these texts and video games—especially action-adventure games, where, Ryan writes, "the player of a game is usually too deeply absorbed in the pursuit of a goal to reflect on the plot that he writes through his actions." Bold also notices that "the game" became a "central motif" to later dime novelists who foregrounded "the operation of rules and the need for decoding" along with "competition" (38). While Bold again sees this as metacommentary on the market conditions of the dimes, I also see it as a reflection of a nascent, more generalized gaming culture evident not only in the capitalist marketplace but also in sporting culture, which are joined in modern video games. In a literary marketplace still dominated by domestic narratives deeply invested in a Christian ethos, Harbaugh's novels notably lack any references to God's will or benevolence. Indeed, *Plucky Phil* is driven by (p)luck. It is not a Christian God, but "fate or fortune" that leads characters to happy ends—even our true woman, Nora Dalton, does not call out to God for succor in her moments of weakness but rather summons "fortune" to her aid (966). Indeed, the characters "thank fortune for this meeting" that reunites good, white characters separated by Native American devices (1012–13). The narrative is similarly invested in gaming metaphors. Phil refuses to be "euchered," while Goldboots asks to be "dealt a better hand," recognizing that "death rakes in the biggest pot" and emphasizing the danger for those who "want to win at this mountain game" (980, 1002, 983, 971). As Phil contemplates, "Fortune may be favoring me [but] she plays queer games in this Indian land" (986). Interestingly, Harbaugh shows himself deeply committed to a sincere, American Christianity in his more respectable texts, such as his popular folk poem, "Trouble in the Amen Corner"; hence his avoidance of any mention of Christianity in the dime novels may mark his efforts not to muddy the waters between serious literature (and life) and fantasy.[10] Regardless of the reason, the consistent gaming metaphors in his dime novels emphasize the frivolous nature of this fiction and, perhaps, contribute to their unreality—though the characters are passionately invested in this game, even paying with their lives in some cases.

Though dime novel Westerns and action-adventure video games might seem light years apart, I conclude that there is, perhaps, something fundamental at the core of each in terms of their masculine experiences of entertainment—a certain simulation of the real that lives in that uncanny valley, "real" enough to engage our emotions and tie into historical circumstance, yet clearly fake enough to allow for simulated violence and the assumption of mobile identities that can toggle between villain and hero. As Brown contends, reading dime Westerns "is a matter of witnessing not just how fact becomes fiction, but also how popular culture becomes mass culture, how legend becomes mass-mediated memory" (34). Reading dime novels through the lens of contemporary video game narratives solidifies that moment of transformation. Teaching the dime novels of Thomas Chalmers Harbaugh and others can test students' interpretive chops, as well as encourage them to thoroughly interrogate notions of literary canon formation. Discussions of Harbaugh inevitably lead students to reveal their own reading practices vis-à-vis contemporary popular literature, as well as their gaming habits. We can talk openly about the value of the different ways that they already read. Ironically, bringing in narrative theory derived from video gaming can help them navigate these texts in a more sophisticated manner, see the relevance of popular nineteenth-century American literature to our own times (for good and ill), and teach them to become more savvy readers of the various narratives they encounter in their daily lives.

Appendix

Appendix

Supplement to Tanglen Essay
Sample Literature Circle Units

⁓

Unit One: National Romance and the Historical Novel

Lydia Maria Child, *Hobomok* (1824)
James Fenimore Cooper, *Last of the Mohicans* (1826)
Nathaniel Hawthorne, *The House of the Seven Gables* (1851)

1. Was your novel popular in its own day? Why or why not? How was your novel critically received in its own day? How has it been evaluated subsequently?
2. How does the novel's depiction of historical events differ from actual historical events? What is the significance of what the author chooses to include, change, or exclude?
3. How does your novel portray the nation's relationship to its past? How does your novel portray the nation's relationship to the future?
4. Are American Indians portrayed as noble savages, vanishing Indians, or both? How does this tie into the author's version of the nation's past and her or his vision for the future?

Unit Two: Literatures of Slavery, Race, and Abolition

Harriet Beecher Stowe, *Uncle Tom's Cabin* (1851–52)
William Wells Brown, *Clotel* (1853)
Harriet Jacobs, *Incidents in the Life of a Slave Girl* (1861)

1. Was your novel popular in its own day? Why or why not? How was your novel critically received in its own day? How has it been evaluated subsequently?
2. How does your text use the specific "elements" of fiction/literature—plot, imagery, character, setting—to structure and create an antislavery argument?
3. What makes your text "literature"? What makes it "propaganda"?
4. How does the race or sex of the author affect the type of argument they make?
5. How would the original audience have received this text? What would have made it persuasive?

Unit Three: Realism, Naturalism, and Social Reform

Elizabeth Stuart Phelps, *The Silent Partner* (1871)
Sarah Winnemucca, *Life among the Piutes* (1883)
Theodore Dreiser, *Sister Carrie* (1900)

1. Was your text popular in its own day? Why or why not? How was your text critically received in its own day? How has it been evaluated subsequently?
2. Kenneth Warren has argued that in the realistic novel "the redemption of the individual lay within the social world," whereas in sentimental fiction "the redemption of the social world lay within the individual" (75–76). How does this distinction function in your group's selection?
3. How might your author respond to William Dean Howells's assertion that American authors should focus on the positive aspects of American life and privilege the "universal" over specific social concerns?

Notes

Introduction: Reading, Pedagogy, and Tainted Lit

1. Leslie Fiedler, "Toward Pop Criticism," 35.

2. Lewis, "High and Low Brows," 272. Carl Little quoted in Berrett, "Mickey Spillane and Postwar America," 7.

3. Krystal, "Easy Writers." For excerpts from the NPR series, see http://www.npr.org/series/104566969/my-guilty-pleasure.

4. Bloom, "Dumbing Down American Readers."

5. Chabon, *Maps and Legends.*

6. Tract #493: "Beware of Bad Books." Ascribed to Rev. R. S. Cook ("Origin and Character of Tracts," *The American Tract Society Documents, 1824–1925* [New York: Arno, 1972]).

7. Jacobs, *The Pleasures of Reading in an Age of Distraction*, 23, 24.

8. Commentators on teaching popular culture in middle and high schools remain especially burdened by the need to argue for its legitimacy; see, as an example, Caralee Adams's "Lessons in Pop." The use of graphic novels is widely discussed in the secondary teaching arena, as is, significantly, the work of Stephen King, which has, among other things, provided the basis for a study of parental influence on teenagers' reading habits (Chandler, "Reading Relationships"). A Stephen King conference and resulting volume of essays published by the National Council of Teachers of English specifically attempted to "use King's writing as a springboard into literacy education issues," particularly for adolescents (see Power, "Reading Stephen King," 6). Though the present volume is concerned with postsecondary literature pedagogies, Randi Tanglen's essay on teaching with literature circles touches on some of the constraints that her college students may face if they become high school teachers in the state of Texas.

9. Bloom, "Can 35 Million Book Buyers Be Wrong? Yes."

"You Will Observe . . .": Letting Lippard Teach

1. I have not been able to locate copies of the novella in its original serial form, a testament to the ephemerality of antebellum print culture and to gaps in the archive that might be incorporated into discussion of the text. See Reynolds, *George Lippard*, 132, and Butterfield, "George Lippard and His Secret Brotherhood," 305, for mention of *'Bel's* serial origins. The novel published by Hotchkiss & Co. was registered in the "Clerk's Office, in the District Court of the District of Massachusetts" by George H. Williams, one of the brothers who published *Uncle Sam*, and the novel had wrappers advertising *Uncle Sam*, solidifying its connection to that paper.

2. Streeby, *American Sensations*, 73. This paragraph is paraphrased from a similar plot summary of the novel that appears in Gniadek, "Seriality and Settlement," 35–36.

3. See Dinius, "Look!! Look!!! at This!!!!"

4. Reynolds, *Beneath the American Renaissance*, 3.

5. Ibid.

6. For a helpful overview of some of these issues and of the place of sensation fiction in American literature, see Shelley Streeby's essay, "Sensational Fiction."

7. The fact that our classroom in Houston, Texas, was less than thirty miles from the San Jacinto battlefield added another layer to the time-space compression depicted in *'Bel of Prairie Eden*. We were reading Lippard's text in a twenty-first-century space that we could easily relate to the geographies of the narrative.

8. Lippard, *'Bel of Prairie Eden*, 115.

9. See the "Introduction" to *Empire and the Literature of Sensation* for helpful background information.

10. Lippard, 142.

11. Goddu, *Gothic America*, 10.

12. Lippard, 118.

13. Ibid., 142, 147.

14. Ibid., 167.

15. Alemán, "The Other Country: Mexico, the United States, and the Gothic History of Conquest," 77.

16. Ibid., 79.

17. See Lippard, 123.

18. Ibid., 186.

19. Ibid.

20. Ibid., 184.

21. For example, F. O. C. Darley's frontispiece illustration for Lippard's best-known novel, *The Quaker City, or The Monks of Monk Hall* (1844), depicts character types that also appear in *'Bel of Prairie Eden*. And it stages those characters in a way that emphasizes themes of voyeurism and concealment. The heavy curtain behind the tableau of characters, full of folds and drawn apart in the middle to expose a

dark, mysterious opening, offers a visual representation of the mysteries and folds of Lippard's narratives. See Streeby, *American Sensations*, 66–73, for discussion of the way that another Lippard novel, *Legends of Mexico* (1847), engages with the visual aesthetic of "war pictures that were staged as panoramas in theaters, reprinted as illustrations in papers, and sold on the street as popular prints" (67).

22. Alemán and Streeby, xvii.

23. For an early introduction to these conversations, see Christopher Castiglia and Russ Castronovo, "A 'Hive of Subtlety': Aesthetics and the End(s) of Cultural Studies."

24. "Sensational fiction is not good literature in an aesthetic sense, but it is a good way to begin to understand the significance of empire-building in nineteenth-century popular and mass culture," write Alemán and Streeby (xxi).

25. Weinstein and Looby, *American Literature's Aesthetic Dimensions*, 4.

"Canons of Nineteenth-Century American Literature": How to Use Literature Circles to Teach Popular, Underrepresented, and Canonical Literary Traditions

I would like to thank Susanne George Bloomfield of the University of Nebraska at Kearney for introducing me to the literature circle format and sharing her materials with me.

1. See Bourdieu.

2. Lack of access to educational and artistic networks for women, African American, and Native American writers has been documented by Brooks, Carby, Tompkins, and other scholars of American literary history.

3. See Baym, Tompkins, and Davidson.

4. Although Davidson's work applies to an earlier period, it is nonetheless relevant to nineteenth-century study, as many of the works she discusses were still being read in the nineteenth century and certainly influenced nineteenth-century audiences. See Alemán and Streeby's collection for several examples of popular serialized and dime novels.

5. Kolodny raises these questions in "The Integrity of Memory."

6. Matthieson's 1941 *American Renaissance* identified Melville, Hawthorne, Whitman, Thoreau, and Emerson as the great authors of the nineteenth century, thereby creating a paradigm for nineteenth-century study still reflected in English department curriculum and syllabi even today.

7. For more information on the development and use of literature circles, see Daniels, *Literature Circles,* as well as Daniels and Steineke, *Mini-Lessons for Literature Circles.*

8. For templates of group member roles and responsibilities, see chapter 7, pp. 107–32, in Daniels's *Literature Circles.*

9. See also "A Brief History of the Reading Group in America" in Laskin and Hughes, *The Reading Group Book.*

10. See Castro, "Texas Education Board Approves Conservative Curriculum Changes by Far-Right" (2010), and Billeaud, "Ariz school's ethnic studies program ruled illegal" (2011).

"One Would Die Rather Than Speak . . . about Such Subjects": Exploring Class, Gender, and Hegemony in Anya Seton's *Dragonwyck*

I would like to thank Elvira Casal and William Thomas for their support and assistance, Samantha Klein Latham for her permission to refer to her excellent course essay, and all of my ENGL 4950 students for their engagement with and insights into the novel.

1. Williams cites the story of Sylvia, who, because of her embrace of "unrealistic" and "sentimental" (495) literature, abandons "her family of widowed mother, a sister, and a brother because they do not measure up to heroic Christianity" (496). While Williams says, "I like Sylvia. She is pretty, gentle, and in most ways kind" (496), it is clear that she proffers the story as a cautionary tale and assumes that her readers will see Sylvia as foolish.

2. See *New Approaches to Popular Romance Fiction* for an overview of the current state of romance scholarship.

3. This refers to the Chicago Review Press edition of the novel.

4. Hebdige's vision of hegemony is not precisely the same as Antonio Gramsci's; John Storey would call it "neo-Gramscian" (*An Introduction* 13–16). In this essay I am focusing on Hebdige's conception for two reasons: first, and most simply, I find his work, like much of the Birmingham School's, compelling, reasonable, and useful. Second, his work is wonderfully teachable and accessible for most students; I often use it in my classes. Therefore, students have these concepts in mind when reading and discussing *Dragonwyck.*

5. While *Dragonwyck* does incorporate many elements of the gothic on both plot and thematic levels, I would argue that it is ultimately not a gothic per se. (As one of my students who is a fan of the genre put it, "I kept waiting for the Gothic, but it wasn't there!") There are even points at which the novel undercuts its own gothic elements and momentary atmospherics. For example, when Miranda first contemplates wearing the Van Ryn family jewels, she is overcome by a wave of "fascinated repulsion" and murmurs, "The last woman to wear this jewel is dead. . . . All these jewels belonged to the dead. That's how they came to me" (227–28). In proper gothic fashion her maid "shiver[s]" and thinks that "[t]he dear lady was almost fearsome, eyeing those baubles as though they were alive and talking in that far away voice" (228), but she then realizes, "Not much sense she was making neither, come to think of it," and responds, "Well, to be sure. . . . Most of the gentry's gear does pass on to others after death" (228).

6. Approaching the novel specifically as a gothic, as Waldman does, could yield another set of readings of Miranda's plight and responses—for example, Michelle Massé's work on the psychosocial dynamics of masochism within the gothic could very productively be brought to bear in a psychoanalytic reading of this novel, and her framing of the political dimensions of the genre provides useful insights for me as well. However, I will be reading the novel's events and dynamics less as articulations of generic patterns than as sites wherein particular sets of social forces and ideologies intersect and do cultural work in the Hebdigian sense. In other words, I am reading the text more as a sociodrama than a psychodrama.

7. According to *College English*'s "The Best Sellers of 1944," *Dragonwyck* was the thirteenth best-selling work of fiction of the year; *Forever Amber* was the sixth.

8. In *Rudeness and Civility*, which explores the relationship between discourses of civility and ideologies of class in nineteenth-century America, John Kasson discusses moments of "courteous aid" that actually "ritualize women's subordination to men" (133). For example, he close-reads a magazine illustration of a man who "carries [a woman's] package and shelters her with an umbrella. . . . In accepting his protection she also subtly yields to his direction and constraint" (133).

9. The novel is set during the Hudson River rent revolts of the 1840s. See David M. Ellis's "Land Tenure and Tenancy in the Hudson Valley, 1790–1860" for background on this political conflict, which the text draws upon in some interesting ways.

10. Massé's reading of similar dynamics in the traditional gothic provides an intriguing perspective on some of Miranda's attitudes:

[Many oppressed women] fully incorporate and perpetuate the cultural split that enables hierarchy. What they resent is not the system that subordinates them, but their own exclusion from its upper reaches. Thus, when possible, they will use their understanding of the Gothic world to achieve what power they can within it. At its worst, this "use" is not subversion or resistance, but complicity. (43)

11. Recognizing that Miranda's youth, beauty, and pliability both highlight her own perceived shortcomings and constitute a threat to her marriage, Johanna treats Miranda like a servant and slights her: for instance, she refers to the Gaansevants as "certainly common people," and Miranda thinks, "Johanna must be aware that she was insulting [Miranda], whose only connection with the Van Ryns was through these same Gaansevants" (45).

12. Even then she tries to rehabilitate Nicholas in her mind, saying, "If it hadn't been for me, it wouldn't have happened. . . . It was the weakness in me touched off the evil in him" (302).

13. Unlike Nicholas, Jeff also recognizes the dynamic of abusing others to feel empowered; upon his return from the Mexican-American War, he confesses that he and his comrades had been "drunk with the ease of conquest, and the childish joy of destruction" (246). He even refuses to hate the soldier who shot him: "He

was a handsome Mexican, had a fine face. . . . For a second we looked right at each other, and I had a crazy feeling of liking him" (247). Jeff's attitudes toward war, democracy, and economics most probably took on additional weight in light of the time of the novel's production and publication; Nicholas's eugenicist positions probably became particularly resonant as well.

14. He also does not object when Boughton, sounding much like Ephraim, calls Miranda a "feather-brained girl" (106).

15. He displays similar attitudes toward the corpulent, aristocratic Johanna, whom he views with "distaste" (128) and is tempted to "laugh at" (128) when she protests his suggestion of eating less for a few days.

16. Waldman attributes such narratives of partnership to changing attitudes toward gender and work in the 1940s (37–38).

17. Waldman notes that the "narrative overthrow of the patriarchal tyrant" and his replacement by a "gentler, more democratic type" (38) may "perhaps undermin[e] the Gothic's subversive potential as critique of male domination . . . [by] suggest[ing] that the [abused] heroine has simply made a bad choice of mate" (36).

18. Students can also critically engage with the dynamics of abuse itself, particularly as it plays out within a cultural matrix. Samantha Klein Latham, for example, extended and developed points raised in our class discussion of Miranda's isolation and silencing in two intriguing ways. First, having established that Nicholas "uses emotion as a weapon and a reward" (4), she argues that while isolation does indeed enable Nicholas's abuse, the latter is also true. For example, in the scene in which Miranda suggests that her mother come to visit, "[h]e reinforces the isolation with 'contemptuous incredulity' [at the idea] that 'made her cheeks burn' (Seton 225). The emotional abuse previously described serves as a tool not only to establish his power but to keep her alone" (6). Second, she notes that "[t]he isolation Miranda experiences with Nicholas is, in some ways, less extreme than the isolation that occurs within the class structure. . . . He attempts to keep her from making friends and seeing family, but she is still able to if he is not around. However, within the class system, Miranda finds herself further isolated because she is unable to fit in anywhere" (7).

19. In fact, we are often able to connect this discussion to our discussions of Grace Metalious's *Peyton Place*, wherein many students miss the fact that Tomas Makris rapes his girlfriend, Constance MacKenzie, because they're positioned to see him as a romantic hero.

20. Azilde, one of Nicholas's forebears, was an abused woman who resisted by imaginatively "retir[ing] into a misty far-off land from which she never tried to return" (95). She laughed at her husband when she learned that he had suffered financial calamity, saying, "[M]isfortune has come to this house of hatred. Always I will laugh at that" (96), and her laughter is heard at various points in the novel. While the spectral forebear is a classic gothic element, Azilde's narrative and her

ghost also serve a specifically political function, weaving together hegemonic structures of gender, class, region, and ethnicity and serving as a pointed reminder that those structures are still very much in operation.

Sneaking It In at the End:
Teaching Popular Romance in the Liberal Arts Classroom

1. Pamela Regis, Web. Romance Listserv communication. Dec. 2011.

2. For an excellent discussion of the reasons romance has been dismissed by critics, see Frantz and Selinger, "Introduction," *New Approaches to Popular Romance Fiction.*

3. At one point I asked a colleague in the Film Studies Department at a similar small liberal arts college who teaches the Intro to Pop Culture course if he would ever consider including a contemporary popular romance—his syllabus currently includes graphic novels, mysteries, sci fi, cyberpunk, cell phone novels, fan fiction, slash fiction, and much more. He's a cultural materialist who'd cut his teeth on the Birmingham School—and he told me that he wouldn't dream of teaching a romance, since romance wasn't a pop culture genre, it was "just trash."

4. Joanne Hollows argues that the dismissal of romance by feminists on feminist grounds (rather than formal grounds) is part of the "critique of romantic love within second wave feminism" (Hollows 68). Kate Millet, Germaine Greer, and Shulamith Firestone all argued (in different contexts) that romance—the discourse of romantic love generally as well as romance fiction—is a tool of patriarchy and keeps women down by instantiating love as women's sole pursuit and value. Post-1980s feminists like Hollows have in their turn critiqued that critique by arguing that, to begin with, romance fiction is not monolithic and, second, readers rarely swallow the whole thing the same way (see Ang; Kaplan; Light). Modleski herself argued that second-wave feminists who denigrated romance novels were simply adopting the masculine subject position and devaluing anything "feminine"—that is, anything related to love, domesticity, marriage, emotion, and so forth. Those critics influenced by Foucault have argued that discourse of romance and romantic love is historically produced ideology and that romance fiction is the best place to observe the workings of that ideology (see Stacey and Pearce 28; also see Pearce, *Romance Writing*, "Introduction").

Chick Lit and Southern Studies

1. On the 2000 Census, for the first time, respondents were given the option of choosing more than one racial designation to describe themselves.

Teaching *Bad Romance*:
Poe's Women, the Gothic, and Lady Gaga

1. See Dayan, "Poe's Women: A Feminist Poe?" (1991); Elbert, "Poe and Hawthorne as Women's Amanuenses" (2004); Rhoads, "Poe's Genre Crossing" (2009); and Hoffman, "Ligeia—Not Me!" (2012).

2. See Winter, *Subjects of Slavery, Agents of Change* (1992). Davis and Alcott's most famous contributions to gothicism were subsequent to Poe's death, however.

3. See Fogel and Quinlan's "Lady Gaga and Feminism" (2011).

4. Recent studies on celebrity culture and middlebrow texts, especially as providing for more nuanced attention to gender performances, include Hammill, *Women, Celebrity, and Literary Culture between the Wars* (2009), and Goldman and Jaffe, *Modernist Star Maps* (2010).

Crossing the Barrier:
An Active-Text Approach to Teaching *Pet Sematary*

1. The most recent incarnation of this debate played out in summer 2012 in the *Los Angeles Review of Books*, starting with Dwight Allen's "My Stephen King Problem: A Snob's Notes" to which Sarah Lagan (also of the *LARB*) responded with "Killing Our Monsters: On Stephen King's Magic."

2. This is a 300-level (LITR310) course called Great Writers, with the writer featured in each respective section varying from one faculty member to another, depending on their areas of interest and expertise.

3. Gage's death in particular horrified King, especially in light of a very similar near-miss with his own son Owen (Vincent 72). This is an anecdote that King relates in introductions to some editions of *Pet Sematary*, so depending on which version(s) students have, teachers may prefer to tell them not to read the introduction before the novel, since this also reveals that Gage will die midway through the book.

4. In a recent section of this course, I organized it in three main thematic units: supernatural horror, technohorror, and real-life horror. This approach provided students with a good sense of the variety of King's writing, gave me the opportunity to include works from both early in his career and more contemporary writing, and include a wide range of different types of King's writing, including short stories, novellas, and novels.

5. Weiss focuses exclusively on the incorporation of King's short stories into the classroom setting, though the pedagogical approaches he discusses could be applied with similar effectiveness to many of King's longer works as well, provided there is class time available for their inclusion.

6. This connection between cultural tension and horror has been discussed extensively, especially in regard to horror films. See, for example, the explosion of "it came from outer space" science fiction and horror films that coincided with the

Cold War tensions of the 1950s, the "final girl" trope through which only virtuous—and usually virginal—young women make it all the way to the end of slasher films of the late twentieth century, and "the disintegration of the idealized family unit [that] could be seen as subtext in many of the horror movies released in the late '60s and '70s" (Eggertson). On the surface of their plots and conflicts, these horror films weren't explicitly about the Cold War, privileged gender roles and behaviors, or the fate of the family, though they explored these high-tension, real-life social issues under the guise of aliens, crazed serial killers, and cannibals. Many excellent scholars have explored these issues, especially as they relate to horror cinema, including Cyndy Hendershot's *I Was a Cold War Monster: Horror Films, Eroticism, and the Cold War Imagination* (2001), Carol Clover's *Men, Women, and Chainsaws: Gender in the Modern Horror Film* (1993), *The Dread of Difference: Gender and the Horror Film* (1996; edited by Barry Keith Grant), and Tony Williams's *Hearths of Darkness: The Family in the American Horror Film* (1996; updated edition, 2014).

7. These infection-inspired horror tales were preceded by a similar strain of novels and films in the 1970s and '80s, coinciding with anxiety surrounding the AIDS virus, including King's *The Stand* (originally published in 1978; uncut version published in 1990). While the historically specific causes of this fear vary—AIDS in the late twentieth century versus the threat of bioterrorism now—the terror and abjection we feel about the vulnerability of our own bodies and immune systems remains a constant source of fear.

8. I have also taught *Pet Sematary* in my Gothic Literature course, where we read both *Frankenstein* and *Pet Sematary* in their entirety to explore the themes of the undead and the monstrous in gothic literature.

9. Another, more subtle text-pairing in addressing the theme of death in *Pet Sematary* is L. Frank Baum's *The Wonderful Wizard of Oz*. Part 3 of King's novel is titled "Oz the Gweat and Tewwible," echoing the pronunciation of Rachel's sister Zelda, who died when Rachel was a child. In *Pet Sematary*, the idea of Oz becomes symbolic of death personified. As King writes, Oz "was waiting to choke you on a marble, to smother you with a dry-cleaning bag, to sizzle you into eternity with a fast and lethal boggie of electricity—Available at Your Nearest Switchplate or Vacant Light Socket Right Now" (375). Oz stands in here for the power and omnipresence of death and while *Pet Sematary* does not correlate quite as directly with Baum as with Jacobs or Shelley, students' familiarity with the *Wizard of Oz* story, either from Baum's book or, more often than not, the 1939 classic film adaptation, allows us to draw this text productively into our conversation as well.

10. This could also provide a productive text-pairing with Greek tragedy, such as Sophocles's *Oedipus Rex*, with its strong themes of prophecy and inescapable fate.

11. All student response are taken from a survey given in my fall 2012 section of Great Writers: Stephen King, which asked students whether they found the text-pairing exercises useful; whether the text-pairings helped them gain a better

or different understanding of the novel and if so, how; and which in-class activities, including text-pairing and the screening of the film adaptation trailer, they found most useful.

12. Pascow's death sets off the theme of death and Louis's responses to it which drive the novel and open the door on the mystery of the Pet Sematary and the burial ground beyond, which Pascow mentions with his dying breaths.

13. This pairing also highlights the significance of Victor Pascow's name, an echo of Shelley's doctor.

14. King argues that there are three key figures in the horror genre, each with a corresponding, canonical text: the Vampire (Bram Stoker's *Dracula*), the Werewolf (Robert Louis Stevenson's *Dr. Jekyll and Mr. Hyde*), and The Thing Without a Name (Mary Shelley's *Frankenstein*) (*Danse Macabre* 51). As King argues, most horror is a variation on these three key figures and "these three are something special. . . . [A]t the center of each stands (or slouches) a monster that has come to join and enlarge what Burt Hatlen calls 'the myth-pool'—that body of fictive literature in which all of us, even the nonreaders and those who do not go to films, have communally bathed" (ibid.)

15. *Frankenstein* is a dynamic example of the active text as well, as are several other gothic classics, including Bram Stoker's *Dracula*, both of which have inspired multiple reimaginings, both literary and popular cultural.

16. The possibility of this repetition haunts the conclusion of *Pet Sematary* as well. As the narrative builds toward its climax, King tells readers that "the house stood empty in the May sunshine, as it had stood empty on that August day the year before, waiting for the new people to arrive . . . as it would wait for other new people to arrive at some future date. . . . And perhaps they would have a dog" (396).

17. Louis's obsession has been fueled by his sense of his own medical authority, which he considers one of the main defining features of his identity, along with his familial roles of husband and father. However, at the end of the novel, he has been stripped of almost all of these means of self-definition. Killing the Gage-thing that has returned from the grave, Louis "slid his fingers expertly down Gage's throat, found the pulse, and held it. He was then a doctor for the last time in his life, monitoring the pulse, monitoring until there was nothing, nothing inside, nothing outside" (402).

18. The film is directed by Mary Lambert and stars Dale Midkiff as Louis, Denise Crosby as Rachel, and Fred Gwynne (best known as Herman Munster in *The Munsters*) as Jud Crandall.

19. Point-by-point comparisons of changes between a novel and its film adaptation are of very limited critical use anyway, creating an inventory of details rather than high-quality critical engagement and discussion. Instead, in addressing literature to film adaptations, it is much more effective to ask students to consider the impact of changes made, as well as key themes in the text that are maintained, negotiated, and transformed in the film and their impact on the film's effectiveness.

20. Given the wealth of film and television adaptations of King's work, a common option I provide students for critical responses and/or research paper assignments is to do a comparison and contrast of the text and the film, one that students tend to enthusiastically embrace.

21. Music is often central to King's fiction; for example, every chapter of *Christine* begins with a rock lyric epigraph. King himself is passionate about music, and until their recent disbanding, he sang and played guitar in a group called the Rock Bottom Remainders, made up of other literary folks, including Dave Barry, Ridley Pearson, and Amy Tan.

The Literature of Attractions: Teaching the Popular Fiction of the 1890s through Early Cinema

Epigraph 1: Frank Norris, "An Opening for Novelists: Great Opportunities for Fiction Writers in San Francisco."

Epigraph 2: Quoted in Tom Gunning, "An Aesthetic of Astonishment: Early Film and the (In)credulous Spectator," 120.

1. Bentley, *Frantic Panoramas*, 3.

2. All quotes from early reviews are found in Ernest Marchand, "1899 Reviews of *McTeague*."

3. Suárez, *Pop Modernism*. Musser, "A Cornucopia of Images," 5.

4. *McTeague*, ed. Donald Pizer, 7.

5. Miller, "The Panorama, the Cinema, and the Emergence of the Spectacular," 36.

6. Singer, "Modernity, Hyperstimulus, and the Rise of Popular Sensationalism," 79.

7. *San Francisco Examiner*, 10 Oct. 1893, 12, quoted in Norris, *McTeague*, 249.

8. Manuscript passage quoted in *McTeague*, 206.

9. "He Was Born for The Rope."

10. Young, "Telling Descriptions," 659.

11. Gunning, "'Primitive Cinema'—A Frame-up? or The Trick's on Us," 3.

12. Doane, *The Emergence of Cinematic Time*, 22.

13. See Gordon, *Why the French Love Jerry Lewis*.

14. Howells, *A Hazard of New Fortunes*, 147.

15. Raczkowski, "The Sublime Train of Sight in *A Hazard of New Fortunes*," 294.

16. Chopin, "The Story of an Hour," 200.

Thomas Chalmers Harbaugh's Dime Novel Westerns and Video Game Narratives

1. *Little Oskaloo* was originally published as no. 17 in the first series of *The Nickel Library*, and *Plucky Phil* was originally published as vol. IX, no. 231 of *Beadle's Half-Dime Library*.

2. Unfortunately, the demand for dimes dried up as literary tastes changed, as did Harbaugh's nest egg, and, sadly, he died in the Miami County poorhouse in 1924.

3. See Nancy Cook's essay, "Reshaping Publishing and Authorship in the Gilded Age" in *Perspectives on American Book History*, as well as Ronald Zboray's work on this issue.

4. Prominent narratological texts in the field are George Landow's *Hypertext: The Convergence of Contemporary Critical Theory and Technology* (1992) (which has been followed by *Hypertext 2.0* and *Hypertext 3.0*) and Janet Murray's *Hamlet on the Holodeck: The Future of Narrative in Cyberspace* (1998). In the ludologist camp are Espen Aarseth's *Cybertext: Perspectives of Ergodic Literature* (1997); Jesper Juul's *Half-Real: Video Games between Real Rules and Fictional Worlds* (2005); Gonzalo Frasca's *Simulation versus Narrative: Introduction to Ludology* (2003); and Markku Eskelinen's *Cybertext Poetics: The Critical Landscape of New Media Literary Theory* (2012).

5. As others have noted, Native American captivity narratives are often at the core of dime novel Westerns, making the genesis of this popular form even older. In *Plucky Phil*, possession of "pretty Nora Dalton, the Pride of Fort McKinley" is the object of the "game" (*Plucky* 1002). Phil Steele, Goldboots, Sitting Bull, and even Policy Pete are all willing to kill for the "white gal" (977). While she initially represents everything the soldiers at Fort McKinley are willing to protect, she holds different value for each of her three main "suitors." Goldboots wants the "beautiful girl and [to] take her to 'Frisco as his wife; he would set coast society wild," and he is willing to keep her "at the muzzle of the revolver and the point of his bowie" in order to possess her and turn her into the "queen of the Pacific slope," thus cementing his place in San Francisco society (1002). He will display her as booty—evidence of his gaming prowess. Though she is in reality from a humble family, Sitting Bull presumes that Nora's beauty "made her the daughter of someone high in authority" and thus she is valuable to him as a tool in negotiating with the white officials poaching his land (1010). In Indian dialect, Sitting Bull explains, "Her never born in common soldier's lodge. By and by her father come to Sitting Bull and say, 'Let the Sioux make their own terms. Give up my child and the Great Father at Washington will put his name to the strong paper.' By and by all this be done, White-Flower" (1010). Once he discovers that her father was no one of very high account and is, in fact, dead, Sitting Bull loses interest in Nora. And Phil needs her to domesticate him.

In *Little Oskaloo*, long-time captive Areotha/White Moccasion is recognized as white by those who meet her. "But you are not an Indian. Your skin is like mine," Harvey Catlett exclaims. And she explains: "'Been Indian long time though,' the girl said with a smile. 'Have Indian mother—the old Madgitwa—in the big Indian village'" (*Little Oskaloo*). And it turns out that her adopted "father" is the villain, John Girty. Girty saves her from the flaming ruins of her western home and keeps her true parentage a secret from her—out of misplaced love for her and a desire to possess her and the tranquility she brings to his home and wolfish spirit. Despite her Indian upbringing, "candor was in her voice and innocence in her soft eyes," and she instinctively feels herself the whites' friend (*Little Oskaloo*). Still, Little Moccasin is tainted by her life with the Native Americans—and her alliance with Jim Girty—and she murders John Darknight, ostensibly to save another young, white woman. Still, hero Harvey Catlett will marry Little Moccasin, thus fulfilling his mission to fully recapture her. Kate Merriweather, another white girl who is captured during the course of *Little Oskaloo*, is purely white and Western—a "peerless beauty"—and thus of value to Girty as a "wife" who will "take[] away all my warlike ambition" and quell the beast within. Apparently, even white women's civilizing power will be depleted after long contact with savagery and must be replenished.

6. In *Playing in the Dark*, Morrison explains how canonical American literature of this era evolves in "response to a dark, abiding, signing Africanist presence" that can reside apart, but is inseparable from, actual black bodies. In attending to the "the way writers peopled their work with the signs and bodies of this presence— one can see that a real or fabricated Africanist presence was crucial to their sense of Americanness" (5–6). Bill Brown adds that dime novel Westerns prioritize the "East-West axis over and against the North-South axis," thus suppressing—or, I suggest, rerouting—black-white racial tensions that emerged in the wake of the Civil War (31).

7. Beginning his text with American Revolutionaries donning Indian disguises to dump tea into Boston Harbor, Deloria writes, "Savage Indians served Americans as oppositional figures against whom one might imagine a civilized national self. Coded as freedom, however, wild Indianness proved equally attractive" (3). While this symbolic function proved particularly important in the early national period, playing Indian has become a way to "represent authenticity in the face of encroaching, modern, urban dangers" (3).

8. Even the author of the dime novel Western goes by many names. Ironically, Slagle is the only modern critic to have written on a Harbaugh novel—though he doesn't seem to know it. In his analysis of *Merciless Matt, or Red Thunderbolt's Secret* (1872), by "Captain Charles Howard," Slagle emphasizes how characters adopt not only physical but also "textual disguises that are much more complex and often figurative" (29). The familiar characteristics of the plot as described by Slagle clearly mark it as Harbaugh's work: vengeance against Indians; a young hero and experienced, older scout; a captive young woman; a mixed-blood or Native character eager to possess the "white" woman. However, Charles Johanssen reveals the many psuedonyms under which Harbaugh wrote, confirming that the dashing-sounding "Captain Charles Howard" is, indeed, the mild-mannered Harbaugh. Harbaugh's many authorial pseudonyms, including Major A. F. Grant and Major S. S. Scott (Johanssen) are all similar: anglicized, militaristic, and fungible. Perhaps Harbaugh was modeling himself on another popular dime novelist of the era, London-born

Captain Frederick Whittaker, who served honorably in the Civil War before turning to literature. Or, like his characters, he was assuming a more violent identity befitting his blood-and-thunder fiction—in this case, a white military man. Harbaugh was deeply invested in the Civil War's late-century commemorative culture, writing patriotic odes to the conflict and touring the country reading them. Only twelve when the war broke out and, then, sixteen at its end, young Harbaugh was too young to serve but clearly old enough to be stirred by its heroics and to slip into authorial personae (Howard, Grant, and Scott) chosen from the ranks of famous Civil War generals.

9. Ryan writes, "Adventure and role-playing games implement the archetypal plot that has been described by Joseph Campbell and Vladimir Propp: the quest of the hero across a land filled with many dangers to defeat evil forces and conquer a desirable object."

10. This popular poem was first published as "For Disturbin' of the Choir" in *The Magazine of Poetry* in 1889 and was immediately and widely anthologized in elocution books and collections of inspirational poetry. It has been set to music and is still performed. At its center is Brother Eyer, an elderly member of the church choir whose heartfelt but "cracked and broken" (9) singing of old-fashioned hymns is ruining the choir's effect. The fashionable congregation, full of the nouveau riche, prides itself on the fact that "We've got the biggest organ, the best dressed choir in town / We pay the steepest sal'ry to our pastor, Brother Brown" (29–30). Unwilling to let Brother Eyer drive away the disgruntled choir, which the church members have paid to "do the singing for us" (46), they tell Brother Eyer, "You'll have to stop your singin', for it flurrytates the choir" (52). Eyer sheds a tear and then immediately drops dead, as the "Master dear had called him to the everlasting chorus" (68). Clearly, this sentimental poem was meant to chide those Christians who were more interested in class mobility and appearances than in sincere worship.

Works Cited

~

Adams, Caralee. "Lessons in Pop: Does Pop Culture Belong in the Classroom?" *Scholastic Instructor*. Holiday 2011, 37–40. Print.

Alemán, Jesse. "The Other Country: Mexico, the United States, and the Gothic History of Conquest." *Hemispheric American Studies*. Ed. Caroline F. Levander and Robert S. Levine. New Brunswick, NJ: Rutgers UP, 2008. Print.

Alemán, Jesse, and Shelley Streeby, eds. *Empire and the Literature of Sensation: An Anthology of Nineteenth-Century Popular Fiction*. New Brunswick, NJ: Rutgers UP, 2007. Print.

———. "Introduction." In Alemán and Streeby, *Empire and the Literature of Sensation*, xiii–xxx. Print.

Allen, Dwight. "My Stephen King Problem: A Snob's Notes." *Los Angeles Review of Books*. Los Angeles Review of Books, 3 July 2012. Web. 28 Jan. 2013.

Ambrose, Susan A., Michael W. Bridges, Michele DiPietro, Marsha C. Lovett, and Marie K. Norman. *How Learning Works: Seven Research-Based Principles for Smart Teaching*. San Francisco: Wiley Bass, 2010. Print.

Ang, Ien. *Living Room Wars: Rethinking Media Audiences*. New York: Routledge, 1995.

Association of American Colleges and Universities. "High-Impact Educational Practices." Web. 27 Mar. 2015. http://www.aacu.org/leap/documents/hip_tables.pdf.

Bad Romance. Dir. Francis Lawrence. Lady Gaga. By Stefani Germanotta and Nadir Khayat. 2009. Performance.

Baldwin, James. "Everybody's Protest Novel." *Notes of a Native Son*. New York: Bantam, 1955. 9–17. Print.

Barnes, Jessica S., and Claudette E. Bennett. *The Asian Population: 2000*. Washington: GPO, 2002. *US Census Bureau*. Web. 15 Jan. 2013.

Baym, Nina. *Woman's Fiction: A Guide to Novels by and about Women in America, 1820–1870*. Ithaca, NY: Cornell UP, 1978. Print.

Bellamy, Edward. *Looking Backward: 2000–1887*. 1887. Ed. Alex MacDonald. Ontario, Canada: Broadview P, 2003. Print.

Bennett, Paula Bernat, Karen L. Kilcup, and Philipp Schweighauser. "Rethinking Nineteenth-Century American Poetry." *Teaching Nineteenth-Century American Poetry*. Ed. Paula Bernat Bennett, Karen L. Kilcup, and Philipp Schweighauser. New York: MLA, 2007. 1–10. Print.

Bentley, Nancy. *Frantic Panoramas: American Literature and Mass Culture, 1870–1920*. Philadelphia: U of Pennsylvania P, 2009. Print.

Berkhofer, Robert F. *The White Man's Indian: Images of the American Indian from Columbus to the Present*. New York: Vintage, 1979. Print.

Berrett, Jesse. "Mickey Spillane and Postwar America." *Scorned Literature: Essays on the History and Criticism of Popular Mass-Produced Fiction in America*. Ed. Lydia Cushman Schurman and Deidre A. Johnson. Westport, CT: Greenwood, 2002. Print.

"The Best Sellers of 1944." *College English* 6.6 (Mar. 1945): 356. *JSTOR*: Middle Tennessee State U. Web.

Billeaud, Jacques. "Ariz schools' ethnic studies program ruled illegal." AP. 27 Dec. 2011. Print.

Bloom, Harold. "Can 35 Million Book Buyers Be Wrong? Yes." *Wall Street Journal* 11 July 2000: A26. Print.

———. "Dumbing Down American Readers." [Op. ed.] *Boston Globe* 24 Sept. 2003. Print.

Bold, Christine. "The Voice of the Fiction Factory in Dime and Pulp Westerns." *Journal of American Studies* 17.1 (Apr. 1983): 29–46. Print.

Bradner, Alexandra. "America's Favorite Joke Is Anything but Funny." *Salon*: n. pag. 7 Jan. 2013. Web. 7 Feb. 2013.

Broek, Michael. "Hawthorne, Madonna, and Lady Gaga: *The Marble Faun*'s Transgressive Miriam." *Journal of American Studies* 46.3 (Aug. 2012): 625–40. Print.

Broomhall, A. F. "Thomas Chalmers Harbaugh." *The Magazine of Poetry: A Quarterly Review*. Vol. 1. Charles Wells Moulton: Buffalo, NY, 1889. 155. Open Library, Oct. 2009. Web. 13 Nov. 2013.

Brown, Bill. "Reading the West: Cultural and Historical Background." *Reading the West: An Anthology of Dime Novel Westerns*. Ed. Bill Brown. New York: Bedford/St. Martin's, 1997. 1–40. Print.

Brown, Novelette. "Obesity." *New Encyclopedia of Southern Culture*. Vol. 22: *Science and Medicine*. Ed. James G. Thomas Jr. and Charles Reagan Wilson. Chapel Hill: U of North Carolina P, 2012. 123–25. Print.

Brown, William Wells. *Clotel: Or, The President's Daughter: A Narrative of Slave*

Life in the United States. 1853. Ed. Robert Levine. New York: Bedford/St. Martin's, 2000. Print.

Buchanan, Carl Jay. "'The Monkey's Paw' and Freud's Three Caskets Theme." *Extrapolation* 48.2 (2007): 408–16. *Academic Search Complete*. Web. 16 Jan. 2013.

Butler, Judith. "Desire." *Critical Terms for Literary Study*. Ed. Frank Lentricchia and Thomas McLaughlin. Chicago: U of Chicago P, 1995. 368–86. Print.

Butterfield, Roger. "George Lippard and His Secret Brotherhood." *Pennsylvania Magazine of History and Biography* 79 (1955). Print.

Cahir, Linda Costanzo. *Literature into Film: Theory and Practical Approaches*. Jefferson, NC: McFarland. 2006. Print.

Castiglia, Christopher, and Russ Castronovo. "A 'Hive of Subtlety': Aesthetics and the End(s) of Cultural Studies." *American Literature* 76.3 (2004): 423–35. Print.

Castro, April. "Texas Education Board Approves Conservative Curriculum Changes by Far-Right." AP. 12 May 2010. Print.

Chabon, Michael. *Maps and Legends: Reading and Writing Along the Borderlands*. San Francisco: McSweeney's, 2008. Print.

Chandler, Kelly. "Reading Relationships: Parents, Adolescents, and Popular Fiction by Stephen King." *Journal of Adolescent & Adult Literacy* 43.3 (Nov. 1999): 228–39. Print.

Chesnutt, Charles. *The Marrow of Tradition*. 1901. Ed. Nancy Bentley and Sandra Gunning. New York: Bedford/St. Martin's, 2002. Print.

Child, Lydia Maria. *Hobomok*. 1824. Ed. Carolyn L. Karcher. *Hobomok and Other Writings on Indians*. New Brunswick, NJ: Rutgers UP, 1986. Print.

Chiles, Nick. "Their Eyes Were Reading Smut." *New York Times*. 4 Jan. 2006. Web. 28 Jan. 2013. http://www.nytimes.com/2006/01/04/opinion/04chiles.html?_r=0.

Chopin, Kate. "The Story of an Hour." *The Awakening and Selected Stories of Kate Chopin*. New York: Signet, 1976. Print.

Clemens, Valdine. *The Return of the Repressed: Gothic Horror from* The Castle of Otranto *to* Alien. Albany: State U of New York P, 1999. Print.

Click, Melissa A., Hyunji Lee, and Holly Willson Holladay. "Making Monsters: Lady Gaga, Fan Identification, and Social Media." *Popular Music and Society* 36.3 (2013): 360–79. Print.

Cook, Nancy. "Reshaping Publishing and Authorship in the Gilded Age." *Perspectives on American Book History: Artifacts and Commentary*. Ed. Scott E. Casper, Joanne D. Chaison, and Jeffrey D. Groves. Amherst: U of Massachusetts P, 2002. 223–54. Print.

Cooper, James Fenimore. *The Last of the Mohicans*. 1826. Ed. John P. McWilliams. New York: Oxford UP, 2009. Print.

Corona, Victor P. "Memory, Monsters, and Lady Gaga." *Journal of Popular Culture* 46.4 (2013): 725–44. Print.

Cranny-Francis, Ann. *Feminist Fictions: Feminist Uses of Generic Fictions.* New York: St. Martin's, 1990. Print.

Crenshaw, Kimberle. "Mapping the Margins: Intersectionality, Identity Politics, and Violence against Women of Color." *Stanford Law Review* 43 (1993): 1241–99. Print.

Crusie, Jennifer. *Welcome to Temptation.* New York: St. Martin's, 2000. Print.

Daniels, Harvey. *Literature Circles: Voice and Choice in Book Clubs and Reading Groups.* 2nd ed. Portland, ME: Stenhouse, 2002. Print.

Daniels, Harvey, and Nancy Steineke. *Mini-Lessons for Literature Circles.* Portsmouth, NH: Heinemann, 2004. Print.

Davidson, Cathy. *Revolution and the Word: The Rise of the Novel in America.* New York: Oxford UP, 1986. Print.

Davisson, Amber L. *Lady Gaga and the Remaking of Celebrity Culture.* Jefferson, NC: McFarland, 2013. Print.

Dayan, Joan. "Poe's Women: A Feminist Poe?" *Poe Studies/Dark Romanticism* 24.1–2 (1991): 1–12. Print.

"Decadent, adj." *Oxford English Dictionary.* 2nd ed. 2012. Web.

Delaney, Martin. *Blake; or The Huts of America.* 1859. Ed. Floyd J. Miller. Boston: Beacon, 1971. Print.

Deloria, Phillip. *Playing Indian.* New Haven, CT: Yale UP, 1998. Print.

Denning, Michael. *Mechanic Accents: Dime Novels and Working Class Culture in America.* New York: Verso, 1987. Print.

Dinerstein, Joel, "Lester Young and the Birth of Cool." *Signifyin(g), Sanctifyin' & Slam Dunking: A Reader in African American Expressive Culture.* Ed. Gena Dagel Caponi. Amherst: U of Massachusetts P, 1999. 239–76. Print.

Dinius, Marcy. "Look!! Look!!! at This!!!!": The Radical Typography of David Walker's *Appeal.*" *PMLA* 126.1 (Jan. 2011): 55–72. Print.

Dixon, Jay. *The Romantic Fiction of Mills and Boon, 1905–1995.* New York: Routledge, 1999. Print.

Doane, Mary Ann. *The Emergence of Cinematic Time: Modernity, Contingency, the Archive.* Cambridge, MA: Harvard UP, 2002. Print.

Dowd, Maureen. "Heels over Hemingway." *New York Times.* 10 Feb. 2007: A15. Print.

Dreiser, Theodore. *Sister Carrie.* 1900. Ed. Ja West, Neda M. Westlake, John C. Berkey, and Alice M. Winters. New York: Penguin, 1981. Print.

Dubino, Jeanne. "The Cinderella Complex: Romance Fiction, Patriarchy, and Capitalism." *Journal of Popular Culture* 27.3 (1993): 103–18.

Dumenico, Simon. "School of Gaga." *Billboard* 19 May 2012. Print.

Durr, Virginia Foster. *Outside the Magic Circle.* Tuscaloosa: U of Alabama P, 1985. Print.

Eggertson, Chris. "100 Years of Horror." *BloodyDisgusting.com*. Bloody Disgusting, LLC, 9 July 2010. Web. 24 July 2014. http://bloody-disgusting.com/editorials/20853/100-years-of-horror-culture-shock-the-influence-of-history-on-horror.

Elam, Diane. *Romancing the Postmodern*. New York: Routledge, 1992. Print.

Elbert, Monika. "Poe and Hawthorne as Women's Amanuenses." *Poe Studies/ Dark Romanticism* 37.1–2 (2004): 21–27. Print.

Elder, Sean. "The Coldest Winter Ever." *Salon.com*. 12 Apr. 1999. Web. 28 Jan. 2013. http://www.salon.com/1999/04/12/souljah/.

Ellis, David M. "Land Tenure and Tenancy in the Hudson Valley, 1790–1860." *Agricultural History* 18.2 (Apr. 1944): 75–82. *JSTOR*. Web. 5 Jan. 2015.

Elmer, Jonathan. "Terminate or Liquidate? Poe, Sensationalism, and the Sentimental Tradition." *The American Face of Edgar Allan Poe*. Ed. Shawn Rosenheim and Stephen Rachman. Baltimore: Johns Hopkins UP, 1995. 91–120. Print.

Farr, Cecilia Konchar. *Reading Oprah: How Oprah's Book Club Changed the Way America Reads*. Albany: State U of New York P, 2005. Print.

Faulkner, William. *Requiem for a Nun*. New York: Random House. Print.

Ferriss, Suzanne, and Mallory Young. *Chick Lit: The New Woman's Fiction*. New York: Routledge, 2006. Print.

Fiedler, Leslie. "Toward Pop Criticism." *What Was Literature? Class Culture and Mass Society*. New York: Simon and Schuster, 1982. 34–37. Print.

Fletcher, Lisa. *Historical Romance Fiction*. Burlington, VT: Ashgate, 2008. Print.

Fogel, Curtis A., and Andrea Quinlan. "Lady Gaga and Feminism: A Critical Debate." *Cross-Cultural Communication* 7.3 (2011): 184–88. Print.

Fowler, Bridget. *The Alienated Reader: Women and Popular Romantic Literature in the Twentieth Century*. New York: Prentice Hall, 1991. Print.

Frantz, Sarah and Eric Murphy Selinger. *New Approaches to Popular Romance Fiction: Critical Essays*. Jefferson, NC: McFarland, 2012. Print.

Frye, Northrup. *The Secular Scripture: A Study of the Structure of Romance*. Cambridge: Harvard UP, 1978. Print.

Fuchs, Barbara. *Romance*. New York: Routledge, 2004. Print.

Fuller, Margaret. *Woman in the Nineteenth Century*. 1845. Ed. Larry J. Reynolds. New York: Norton, 1997. Print.

"Games: Improving the Economy." *Games: Improving What Matters*. Entertainment Software Assocation, 2012. Web. 12 Sept. 2013. Print.

Genz, Stéphanie. "Teaching Gender and Popular Culture." *Teaching Gender*. New York: Palgrave Macmillan, 2012. 122–37. Print.

Genz, Stéphanie, and Benjamin A. Brabon. *Postfeminism: Cultural Texts and Theories*. Edinburgh: Edinburgh UP, 2009. Print.

Gilfillan, George. *Galleries of Literary Portraits: Poets, French Revolutionists, Novelists*. Edinburgh: J. Hogg, 1856. Print.

Gill, Rosalind, and Elena Herdieckerhoff. "Rewriting the Romance: New Femininities in Chick Lit?" *Feminist Media Studies* 6.4 (2006). Print.

Gilman, Charlotte Perkins. *The Yellow Wallpaper*. 1892. Ed. Dale M. Bauer. New York: Bedford/St. Martin's, 1998. Print.

Gniadek, Melissa. "Seriality and Settlement: Southworth, Lippard, and *The Panorama of the Monumental Grandeur of the Mississippi Valley*." *American Literature* 86.1 (2014): 31–59. Print.

Goade, Sally, ed. *Empowerment vs. Oppression: Twenty-First Century Views of Popular Romance Novels*. Cambridge: Cambridge Scholars Publishing, 2007. Print.

Goddu, Teresa A. *Gothic America: Narrative, History, and Nation*. New York: Columbia UP, 1997. Print.

Goldman, Jonathan, and Aaron Jaffe. *Modernist Star Maps*. Burlington, VT: Ashgate, 2010. Print.

Gordon, Rae Beth. *Why the French Love Jerry Lewis: From Cabaret to Early Cinema*. Stanford, CA: Stanford UP, 2002. Print.

Graham, Allison. *Framing the South: Hollywood, Television, and Race during the Civil Rights Struggle*. Baltimore: Johns Hopkins UP, 2001. Print.

Gramsci, Antonio. *The Antonio Gramsci Reader: Selected Writings 1916–1935*. Ed. David Forgacs. New York: NYU P, 2000. Print.

Gray, Richard J., II, ed. *The Performance Identities of Lady Gaga: Critical Essays*. Jefferson, NC: McFarland, 2012. Print.

Griffin, Larry J. "Southern Distinctiveness, Yet Again, or, Why America Still Needs the South." *Southern Cultures* 6.3 (2000): 47–72. Rpt. in *Southern Cultures: The Fifteenth Anniversary Reader, 1993–2008*. Ed. Harry L. Watson and Larry J. Griffin. Chapel Hill: U of North Carolina P, 2008. 3–21. Print.

"Grotesque, n. and adj." *Oxford English Dictionary*. 2nd ed. 2012. Web.

Gunning, Tom. "An Aesthetic of Astonishment: Early Film and the (In)credulous Spectator." Rpt. in *Viewing Positions: Ways of Seeing Film*. Ed. Linda Williams. New Brunswick, NJ: Rutgers UP, 1995. Print.

———. "The Cinema of Attraction[s]: Early Film, Its Spectator and the Avant-Garde." *Cinema of Attractions Reloaded*. Ed. Wanda Strauven. Amsterdam: Amsterdam UP, 2006. Print.

———. "'Primitive Cinema'—A Frame-up? or The Trick's on Us." *Cinema Journal* 28.2 (Winter 1989). Print.

Halberstam, J. Jack. *Gaga Feminism: Sex, Gender, and the End of Normal*. Boston: Beacon, 2012. Print.

Hall, Stuart. "Notes on Deconstructing the Popular." In *Cultural Theory and Popular Culture: A Reader*. Ed. John Storey. New York: Prentice Hall, 1998. 442–53. Print.

Hammill, Faye. *Women, Celebrity, and Literary Culture between the Wars*. Austin: U of Texas P, 2009. Print.

Harbaugh, Thomas Chalmers. "For Disturbin' of the Peace." *The Magazine of Poetry: A Quarterly Review*. Vol. 1. Buffalo, NY: Charles Wells Moulton, 1889. 155–56. Open Library, Oct. 2009. Web. 13 Nov. 2013.

———. *Little Oskaloo, or the White Whirlwind*. New York: Periodical Printing, 1877. Kindle.

———. *Plucky Phil, of the Mountain Trail; or, Rosa, the Red Jezebel, a Tale of Siouxdom*. 1881. *Popular American Literature of the 19th Century*. Ed Paul C. Gutjahr. New York: Oxford UP, 2001. 963–1021. Print.

Harrington, C. Lee., and Denise Bielby. *Popular Culture: Production and Consumption*. Boston: Blackwell, 2000.

Harzewski, Stephanie. *Chick Lit and Postfeminism*. Charlottesville: U of Virginia P, 2011. Print.

Hawthorne, Nathaniel. *The Blithedale Romance*. 1852. Ed. Annette Kolodny. New York: Penguin, 1983.

———. *The House of the Seven Gables*. 1851. Ed. Robert Levine. New York: Norton, 2005. Print.

———. *The Scarlet Letter and Other Writings*. Ed. Leland S. Person. New York and London: Norton, 2005. Print.

"He Was Born for The Rope." *San Francisco Examiner* 14 Oct. 1893: 8. Rpt. in Norris, *McTeague*, ed. Donald Pizer. 256. Print.

Hebdige, Dick. *Subculture: The Meaning of Style*. London: Methuen, 1979. Print.

Heinecken, Dawn. "Changing Ideologies in Romance Fiction." *Romantic Conventions*. Ed. Anne K. Kaler and Rosemary E. Johnson-Kurek. Bowling Green, OH: Bowling Green State U Popular P, 1999. 149–72. Print.

Hickey, Dave. *Air Guitar: Essays on Art and Democracy*. Los Angeles: Art Issues, 1997. Print.

Hoffman, Daniel. "Ligeia—Not Me! Three Women Writers Respond to Poe." *Poe's Pervasive Influence*. Ed. Barbara Cantalupo. Bethlehem: Lehigh UP, 2012. 117–25. Print.

Hollander, Paul. "Michael Jackson, the Celebrity Cult, and Popular Culture." *Society* 47.2 (2010): 147–52. Print.

Hollows, Joanne. *Feminism, Femininity and Popular Culture*. Manchester: Manchester UP, 2000. Print.

hooks, bell. *Black Looks: Race and Representation*. Boston: South End, 1992. Print.

———. *Killing Rage: Ending Racism*. New York: Henry Holt, 1995. Print.

———. *Outlaw Culture: Resisting Representations*. New York: Routledge, 2006. Print.

———. *Teaching Critical Thinking: Practical Wisdom*. New York: Routledge, 2010. Print.

———. *Writing Beyond Race: Living Theory and Practice*. New York: Routledge, 2012. Print.

Horkheimer, Max, and Theodor Adorno. *The Dialectic of Enlightenment*. New York: Continuum, 1989. Print.

"Horror, n." *Oxford English Dictionary*. 2nd ed. 2012. Web.

Howe, Julia Ward. *The Hermaphrodite*. c. 1840. Ed. Gary Williams. Lincoln: Nebraska UP, 2009. Print.

Howells, William Dean. *A Hazard of New Fortunes*. 1890. New York: Modern Library, 2002. Print.

Jackson, Christine A. *The Tell-Tale Art: Poe in Modern Popular Culture*. Jefferson: McFarland, 2012. Print.

Jackson, Kennell. "Introduction: Traveling While Black." *Black Cultural Traffic: Crossroads in Global Performance and Popular Culture*. Ed. Harry Elam Jr. and Kennell Jackson. Ann Arbor: U of Michigan P, 2005. 1–39. Print.

Jacobs, Alan. *The Pleasures of Reading in an Age of Distraction*. Oxford UP, 2011. Print.

Jacobs, Harriet. *Incidents in the Life of a Slave Girl*. 1859. Ed. N. I. Painter. New York: Penguin, 2000. Print.

Jacobs, W. W. "The Monkey's Paw." *The Oxford Book of English Ghost Stories*. Ed. Michael Cox and R. A. Gilbert. Oxford: Oxford UP, 1986. 180–89. Print.

Jenkins, Henry. "Game Design as Narrative Architecture." Henry Jenkins Publications, Department of Comparative Media Studies, MIT, 2010. Web. 4 Sept. 2013.

Johanssen, Albert. "Harbaugh, Thomas C." *The House of Beadle and Adams and Its Dime and Nickel Novels: The Story of a Vanished Literature*. Norman: U of Oklahoma P, 1950. Northern Illinois U, 2010. Web. 4 Sept. 2013.

"Juliette." *Exploregeorgia.org*. Georgia Department of Economic Development, n.d. Web. 6 Feb. 2013.

Kaler, Anne K., and Rosemary E. Johnson-Kurek, eds. *Romantic Conventions*. Bowling Green, OH: Bowling Green State U Popular P, 1999. Print.

Kaplan, Cora. *Sea Changes*. London: Verso, 1986. Print.

Kasson, John F. *Rudeness and Civility: Manners in Nineteenth-Century Urban America*. New York: Hill and Wang, 1990. Print.

Katie. "On R. Kelly, Lady Gaga, and Redemption Narratives: A Conversation with Salamishah Tillet, Ph.D." *Feministing*. 22 Nov. 2013. Web. 1 Aug. 2014. http://feministing.com/2013/11/22/on-r-kelly-lady-gaga-and-redemption-narratives-a-conversation-with-salamishah-tillet-ph-d/.

King, Stephen. *Danse Macabre*. New York: Berkley, 1981. Print.

———. *Pet Sematary*. New York: Doubleday, 1983. Print.

Klein Latham, Samantha. "Abusive Class: The Juxtaposition of Class Rigidity and Abusive Relationships in *Dragonwyck*." 4 Oct. 2011. TS.

Kolodny, Annette. "The Integrity of Memory: Creating a New Literary History of the United States." *American Literature* 57 (1985): 291–307. Print.

Korda, Michael. *Making the List: A Cultural History of the American Bestseller, 1900–1999*. New York: Barnes and Noble, 2001. Print.

Krentz, Jayne Ann, ed. *Dangerous Men and Adventurous Women*. Philadelphia: U of Pennsylvania P, 1992. Print.

Krystal, Arthur. "Easy Writers." *New Yorker* 28 May 2012: 81. Print.

Lagan, Sarah. "Killing Our Monsters: On Stephen King's Magic." *Los Angeles Review of Books*. 17 July 2012. Web. 28 Jan. 2013.

The Language of Literature, Grade 11, American Literature. Boston: Houghton Mifflin Harcourt, 2006. Print.

Laskin, David, and Holly Hughes. "A Brief History of the Reading Group in America." *The Reading Group Book: The Complete Guide to Starting and Sustaining a Reading Group*. Ed. David Laskin and Holly Hughes. New York: Plume, 1995. 1–17. Print.

Lauter, Paul. "Early Nineteenth Century 1800–1865." *The Heath Anthology of American Literature*. Vol. B: *Early Nineteenth Century: 1800–1865*. 6th ed. Ed. Paul Lauter. Boston: Houghton Mifflin, 2009. 1443–73. Print.

LeBesco, Kathleen. *Revolting Bodies? The Struggle to Redefine Fat Identity*. Amherst: U of Massachusetts P, 2004. Print.

Lester, Paul. *Lady Gaga: Looking for Fame: The Life of a Pop Princess*. London: Omnibus, 2010. Print.

Lewis, C. S. "High and Low Brows." 1939. Rpt. in Lewis, *Selected Literary Essays*. Ed. Walter Hooper. Cambridge: Cambridge UP, 1969. 266–79. Print.

Light, Alison. "Returning to Manderley: Romance Fiction, Female Sexuality, and Class." *Feminist Review* no. 16 (Summer 1984): 7–25. Print.

Lippard, George. *'Bel of Prairie Eden*. In Alemán and Streeby, *Empire and the Literature of Sensation*. Print.

Lockwood, Cara. *Dixieland Sushi*. New York: Downtown, 2005. Print.

Lynch, Annette. *Porn Chic: Exploring the Contours of Raunch Eroticism*. London: Berg, 2013. Print.

Magistrale, Tony. *Hollywood's Stephen King*. New York: Palgrave Macmillan, 2003. Print.

Makinen, Merja. *Feminist Popular Fiction*. Hampshire, UK: Palgrave, 2001. Print.

Marchand, Ernest. "1899 Reviews of *McTeague*." Rpt. in Norris, *McTeague*, ed. Donald Pizer. 1–5. Print.

Massé, Michelle. *In the Name of Love: Women, Masochism, and the Gothic*. Ithaca: Cornell UP, 1992. Print.

Matthieson, F. O. *American Renaissance: Art and Expression in the Age of Emerson and Melville*. New York: Oxford UP, 1941. Print.

McGrath, Ben. "The Radical—Why Do Editors Keep Throwing 'The Boondocks' off the Funnies Page?" *New Yorker*. 19 Apr. 2004. Web. 17 July 2014. http://www.newyorker.com/archive/2004/04/19/040419fa_fact2?currentPage=all.

McGruder, Aaron. *A Right to Be Hostile*. New York: Three Rivers, 2003. Print.

———. *Because I Know You Don't Read the Newspapers*. Kansas City: Andrews McMeel, 2000. Print.

———. *Fresh for '01 . . . You Suckas!* Kansas City: Andrews McMeel, 2001. Print.

McPherson, Tara. *Reconstructing Dixie: Race, Gender, and Nostalgia in the Imagined South*. Durham, NC: Duke UP, 2003. Print.

Melville, Herman. *Benito Cereno*. 1855. Ed. Wyn Kelly. New York: Bedford, 2006. Print.

Metalious, Grace. *Peyton Place*. 1956. Boston: Northeastern UP, 1999. Print.

Miller, Angela. "The Panorama, the Cinema, and the Emergence of the Spectacular." *Wide Angle* 18.2 (1996): 36. Print.

Mills, David. "Sister Souljah's Call to Arms." *Washington Post*. 13 May 1992. Web. 17 July 2014. http://pqasb.pqarchiver.com/washingtonpost/access/74018923. html?dids=74018923:74018923&FMT=ABS.

Modleski, Tania. *Loving with a Vengeance: Mass Produced Fantasies for Women*. 1982. New York: Routledge, 2007. Print.

Morrison, Toni. *Playing in the Dark: Whiteness and the Literary Imagination*. Cambridge, MA: Harvard UP, 1992. Print.

Musser, Charles. "A Cornucopia of Images: Comparison and Judgment across Theater, Film, and the Visual Arts during the Late Nineteenth Century." *Moving Pictures: American Art and Early Film, 1880–1910*. Ed. Nancy Mowll Matthews with Charles Musser. Manchester, VT: Hudson Hills, 2005. Print.

Naughton, Julie, and Pete Born. "Lady Gaga on What Drives Her." *WWD*. 18 Feb. 2011. Web. 25 Jan. 2013. http://www.wwd.com/eye/people/ lady-gaga-on-what-drives-her-3504137.

Norris, Frank. "An Opening for Novelists: Great Opportunities for Fiction Writers in San Francisco." *San Francisco Wave* (22 May 1897): 2. Rpt. in *McTeague*, ed. Donald Pizer. 249. Print.

———. *McTeague*. 1899. Ed. Donald Pizer. New York: Norton, 1997. Print.

Paizis, George. *Love and the Novel: The Poetics and Politic of Romantic Fiction*. New York: St. Martin's, 1998. Print.

Pearce, Lynne, and Jackie Stacey. *Romance Revisited*. New York: NYU P, 1995. Print.

Perea, Juan F. "The Black/White Binary Paradigm of Race." *Critical Race Theory: The Cutting Edge*. Eds. Richard Delgado and Jean Stefancic. Philadelphia: Temple UP, 2000. 344–53. Print.

Person, Leland S. "Poe and Nineteenth-Century Gender Constructions." *A Historical Guide to Edgar Allan Poe*. Ed. J. Gerald Kennedy. New York: Oxford UP, 2000. 129–66.

Pharr, Mary Ferguson. "A Dream of New Life: Stephen King's *Pet Sematary* as a Variant of *Frankenstein*." *The Gothic World of Stephen King: Landscape of Nightmares*. Ed. Gary Hoppenstand and Ray B. Browne. Bowling Green, OH: Bowling Green State U Popular P, 1987. 115–25. Print.

Phelps, Elizabeth Stuart. *The Gates Ajar*. 1868. Rpt. as *Three Spiritualist Novels by Elizabeth Stuart Phelps: The Gates Ajar (1868), Beyond the Gates (1883), and The Gates Between (1887)*. Ed. Nina Baym. Urbana: U of Illinois P, 2000. Print.

———. *The Silent Partner*. 1871. Rpt. as *The Silent Partner: Including "The Tenth of January."* Ed. Mary Jo Buhle and Florence Howe. New York: Feminist P at CUNY, 1993. Print.

Phillips, Susan Elizabeth. *Nobody's Baby but Mine*. New York: William Morrow, 2012. Reprint.

Poe, Edgar Allan. "Lenore." *Pioneer* 1 (Feb 1843): 60–61. Print.

———. *The Selected Writings of Edgar Allan Poe*. Ed. G. R. Thompson. New York : Norton, 2004. Print.

Power, Brenda Miller. "Reading Stephen King: An Ethnography of an Event." *Reading Stephen King: Issues of Censorship, Student Choice, and Popular Literature*. Ed. Brenda Miller Power, Jeffrey D. Wilhelm, and Kelly Chandler. Urbana, IL: NCTE, 1997. 3–12.

Raczkowski, Christopher. "The Sublime Train of Sight in *A Hazard of New Fortunes.*" *Studies in the Novel* 40.3 (Fall 2008). Print.

Radway, Janice. *Reading the Romance: Women, Patriarchy, and Popular Literature*. Chapel Hill: U of North Carolina P, 1984. Print.

Regis, Pamela. *A Natural History of the Romance*. Philadelphia: U of Pennsylvania P, 2007. Print.

Reynolds, David S. *Beneath the American Renaissance: The Subversive Imagination in the Age of Emerson and Melville*. 1988. Oxford: OUP, 2011. Print.

———. *George Lippard*. Boston: Twayne, 1982. Print.

Rhoads, Bonita. "Poe's Genre Crossing: From Domesticity to Detection." *Poe Studies* 42.1 (Oct. 2009): 14–40. Print.

Rice, Almah Lavon. "The Rise of Street Literature. " *Colorlines*. 4 June 2009. Web. 27 June 2012. http://colorlines.com/archives/2009/06/the_rise_of_street_literature.html.

Richards, Eliza. *Gender and the Poetics of Reception in Poe's Circle*. Cambridge : Cambridge UP, 2004. Print.

———. "Women's Place in Poe Studies." *Poe Studies* 33.1–2 (2000): 10–14. Print.

Roberts, Nora. *The Search*. New York: Jove Books, 2010. Print.

"Romance, n. and adj." *Oxford English Dictionary*. 3rd ed. 2012. Web.

Ryan, Marie-Laure. "Beyond Myth and Metaphor—The Case of Narrative in Digital Media." *Game Studies: The International Journal of Computer Game Research* 1.1 (July 2001): n. pag. Web.

Sears, John. *Stephen King's Gothic*. Series ed. Andrew Smith and Benjamin F. Fisher. Cardiff: U Wales P, 2011. Print. Gothic Literary Studies.

Sedgwick, Catherine Maria. *Hope Leslie*. 1827. Ed. Carolyn L. Karcher. New York: Penguin, 1998. Print.

Selinger, Eric Murphy. "Rereading the Romance." *Contemporary Literature* 48.2 (Summer 2007). Print.

Seton, Anya. *Dragonwyck.* 1944. Chicago: Chicago Review, 2005. Print.

Shelley, Mary. *Frankenstein.* Ed. Johanna M. Smith. Series ed. Ross C. Martin. Boston: Bedford/St. Martin's, 2000. Case Studies in Contemporary Criticism, 2nd ed. Print.

Showalter, Elaine. *Sister's Choice: Tradition and Change in American Women's Writing.* Oxford: Oxford UP, 1991. Print.

Simon, Richard Keller. *Trash Culture: Popular Culture and the Great Tradition.* Berkeley: U of California P, 1999. Print.

Simons, Jan. "Narrative, Games, and Theory." *International Journal of Computer Game Research* 7.1 (Aug. 2007): n. pag. Web.

Singer, Ben. "Modernity, Hyperstimulus, and the Rise of Popular Sensationalism." *Cinema and the Invention of Modern Life.* Ed. Leo Charney and Vanessa Schwartz. Berkeley: U of California P, 1995. Print.

Sister Souljah. *The Coldest Winter Ever.* Special Collection ed. 2005. New York: Washington Square, 1999. Print.

Slagle, Jefferson D. "The Heirs of Buffalo Bill: Performing Authenticity in the Dime Western." *Canadian Review of American Studies/Revue canadienne l'études américaines* 39.2 (2009): 19–38. Print.

Snitow, Ann, ed. *Powers of Desire.* Monthly Review, 1983. Print.

Southgate, Martha. "Someday We'll All Be Free: Considering Post-Oppression Fiction." *Contemporary African American Literary Canon: Theory and Pedagogy.* Ed. Lovalerie King and Jocelyn Moody. Bloomington: Indiana UP, forthcoming. Print.

———. "Writers Like Me." *New York Times.* 1 July 2007. Web. 6 July 2014. http://www.nytimes.com/2007/07/01/books/review/Southgate-t.html?_r=0.

Southworth, E.D.E.N. *The Hidden Hand, or, Capitola the Madcap.* 1859. Ed. Joanne Dobson. New Brunswick, NJ: Rutgers UP, 1988. Print.

Stimpson, Catharine R. "Reading for Love: Canons, Paracanons, and Whistling Jo March." *New Literary History* 21 (1990): 957–76. Print.

Storey, John. *Cultural Studies and the Study of Popular Culture.* 2nd ed. Athens: U of Georgia P, 2003. Print.

———. *An Introduction to Cultural Theory and Popular Culture.* 2nd ed. Athens: U of Georgia P, 1998. Print.

Stowe, Harriet Beecher. *Uncle Tom's Cabin.* 1852. Ed. Elizabeth Ammons. New York: Norton, 1994. Print.

Strauss, Neil. *Everyone Loves You When You're Dead: Journeys into Fame and Madness.* New York: HarperCollins, 2011. Print.

Streeby, Shelley. *American Sensations: Class, Empire, and the Production of Popular Culture.* Berkeley: U of California P, 2002. Print.

———. "Sensational Fiction." *A Companion to American Fiction, 1780–1865*. Ed. Shirley Samuels. Malden, MA: Blackwell, 2004. 179–89. Print.

Strengell, Heidi. *Dissecting Stephen King: From the Gothic to Literary Naturalism*. Madison: U of Wisconsin P, 2005. Print.

Suárez, Juan A. *Pop Modernism: Noise and the Reinvention of the Everyday*. Chicago: U of Illinois P, 2007. Print.

Suddath, Claire. "Why Are Southerners So Fat?" *Time*. 9 July 2009. Web. 29 July 2014.

Suellentrop, Chris. "War Games." *New York Times* 12 Sept. 2010: MM62. Print.

Thigpen, David E. "Literary Yearnings: Rock Stars and the Authors Who Love Them." *Time* 148.3 (1996): 75. *Academic Search Complete*. Web. 16 Jan. 2013.

"Thomas Chalmers Harbaugh." *1909 History Miami County*. Troy Historical Society (Ohio), n.d. Web. 5 Sept. 2013.

"Thomas Harbaugh." *1900 Biog. Hist. Miami Co. Ohio*. Troy Historical Society (Ohio), n.d. Web. 5 Sept. 2013.

Tompkins, Jane. *Sensational Designs: The Cultural Work of American Fiction, 1790–1860*. New York: Oxford UP, 1985. Print.

Touré. *Who's Afraid of Post-Blackness? What It Means to Be Black Now*. New York: Simon & Schuster, 2011. Print.

Tract #493: "Beware of Bad Books." *Tracts of the American Tract Society: General Series (Vol. 12)*. Exact date unknown. Web. http://greatchristianlibrary. blogspot.com/2010/04/tracts-of-american-tract-society-tracts.html. 3 Jan. 2015.

"Twenty-Nine Fatal Wounds." *San Francisco Examiner* 10 Oct. 1893: 12. Rpt. in Norris, *McTeague*, ed. Donald Pizer. Print.

US Census Bureau. "Table 1. Urban and Rural Population: 1900 to 1990." *Census. gov*. US Census Bureau, Oct. 1995. Web. 1 Feb. 2013.

Vincent, Bev. *The Stephen King Illustrated Companion*. New York: Metro Books, 2009. Print.

Waldman, Diane. "'At last I can tell it to someone!': Feminine Point of View and Subjectivity in the Gothic Romance Film of the 1940s." *Cinema Journal* 23.2 (Winter 1983): 29–40. *JSTOR*. Web. 22 May 2014.

Warren, Kenneth. *Black and White Strangers: Race and American Literary Realism*. Chicago: U of Chicago P, 1995. Print.

Watson, Daphne. *Their Own Worst Enemies: Women Writers of Women's Fiction*. Pluto, 1995. Print.

Weber, Brenda R. "Teaching Popular Culture through Gender Studies: Feminist Pedagogy in a Postfeminist and Neoliberal Academy?" *Feminist Teacher* 20.2 (2010): 124–31.

Weinstein, Cindy, and Christopher Looby, eds. *American Literature's Aesthetic Dimensions*. New York: Columbia UP, 2012.

Weiss, M. Jerry. "A Teacher's Guide to the Signet Editions of Selected Short Horror Stories of Stephen King." *Penguin.com*. Series ed. W. Geiger Ellis and Arthea J. S. Reed. Penguin/Random House, 2014. Web. 24 July 2014.

Williams, Elizabeth. "Teaching Judgment of Prose Fiction." *English Journal* 47.8 (Nov. 1958): 495–99. *JSTOR*. Web. 28 Dec. 2012.

Williams, Noelle. "Is Lady Gaga a Feminist or Isn't She?" *Ms.* 11 Mar. 2010. Web. 1 Jun. 2014. http://msmagazine.com/blog/2010/03/11/is-lady-gaga-a-feminist-or-isnt-she/.

Wilson, Cheryl A. "Chick Lit in the Undergraduate Classroom." *Frontiers: A Journal of Women Studies* 33.1 (2012): 83–100. Print.

Windsor, Kathleen. *Forever Amber*. 1944. Chicago: Chicago Review, 2000. Print.

Winnemucca, Sarah. *Life among the Piutes: Their Wrongs and Claims*. 1883. Ed. Catherine S. Fowler. Reno: U of Nevada P, 1994. Print.

Winter, Kari J. *Subjects of Slavery, Agents of Change: Women and Power in Gothic Novels and Slave Narratives, 1790–1865*. Athens: U of Georgia P, 1992. Print.

Woodward, C. Vann. "The Search for Southern Identity." *The Burden of Southern History*. Baton Rouge: Louisiana State UP, 1960. 3–25. Print.

Worden, Daniel. "Masculinity for the Million: Gender in Dime Novel Westerns." *Arizona Quarterly* 63.3 (Autumn 2007): 35–60. Print.

Young, Kevin. "Broken Tongue: Paul Laurence Dunbar, His Descendants, and the Dance of Dialect." *The Grey Album: On the Blackness of Blackness*. Minneapolis: Graywolf, 2012. 89–132. Print.

Young, Paul. "Telling Descriptions: Frank Norris's Kinetoscopic Naturalism and the Future of the Novel, 1899." *Modernism/Modernity* 14.4 (Nov. 2007). Print.

Zboray, Ronald. "Antebellum Reading and the Ironies of Technological Innovation." *American Quarterly* 40.1 (Mar. 1988): 65–82. Print.

Contributors

~

ALISSA BURGER is an associate professor at the SUNY Delhi, where she teaches English and humanities courses, including a single-author seminar on Stephen King. She is the author of *The Wizard of Oz as American Myth: A Critical Study of Six Versions of the Story, 1900–2007* and editor of the collection *The Television World of Pushing Daisies: Critical Essays on the Bryan Fuller Series.*

JANET G. CASEY is professor of English and director of the First Year Experience at Skidmore College, where she also teaches courses in American studies (notably American Bestsellers and Popular Culture and Magazines and Modernity). She is a core (i.e., founding) member of the Middlebrow Research Network. Her books include *Dos Passos and the Ideology of the Feminine* (Cambridge UP, 1998) and *A New Heartland: Women, Modernity, and the Agrarian Ideal in America* (Oxford UP, 2009). She has also edited *The Novel and the American Left: Critical Essays on Depression-Era Fiction* (U of Iowa P, 2004).

MICHAEL DEVINE is assistant professor of English at SUNY Plattsburgh. His work on early cinema, literature, and the arts has appeared in *American Literature* and *Adaptation*. He has forthcoming essays on Stephen Crane's literature of attractions and Martin Scorsese's *Hugo*.

MELISSA GNIADEK is an assistant professor in the Department of English at the University of Toronto. She previously taught at Rice University. Her current projects involve temporalities of settlement in US contexts and the Pacific "at home" in nineteenth-century America. Her work has appeared in *American Literature, J19: The Journal of Nineteenth-Century Americanists*, the *Journal of New Zealand Literature*, and the *International Journal of Francophone Studies*.

JOLENE HUBBS is an associate professor of American studies at the University of Alabama, where she teaches and writes about Southern literature and culture. Her articles on Charles Chesnutt, William Faulkner, and Flannery O'Connor have appeared in such journals as *Mississippi Quarterly* and *American Literary Realism*.

LISA LONG is professor of English and chair of the Division of Arts and Letters at North Central College in Naperville, Illinois. Her books include *White Scholars/African American Texts* (Rutgers UP, 2005) and *Rehabilitating Bodies: Health, History, and the American Civil War* (U of Pennsylvania P, 2004). She has also published broadly on nineteenth- and twentieth-century American women writers, pedagogy, and African American and Southeast Asian American literatures in such journals as *American Literature, American Literary History, College English, Twentieth-Century Literature,* and *Legacy*.

ANTONIA LOSANO is associate professor of English and American literatures at Middlebury College, where she teaches Victorian literature, gender studies, and literary theory. Currently she is at work on a book manuscript exploring the role of animals in popular romance fiction.

DEREK MCGRATH received his doctoral degree in English literature from Stony Brook University. His courses are based around applying older nineteenth-century texts as they speak to current cultural issues and tracing their adaptations within emerging literary and digital forms. His chapter is adapted from an address he was invited to deliver to the Poe Room at New York University.

RICHARD SCHUR is professor of English and director of the Law and Society Program at Drury University in Springfield, Missouri. He is the author of *Parodies of Ownership: Hip-Hop Aesthetics and Intellectual Property Law* (U of Michigan P) and coeditor of *African American Culture and Legal Discourse* (Palgrave Macmillan). His research focuses on African American culture, popular music, and law. He also is cohost of the *New Books in Popular Music* podcast at http://newbooksinpopmusic.com.

RANDI LYNN TANGLEN is associate professor of English at Austin College in Sherman, Texas. Her work has previously appeared in *Western American Literature* and *Tulsa Studies in Women's Literature*.

KATHLEEN M. THERRIEN is an associate professor of English at Middle Tennessee State University, where she teaches courses in nineteenth- and twentieth-century American literature, women writers, and popular literature.

Index